World Englishes
Implications for international communication and English language teaching

World Englishes
Implications for international communication and English language teaching

ANDY KIRKPATRICK

Hong Kong Institute of Education

CAMBRIDGE
UNIVERSITY PRESS

CAMBRIDGE UNIVERSITY PRESS
Cambridge, New York, Melbourne, Madrid, Cape Town,
Singapore, São Paulo, Delhi, Tokyo, Mexico City

Cambridge University Press
The Edinburgh Building, Cambridge CB2 8RU, UK

www.cambridge.org
Information on this title: www.cambridge.org/9780521616874

First published 2007
Reprinted 2011

Printed in the United Kingdom at the University Press, Cambridge

A catalogue record for this publication is available from the British Library

ISBN 978-0-521-61687-4 Paperback
ISBN 978-0-521-85147-3 Hardback

Contents

To Mum, Lyn, Ian and Helen

Acknowledgements

The author

A great many people have helped in the writing of this book, not least the many students I have been privileged to teach. I would like to make particular mention of recent doctoral students including Zi Adnan, James McLellan, David Prescott, Helen Singleton, Rusdi Taib, Glenn Toh and Xu Zhichang. Their scholarship continues to be a great source of stimulation.

I also need to thank other friends who so generously offered their time and voices – Karen Higgins, Marion Johnston, Thiru Kandiah, KC, KT, 'tope Omoniyi, Sivanes Phillipson and Claudia Sullivan – and all the others whose voices are also recorded here, including Budi, Dalvindar, Erlinda, Janet, Myint, Phan, Phuong, Setya, Shwe Oo, Tirote, Un and Yusniza.

I would also like to thank the Cambridge editorial team who have been such a pleasure to work with, in particular Jane Walsh, Alison Sharpe, Clive Rumble, Michelle Simpson and Sylvia Goulding.

The publishers

The author and publishers are grateful to the following for permission to reproduce copyright material. While every effort has been made, it has not always been possible to identify the sources of all the material used, or to contact the copyright holders. If any omissions are brought to our notice, we will be happy to include the appropriate acknowledgements on reprinting.

Penguin Group (UK) for permission to use a number of small extracts taken from Crystal, D. (2004) *The Stories of English*. Penguin Allen Lane, 2004. © David Crystal, 2004.

Oxford University Press for permission to use a number of small extracts taken from Birchfield, R. (1986) *The English Language*, Oxford: Oxford University Press.

Multilingual Matters for permission to use the extracts on p35 and pp177–8 taken from Phillipson, R. (1997) 'Realities and Myths of Linguistic Imperialism' *Journal of Multilingual and Multicultural Development*, Vol 18: 3, 1997, pp238–48.

Leopard Magazine for permission to use the cartoon 'Councillor Swick' on p50 taken from Issue No. 314, April 2005. Used by kind permission of *Leopard* Magazine.

Mainstream Publishing for permission to use short quotes by Kynoch on p52, taken from Kay, B. (1986) *Scots: The Mither Tongue*, Edinburgh: Mainstream Publishing Co.

Cambridge University Press for permission to use the extract on p61 taken from McArthur, T. (1998) *The Shapes of English*, Cambridge: Cambridge University Press.

Cambridge University Press for permission to use the extracts on pp85, 86 and 93: taken from Mehrotra, R. R. (2003) 'A British Response to some Indian English Usages', *English Today*, vol 19: 3, pp19–25.

Pearson Education for permission to use extracts on pp103, 109–11 and 116 taken from Schmied, J. J. (1991) *English in Africa: An Introduction*. New York, Longman.

Ken Saro-Wiwa's estate for kind permission to use the extract on pp113–14 taken from Saro-Wiwa, K. *Sozaboy*, © Ken Saro-Wiwa Literary Estate.

Dr James McLellan for kind permission to use the quotes on pp127–8: The first quote posting date 18/8/2001, Brudirect ("Have your Say") forum, http://www.bruneidirecthys.net/hys/index.php, the second quote posting date 3/12/2001, Bruclass forum, http://www.bruclass.com/ (Asian Community).

Macquarie Dictionary for permission to use the table on p131, Gonzalez, A. 'The vowel and consonant sounds of cultivated Philippine English'; p142, Butler, S. 'Five Criteria', taken from Bautista, M. L. S. (ed.) (1997) *English is an Asian Language: The Philippine Context*, Sidney, Australia: Macquarie Library Pty Ltd.

Blackwell Publishing for permission to use the adapted table on p145 taken from Adamson, B. (2002) 'The historical role and status of the English Language in China', *World Englishes Vol 2, No 2*.

Marc Xu Zhichang for kind permission to use the extracts on pp148–9 taken from the thesis by Zhichang Xu (2005) *Chinese English: What is it and is it to become a regional variety of English?*, Perth, Australia: Curtin University.

Random House Group for permission to use the extract on pp150–51 Ha Jin (2000) *In the Pond*, New York: Vintage.

The Australian Broadcasting Corporation for permission to use the recording and the transcript on pp208–10 MacNamarra, I. 'Australia all over', first broadcast 7 March 2003 on ABC Local Radio. Reproduced by permission of the Australian Broadcasting Corporation and ABC Online © 2003 ABC. All rights reserved. For the recording and transcript on p210 'Children of the Bush', interview with John Williamson, first broadcast on ABC Radio National. Reproduced by permission of the Australian Broadcasting Corporation and ABC Online © 2007 ABC. All rights reserved;

Matthews Music Pty Ltd for permission to use the three lines of lyrics on p210 by Williamson, J. (1986) '*True Blue*'. © Emusic Pty Ltd (APRA). www.johnwilliamson.com.au.

Yasmine Gooneratne for kind permission to use the poem on pp211–12 'Menika', and for the poem on pp212–14:'The Lizard's Cry', both from Gooneratne, Y. (1972) *The Lizard's Cry and Other Poems*, published privately in Kandy, Sri Lanka.

Asia2000 Ltd. for permission to use the poem on p225 'Yellow flowers on a battlefield', by Agnes Lam, for the poem on p226 'Hong Kong Riots, 1967', by Louise Ho, and for the poem on p226 'End of an era', by Louise Ho.

Pieta O'Shaughnessy for permission to use the recording and transcript on pp215–17, 'Interview with a Soweto Flying Squad (SFS) Policeman. Interview on Curtin Radio, Curtin University, Perth, Australia. Used by permission of Pieta O'Shaughnessy;

'tope Omoniyi for permission to use the recording and transcript of four poems on pp217–20, 'Let them who have ears hear', 'I do not know anymore', 'Midwives or a deluge?' and 'The Dogs of Baidoa' taken from Omoniyi, 'tope. (2001) *Farting Presidents and Other Poems,* Lagos, Nigeria: Kraft Books Ltd.

Cover design: Michael Stones. Text design: Dale Tomlinson.

Introduction

All over the world people in ever-increasing numbers are using more and more varieties of English. English has now become the language of international communication. Perhaps the most remarkable fact behind this increasing use of English is that the majority of English speakers are now multilingual people who have learned English and who use English to communicate with fellow multilinguals. There are many more speakers of World Englishes and people who use English for international communication than there are native speakers of it. This book will consider the implications for international communication and English language teaching of this extraordinary growth in the varieties of English and in the numbers of English speakers.

Courses in World Englishes are becoming ever more popular and are seen, especially among ELT practitioners and professionals, as relevant for those who plan to become English language teachers. Indeed, one noted scholar has suggested that no TESOL development course should be without a course in World Englishes (Görlach, 1997). There are a number of excellent introductory texts to World Englishes, of which Kachru's *The Other Tongue* (1982/92) remains an outstanding example. McArthur's *The English Languages* (1998) and his *Oxford Guide to World Englishes* (2002) provide extremely valuable background and reference materials. Görlach (1991) and Schneider (1997) have both edited series on World Englishes. Melchers' and Shaw's (2003) book *World Englishes* offers a useful introduction, and Jenkins (2005) is an excellent resource that provides a summary of current developments and key debates. There are also a number of texts that focus on one variety of 'World English'. For example, Hong Kong University Press is currently publishing a series on Englishes in Asia (Adamson, 2004; Stanlaw, 2004; Kachru, 2006).

This book differs from all the above in that it aims to describe selected varieties of World Englishes and then discusses the implications of these varieties for English language learning and teaching in specific contexts. In this way, the text describes selected varieties of World Englishes for an audience of English language teachers and teacher trainers. It also considers and compares international contexts in which English is used as a *lingua franca*. In particular, the book hopes to be both relevant and useful to so-called non-native speaker teachers, who make up the overwhelming majority of English language teachers worldwide (Braine, 1999). It stresses the importance and validates the roles and contributions of multilingual and multicultural English language teachers who may be either speakers of a nativised model of English, such as Singaporean, or non-native speaker teachers who use English primarily as a *lingua franca* with fellow non-native speakers, as will the great majority of their students. In this context it argues that native speaker and nativised varieties of English have developed in comparable ways.

The book is aimed primarily at ELT professionals and trainee teachers undertaking TESOL training throughout the world. It also aims to become an important text on World Englishes for undergraduate and postgraduate students of World Englishes.

The book is divided into three sections. Part A (Chapters 1–3) introduces readers to relevant key sociolinguistic and linguistic concepts, and provides a brief background history of the development of World Englishes. Part A thus offers readers an introduction to basic concepts that are developed throughout the book.

Part B (Chapters 4–11) provides a description of the linguistic features of selected varieties of World Englishes, including examples from phonology, lexis, syntax, discourse and pragmatic norms. Each chapter describes the socio-political features of the variety and typically includes the historical background leading to the development of that variety, its current status, the attitudes that speakers of the variety and 'outsiders' have to the variety under discussion, and its current roles and functions in the society *vis-à-vis* other languages spoken in the community. Each of the chapters in Part B also provides spoken and written examples of the relevant variety in real use, including, where appropriate, samples from literature written in the variety. Examples which are spoken or read by speakers of their respective varieties can be heard on the accompanying CD, allowing readers to listen to how these different varieties actually sound in real life. Transcripts of the recordings are provided in the appendix.

It would be impossible to include all the current varieties of English. I have chosen to start with a description of three so-called native speaker varieties – British, American and Australian – and then describe varieties from the Indian subcontinent, Africa and from East and South-East Asia. As the reader will discover, all these varieties themselves represent a range of different varieties, so that British English, for example, is actually a range of British Englishes. I have also included a description of English when it is used as a *lingua franca* and considered its role as a *lingua franca* in Europe.

Part C considers the controversies and debates associated with the emergence of new varieties of English and their existence alongside more established varieties. Issues that are covered here include the question of which model or variety of English is the most appropriate for which context. The relative roles of native and non-native speaker teachers are considered and the recognition of the importance of multilingual and multicultural ELT teachers is stressed.

Five key themes underpin the book:

(a) that variation is natural, normal and continuous – and that ELT professionals must establish a tolerance and understanding of variation;

(b) that, while prejudice against varieties is likely to occur, these prejudices are simply that – prejudices;

(c) that the differences between all varieties, both native and nativised, are similar and comparable;

English that was a truly mongrel language, made up of a mixture of Latin, Greek, French, Germanic and Anglo-Saxon forms.

If it is difficult to find rational criteria for classifying varieties of English as native; it is easier to classify them as nativised. I suggest that the difference between varieties of English can be explained by the fact that they are all nativised. By a nativised variety I therefore mean a variety that has been influenced by the local cultures and languages of the people who have developed the particular variety. Other terms for this phenomenon include acculturation and indigenisation. A nativised, accultured or indigenised variety of English is thus one that has been influenced by the local cultures in which it has developed. By this definition all varieties of English that are spoken by an identifiable speech community are nativised. Thus, varieties of British English are as nativised as varieties of Philippino English.

The distinction between native and nativised varieties can become important, however, in contexts where a so-called native variety, such as British or English, is set against a so-called nativised variety, such as Malaysian English. In the context of English language teaching, some people may argue that British English provides a better model than Malaysian English because it represents 'proper' English. But it is important to remember that both these varieties are nativised in the sense that they reflect their own cultures. The Malaysian variety of English is different from the British variety precisely because it reflects local cultures. The British variety is different from the Malaysian variety because it reflects British culture. So, if people choose British English as the model, they are also, wittingly or unwittingly, allowing British culture to seep into their learning of English.

I shall consider the issues surrounding the question of which variety to choose for language teaching in specific contexts in Part C. But I want to stress here that there is no need to worry if you feel that you speak a nativised variety and therefore the variety you speak is somehow worse and less pure than the 'native' variety spoken by someone else. It isn't. All varieties are nativised. By the same token, there is no justification in assuming that the 'native' variety you speak is somehow better and purer than the nativised variety spoken by someone else. It isn't. By the definition adopted here, you also speak a nativised variety.

This leaves the definition of English as a Lingua Franca (ELF). A *lingua franca* is the common language used by people of different language backgrounds to communicate with each other. *Lingua francas* can be used both within countries and internationally. In Indonesia, the national language, *Bahasa Indonesia*, is used as a national *lingua franca* to provide the many different peoples of Indonesia with a common language in which to communicate with each other. In China, Mandarin or *Putonghua*, the 'common language', is used as a *lingua franca* to allow speakers of different Chinese dialects to communicate with each other. In countries of East Africa, where many different languages are spoken, *Ki-Swahili* is used as the *lingua franca* or common language. In Part B of the book, I compare the international use of ELF within the European Community and within the Association of South-East Asian Nations (ASEAN). In both cases, people who are not born as English speakers have learned English in order to be able to communicate with other people in these communities. In the ASEAN community, therefore, a Thai and an Indonesian may choose to communicate with each other using English as their *lingua franca* or common language.

1.2   The native speaker vs the non-native speaker

Many scholars have attempted over many years to provide workable and rational distinctions between 'a native speaker' and 'a non-native speaker' and many others have argued that it is impossible to provide workable and rational distinctions between these two terms (Davies, 2003). Swales (1993) argues that it no longer makes any sense to differentiate between native and non-native speakers. White and Genesee (1996) have provided evidence to show that the linguistic ability of the near-native speaker is indistinguishable from the linguistic ability of the native speaker. Medgyes, on the other hand, insists that 'the native English speaker teacher and the non-native English speaker are two different species' (1994: 27).

In the contexts of World Englishes, the real problem is caused by many people believing that native speakers are necessarily better at speaking English than non-native speakers, and that native speakers are necessarily better at teaching English than non-native speakers. In this book, I shall argue that neither of these beliefs can be supported.

Other terms are also used to try and capture the distinction between a native and a non-native speaker. Examples include 'a mother tongue speaker', 'a first language speaker' vs 'a second language speaker' vs 'a foreign language speaker'. Bloomfield (1933) defines a native language as one learned on one's mother's knee, and claims that no one is perfectly sure in a language that is acquired later. 'The first language a human being learns to speak is his native language; he is a native speaker of this language' (1933: 43). This definition equates a native speaker with a mother tongue speaker. Bloomfield's definition also assumes that age is the critical factor in language learning and that native speakers provide the best models, although he does say that, in rare instances, it is possible for a foreigner to speak as well as a native. 'One learns to understand and speak a language by hearing and imitating native speakers' (quoted in Hockett, 1970: 430).

The assumptions behind all these terms are that a person will speak the language they learn first better than languages they learn later, and that a person who learns a language later cannot speak it as well as a person who has learned the language as their first language. But it is clearly not necessarily true that the language a person learns first is the one they will always be best at, as the examples below will show. The names given are pseudonyms.

Claire was born in Sicily and migrated to Australia when she was eight. As a child she learned Sicilian as her first language/mother tongue and standard Italian as a second language. When she arrived in Australia, she started to learn English. She is now 40 and has been in Australia for more than 30 years. The language that she learned third, from the age of eight, is the language that she is now best at. Her second-best language is Standard Italian and her third is Sicilian. In other words, what was her first language and mother tongue is now a language that she does not speak as well as the other languages she speaks. She is a so-called native speaker of Sicilian but one who does not speak it well. She is a so-called non-native speaker of English, but speaks it fluently. The language she speaks best is a language that she only started to learn once she was eight. Claire is by no means an unusual example. There are many people who have what I shall call a 'shifting L1'. Indeed in immigrant communities it is common. It is also common in multilingual societies, as the following example from Nigeria shows.

A Nigerian couple are both Yoruba speakers. They have two children, both of whom are first language or mother tongue speakers of Yoruba. The family then moves to Northern Nigeria, where the dominant language is Hausa. Although the parents speak Yoruba at home, the children refuse to speak it, preferring to speak the Hausa that their school friends all speak. Like many children everywhere, they do not want to appear to be different, but want to fit in and identify with their peers at school. In addition, they learn to speak English at school, the language of education. The children then grow up speaking both Hausa and English better than they speak Yoruba. In describing their language level, does it make any sense to say that these children are native speakers of Yoruba? Does it make any sense to say they are non-native speakers of English?

Earlier I mentioned Indonesia as an example of a multilingual nation that has adopted the use of Bahasa Indonesia as its national language and *lingua franca*. There are literally millions of people in Indonesia who have grown up with a particular mother tongue, be it Bugis or Javanese or Balinese, and then learned Bahasa Indonesia at school. They have then travelled from their home villages into towns in different parts of Indonesia – for education, for marriage or, most commonly, in search of work – and Bahasa Indonesia has become the language that they are best at. They represent common examples of people with shifting L1s.

A reason why all these terms now appear unsatisfactory may be that they were coined by linguists who grew up in monolingual societies where both parents and the community as a whole all spoke the same language. They assumed that these societies represented the norm and that other languages were 'foreign' languages that you might need to learn if you travelled overseas. Indeed, Bloomfield's work on language teaching (see Hockett, 1970: 426–38) was aimed at the teaching of foreign languages to the American military where native speakers of these foreign languages, known as 'informants', were used alongside American instructors. Interestingly, this model still operates in Japan, where native-speaking Americans and others work with Japanese English language teachers in the classroom in an attempt to get Japanese learners to produce American English.

In fact, however, monolingual societies are less common than multilingual societies, where the concepts 'native' speaker and 'mother tongue' speaker make little sense as people find it very difficult to answer the apparently simple question, 'What is your mother tongue?' A good example of someone who found this question impossible to answer is Jane, who grew up in Brunei, the daughter of two Chinese migrants. As a child she learned two Chinese dialects (Hakka and Fuzhou, literally her mother tongue) from her parents, Mandarin from a special Chinese school and family friends, and English and Malay at school. She is now in her thirties and says that English is her best language, with Malay and Mandarin vying for second place. She has forgotten most of her Fuzhou and Hakka.

Another problem with the term 'native speaker' crops up with bilingual children. Can, for example, a bilingual child be a native speaker of two languages? Davies defines full bilingualism as the acquisition of 'linguistic and communicative competence in two or more languages' (1991: 98). But linguistic and communicative competence are both hard to define. As Davies says, a native-speaking speaker of English from England may lack communicative competence in Australia. I would add that a native speaker of English who had lived all his life in the south of England might lack communicative competence in the north of England. I would also add that these speakers may not possess the rules of linguistic competence in these situations either. English speakers brought up in London will not know the linguistic rules of the Australian variety of English. There is no reason why they should know the communicative and linguistic rules specific to the varieties of English that are not their own.

For the purposes of this book, the terms 'native speaker' or 'mother tongue speaker' are not precise enough to be helpful. Indeed, as they are often associated with relative competence, they can be prejudicial. For example, government officials, owners of language schools and students often say they want native speakers of English, as they feel these people are better teachers and provide better models. As a result, untrained people can potentially be employed as English language teachers ahead of well-trained and competent local teachers solely on the grounds that they are native speakers.

In the context of World Englishes, therefore, these terms should be avoided. A possible option is to use the term 'L1' or 'first language', but in the sense of the language that the speaker is most proficient in and not in the sense of the language that the speaker learned first. Rampton (1990) has suggested the term 'expert user'. This is a useful term in that expertise can be assigned to distinct categories. A person might be an expert speaker but a poor writer, for example. In the context of language teaching, Cook (1999) has proposed that we should use successful L2 learners rather than native speakers as models for the L2 learner. I shall return to these notions of native speakers, non-native speakers and expert users in Part C when I consider the implications of World Englishes for language teaching and international communication.

1.3   The functions of language and the 'identity–communication continuum'

A recurrent point that will be made in this book is that people are normally able to speak more than one variety of a language and will choose the variety they speak depending on the context in which they find themselves and the functions they want the variety to perform. Language has three major functions. The first is communication – people use language to communicate with one another. The second is identity – people use language to signal to other people who they are and what group(s) they belong to. The third, which is closely related to identity, is culture – people use language to express their culture.

Each of these functions may require a different variety or register and these functions may, at times, be at odds with each other. For example, the communicative function will often require the diminishing of the identity function. Conversely, when identity is the primary function of language use, the variety chosen by the speaker may not be intelligible to speakers outside that particular group. As Crystal has pointed out, 'the two functions can be seen as complementary, responding to different needs' (2003: 22). I shall give a number of examples of this in Part B so here I will give only one. Let us imagine that an Australian businessman travels to Singapore to talk to his counterparts there. It is likely that the major function that he will want his language to fulfil is the communicative function. He will then take care to edit out specific Australianisms from his speech and try to make his accent sound less 'Australian', so that his Singaporean colleagues can understand what he says. Now let us imagine that the Australian's mobile phone rings and it is his son calling from their home in Australia. It is very likely that the identity and cultural functions of language will become more important. This will mean that, when speaking to his son, the Australian will use far more Australian-specific vocabulary and cultural references and that his accent will immediately sound more Australian.

It is important to understand how these functions of language influence the type of language we use. People who complain, for example, that Singaporeans who speak Singlish do not speak proper English fail to understand that language serves these different functions and that the variety of language spoken will differ depending on the function it is serving. When Singaporeans are together and talking about something local that is culturally important to them – let's say food, for example – it is only natural that the variety of English that they choose will be a broad, informal variety as it is this variety that is best at signifying identity and culture. This does not mean that these Singaporeans can only speak in this way, any more than it means an Australian or an American can only speak in a highly localised variety of English. As soon as those Singaporeans travel overseas or meet with people from different cultures in Singapore or move into a more formal setting, they will need to use language for its communicative function. Thus the Singapore English they speak will be of a more formal or educated variety.

The link between function and variety can be represented on a continuum representing two of the functions of language, called the 'identity–communication continuum' (Kirkpatrick, 2006c). I call one end of the continuum 'communication' because being intelligible and getting your meaning across is the most important aspect of the communicative function. More standard or educated varieties are likely to be better suited for communication. Broad, informal varieties or job- and class-specific registers are likely to be better suited for signifying identity. Figure 1 (overleaf) shows how the continuum works.

We can see this continuum in another way. The fewer people who are involved in an act of communication and the closer the social distance between them, the greater the identity function of their speech will be. A good example of this is families, as they often speak a sort of special language that can only be understood by other family members. On the other hand, the more people who are involved and the greater the social distance between them, the greater the intelligibility function of their speech will be in any act of communication. An example of this might be an international conference. It becomes apparent that these functions can provide a possible tension or contradiction between them. For example, using a variety that advertises a person's identity might well mean using a variety that other people

Figure 1: The identity–communication continuum

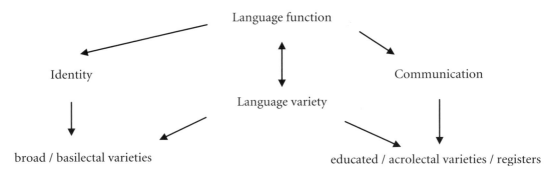

may not understand. This is common in all societies. Consider, for example, the language teenagers use, or the language of people who are particularly proud to come from a certain district, or belong to a certain profession. If they use these varieties with people outside their group, they can be impossible to understand. Of course, this may be deliberate. Some teenagers, for example, are keen to ensure that their variety is not understood by others.

To be successful, a variety of English will need to be able to fulfil each of these three functions. This means that any variety of English itself comprises a number of varieties. This may seem confusing, but it is important to understand that language variation is both normal and natural. The idea that there is some form of fixed standard of a language that everyone who speaks the language always uses in exactly the same way leads people to misunderstand how language works in real life. At an individual level there is variation, as each of us speaks our own language in our own ways. This explains why we can identify a friend who is speaking on the phone even when we cannot see them. Their pronunciation and accent is unique to them. At a functional level, we have seen how we choose a particular variety of language depending on the function we want the variety to fulfil. At a contextual level, we have seen how the situation will determine the variety or register of language we use. There is a great difference between the language people use in formal situations and the language they use in very informal situations. And consider how different the languages of poetry, preaching, joking, lecturing and swearing are. Interactional and social factors can determine why people use the variety or variation they do (Cheshire, 2003).

The different varieties of a language have been classified in various ways. For example, Australian English has been classified on a continuum with a broad variety at one end of the continuum and an educated or cultivated variety at the other. As shown in Figure 1 above, the broad variety often serves the function of identity and the educated variety the function of communication. The general variety of Australian English operates somewhere along the middle of the continuum. Other languages – Singapore English is a good example – have been similarly classified, but using the terms 'basilectal', 'mesolectal' and 'acrolectal' (Platt and Weber, 1980), corresponding to broad, general and educated respectively. In this book we shall use the terms 'broad', 'general' and 'educated', and the terms 'informal' and 'formal', rather than 'basilectal', 'mesolectal' and 'acrolectal', because the latter three terms are often equated with 'bad', 'not so bad' and 'good'. For example, some people refer disparagingly to the basilectal variety of Singapore English as Singlish. I describe Singapore English in detail in Chapter 9, so here I will simply point out that Singlish is actually the broad variety of Singapore English and, as I indicated above, is the appropriate variety to use in the right context and for the right function.

So, not only do people usually speak more than one variety of a language, all language is characterised by variation. I shall describe how this variation is realised in individual varieties of English in Part B and discuss the implications of the existence of variation for international communication and language teaching in Part C.

The reader will have noted the use of the term 'register' alongside the term 'variety' above. Register is often associated with particular types of employment. For example, lawyers will use legal register when talking about the law and doctors may use medical register when talking about medicine. In this context, register is an important marker of professional identity.

1.4   Pidgins vs creoles vs varieties of Englishes

Pidgins are languages that are born after contact between at least two other languages. As many pidgins developed during the period of empire and international trade, one of the language 'parents' was frequently a European language such as French or English, and the other language parent was the language of the people with whom the Europeans were trading or whom they were colonising. Usually one of the languages provided the majority of vocabulary items and the other provided the grammatical structure. When pidgins become learned as a mother tongue, they become known as creoles. I am not going to discuss pidgins and creoles and contact languages as such in this book in any depth. There are many excellent books on the topic that the interested reader can refer to (see Holm, 1989, 2000; Clyne, 2003). Here I want to suggest that varieties of English are not very different from pidgins and creoles. I agree with Mufwene when he says 'native Englishes, indigenised Englishes and English pidgins and creoles have all developed by the same kind of natural restructuring processes' (2001: 113). I shall argue that the main difference between them is simply one of degree. As I pointed out in 1.1 above, all varieties of English have been influenced by contact with other languages and have adopted vocabulary items from local languages. For example, 'kangaroo', 'koala' and 'boomerang' are all words of Australian English which have been taken from Australian Aboriginal languages. And, as we shall see in Part B, the linguistic structures of varieties of English can be influenced by local languages. So it is hard to provide linguistic criteria that distinguish creoles from varieties of English. Some people have suggested that intelligibility is one criterion for distinguishing between a pidgin and a variety of English and, as I shall show in Chapter 3, Widdowson (1997) argues that some varieties of English are actually different languages because they are mutually unintelligible. But intelligibility is not a reliable criterion to use because many broad varieties of English are incomprehensible to speakers of other varieties. This is sometimes true of varieties of British English. The English spoken by the people of

Newcastle, for example, is notoriously hard for other English people to understand. I look at different varieties of British English in Chapter 4. So, intelligibility is not a foolproof criterion for distinguishing between a pidgin and a variety.

In Section 1.1, I suggested prejudice as a possible explanation for making a distinction between native and nativised varieties of English. Prejudice is another possible reason why some people distinguish creoles from varieties of English. As these languages had developed from a mix of languages, pidgins and creoles were traditionally seen as inferior languages and discriminated against in the same way that children of mixed marriages have traditionally been discriminated against. Yet, we now know that all languages develop as a result of contact with other languages and the only difference is the degree of contact and influence. The description of specific varieties of English in Part B will provide evidence that all varieties of English develop following similar processes and influences.

As I have argued above that prejudice plays an important role in the way people make judgments about languages and varieties, I now discuss the notion of linguistic prejudice in more depth.

1.5   Linguistic prejudice

However much we may protest, we are all likely to be linguistically prejudiced in some way, positively or negatively. For example, research shows that speakers of so-called native speaker varieties of English are prejudiced either for or against other native speaker varieties of English. In what remains a seminal work, Giles and Powesland (1975) reviewed research into linguistic prejudice and I review two of Giles' own studies into linguistic prejudice below.

In the first study Giles investigated reactions of British school children to a variety of English accents. Children listened to a variety of accents and made judgments about the speakers. These accents included the educated accent known as Received Pronunciation or RP, and a number of rural and urban accents, including the accent of Birmingham, a city in the English Midlands. Giles discovered that people who spoke with a standard British English RP accent were considered to be the most intelligent or competent and that those who spoke with a Birmingham accent were considered to be the least intelligent. On the other hand, he discovered that people thought that those who had accents similar to their own, no matter whether these were rural or urban speakers, and sounded more like themselves were considered more honest and warmer.

A second piece of research studied people's responses to arguments given in different varieties of English. Having ascertained the attitudes towards capital punishment of a selection of 17-year-olds, arguments against capital punishment were given to them. The arguments were given as a written transcript and in four different accents. These accents were: RP; Welsh (the variety of English spoken in Wales); Somerset (a mainly rural county – province, state or prefecture – in the south-west of England); and the accent of Birmingham. As we saw above, earlier research had shown that RP was considered the most prestigious of these accents and Birmingham the least. In this study, the children considered that the arguments given in RP were more intelligent than the arguments given in the regional accents. However, they found the arguments given in regional accents were more persuasive, as only regional voices 'were effective in producing a significant shift in subjects' attitudes; the typescript and the RP guise did not' (1975: 94).

This is a fascinating result because it suggests that people can sound intelligent to other people but not necessarily be effective or persuasive in their arguments. At the same time, people who are not thought to be intelligent can be persuasive. Not even the most famous are spared. In Chapter 5, I shall discuss this in the context of the United States and here give just one example from the chapter. Before Bill Clinton became President of the United States and was Governor of the State of Arkansas a reporter asked him:

'Governor Clinton, you attended Oxford University in England and Yale Law School in the Ivy League, two of the finest institutions of learning in the world. So how come you still talk like a hillbilly?'

(Lippi-Green, 1997: 210–12)

You might stop to consider these findings in the light of your own experience. Which accent in your country do people think shows intelligence? Are there some people who speak with accents that are associated with a lack of education or sophistication?

If we think that one accent somehow sounds more or less intelligent than others, it shows we are linguistically prejudiced. And, I'm afraid to say, we all are. The fact that prejudices change provides further evidence that the preference for particular varieties over others is based on prejudice. If we take Britain as an example, there has recently been a significant change in perception of which variety is valued. The prestige of RP has been reduced, while the prestige associated with speaking a type of Black English has risen. Twenty years ago, the position was precisely the reverse. Social and cultural change is the main reason for this shift in preference and prestige.

We can see a similar trend internationally. Twenty years ago, British English was considered the prestige accent in China and the model that most students wanted to imitate. Today, American English is the variety that the majority of students want to learn (Kirkpatrick and Xu Xi, 2002). Tomorrow it may be a Chinese variety of English. We consider the implications of these preferences and prejudices in detail in Parts B and C. Here I want to stress that we cannot ignore prejudice as a fundamental cause for shaping our views about language. It is a major cause for distinguishing between a native variety of English and a nativised one, for thinking that one variety or accent of English is better than another and for thinking that pidgins and creoles are inferior in some way to other languages. In the context of World Englishes, it is important to realise the role that prejudice can play in making judgments about different varieties – and therefore about the personalities or intelligence of the speakers of those varieties – and to try and ensure that any judgments we make can be supported rationally.

I shall come back to the issues I have discussed here in Parts B and C. In Chapter 2, I move on to describe and define the key linguistic terms I shall be using in my description of the World Englishes presented in Part B.

2 **Key linguistic terms**

In this chapter, I explain to those readers who may not be familiar with basic linguistics the key linguistic terms I use in the book and give examples of the linguistic features I will be describing. I take most of the examples from British English but supplement these with examples from other varieties. These features will be considered under the separate subheadings of

2.1 Phonology and pronunciation
2.2 Vocabulary
2.3 Morphology and syntax
2.4 Cultural conventions and schemas

2.1 **Phonology and pronunciation**

I shall first describe and give examples of consonant and vowel sounds and then move on to consider stress patterns and timing. I shall use the symbols of the International Phonetic Alphabet (IPA) to indicate the consonant and vowel sounds, as the IPA is still the most frequently used system in the majority of countries represented in this book. In this section I also make reference to Received Pronunciation (RP) because, although RP is used by a small minority of speakers of a certain variety of British English, it remains a common target for learners of English. I shall argue later, however, that RP is actually both an unrealistic and inappropriate model of pronunciation for the vast majority of learners of English.

All varieties of English are notorious for being difficult to pronounce. By this people mean that it is often impossible to predict how a word will be pronounced by looking at the way it is spelt. One has sympathy for learners when confronted with words like 'rough', 'though', 'thorough', 'through' and 'cough', as each of these 'ou' vowel sounds are pronounced differently in Standard British English. And while different varieties of English have different pronunciations, this mismatch between spelling and pronunciation exists in all of them.

One major reason for this mismatch is that individual consonants and vowels can be pronounced in different ways. It is important to remember that there is a distinction between a consonant and a consonant sound and between a vowel and a vowel sound. For example 'c' is a consonant of English but it can be pronounced in different ways. The 'c' consonant of the word 'cat' is actually pronounced /k/, but in mice it is pronounced /s/. This means that there are more consonant sounds than there are consonants in English. The 'g' consonants in 'George' and 'good' provide a further example of this. The consonant sound of both the 'g' sounds in 'George' is /dʒ/, but in 'good' it is /g/.

If this is true of consonants, it is much more true of vowels. A single vowel may have a range of possible vowel sounds. Consider the vowel 'o' in the following words: 'pot', 'coke' and 'bow' (incline the head or body in a show of respect). Each 'o' is pronounced quite differently in Received Pronunciation or RP, to give /pɒt/, /koʊk/ and /baʊ/ respectively. To make it more confusing, 'bow' as in 'bow and arrow' has the same vowel sound as 'coke', /boʊ/. Also note that the apparently single vowel 'o' is pronounced as a diphthong in the words 'coke' and 'bow'. A diphthong is a sound which moves or glides from one vowel sound to another.

Varieties of English differ markedly from each other in the way they pronounce words, especially vowels. In my variety of English, the word 'poor' is pronounced /pɔː/ and the 'r' is not sounded, but in varieties of Scottish English (and others) the vowel sound is pronounced as a diphthong and the 'r' is sounded to give /pʊər/ And, as hinted at above, we have to be careful in using the term 'Received Pronunciation'. RP was originally so-called because it was the accent that children who were educated in private schools in Britain were taught to use. This was at a time when localised accents or varieties of English were considered inferior. Today, however, RP no longer carries the prestige it once did, and many more English people now proudly speak in localised accents. At the same time, the current 'non-localised accent' of British English has actually shifted away from the pronunciation of original RP, which is now referred to as 'marked RP'. So, when I refer to RP here, I am referring to an idealised or marked RP.

A well-known difference between RP and the broad variety of Australian English can be seen in the pronunciation of the words 'main' and 'mine'. In RP these are pronounced /meɪn/ and /maɪn/ respectively, while in broad Australian both sound more like /maɪn/. The broad variety of Australian English more or less dispenses with the /eɪ/ diphthong. These examples show that there are significant differences in pronunciation even between so-called native speaker varieties of English. A different pronunciation does not necessarily mean a wrong pronunciation therefore.

In RP the word 'bath' is pronounced with a long 'a' as /bɑːθ/, while in many other varieties it sounds more like /bæθ/. This brings us to the sound that probably causes learners of English more trouble than any other and that is the 'th' sound /θ/ and its voiced partner /ð/. In RP, these sounds distinguish certain noun and verb pairs so we get the voiceless nouns such as /bɑːθ/ (bath) and /maʊθ/ (mouth) and their voiced verbs /beɪð/ (bathe) and /maʊð/ (mouth). RP also has the /θ/ sound at the beginning of the words in 'thirty-three', but not all varieties of English do. For example, Irish and certain varieties of American English use sounds that are closer to a /t/ in these words. RP has /ð/ in a word like 'mother' but in other varieties the /ð/ sound is more like a /d/ sound. So I feel sorry for poor learners of English who spend hours of classroom time trying to master the RP sounds of /θ/ and /ð/, as these are difficult sounds to learn if they do not exist in your own language and, it turns out, they are not used in many varieties of English anyway. I shall discuss the implications of World Englishes for language teaching in Part C, but here will mention a valuable book by Jenkins (2000) in which she considers which sounds of English are important for non-native speakers to master and which they can happily ignore if they wish to be intelligible to fellow non-native speakers of English. A useful term in this context is 'functional load'. This defines the relative meaning-load a sound may carry. For example, it has been shown that the distinction between the two RP vowel sounds in 'hip' and 'heap' [/hɪp/ and /hiːp/ respectively] is important, as these two vowel sounds are the sole distinguishing features or difference between a large number of RP sounds. These sounds are thus said to carry a high or heavy functional load, while the contrast between the vowel sounds /ʊ/ and /uː/ as in RP 'pull' and 'pool' do not carry such a high functional load. Again we must be careful, because vowel sounds that carry high functional loads in, for example, Standard American English may well carry a lower functional load in other varieties of English.

The point I want to stress is that speaking and learning English does not necessarily mean speaking and learning RP or Standard American. There are many varieties of English and they all have their own characteristics, which include pronunciations that may be specific to them. To reiterate a theme of this book, variation is natural, common and normal.

There is no doubt that one cause of the differences in pronunciations of varieties of English is the other languages that the speakers of those varieties speak. A first language may influence the way a second language is pronounced. I shall describe these influences in Part B and here just give some examples. The first example concerns consonant clusters. The term 'consonant cluster' is used when two or more consonant sounds occur side by side. The word 'skyscraper' has two consonant clusters. The first are the /sk/ sounds at the beginning of the word and the second the /skr/ sounds in the middle of the word. Incidentally, note how the two consonants 'k' and 'c' are both pronounced /k/ here. Consonant clusters do not exist in all languages. Many languages are made up of sounds that follow a consonant–vowel–consonant–vowel (CVCV) pattern. People who speak such languages may therefore slip in a vowel sound between each consonant so that /sk/ becomes something like /səkə/ and /skr/ becomes /səkərə/. This explains why the word 'strike', which has the three-consonant sound cluster 'str', is pronounced something like /sətəraɪkə/ by Japanese speakers of English, as Japanese is a CV language.

It is important to note that many varieties of English slip in an extra vowel, usually a 'schwa' /ə/in certain contexts. For example, these occur in Irish and Australian Englishes, speakers of which may say the words 'film' and 'known' as /fɪləm/ and /noʊwən/ respectively, in contrast to RP /fɪlm/and /noʊn/.

When consonant clusters occur at the ends of words, as often happens with English past tense and plurals for example, it is possible that speakers of languages that do not have consonant clusters will simplify the endings to a single consonant sound in their varieties of English. Thus /wɔːkt/ (walked) may become /wɔːk/ (walk), or even /wɒʔ/, with a glottal stop as the final sound, and /bʊks/ (books) become /bʊk/ (book). Speakers of many native varieties of English also do this, especially when a word ending in a consonant cluster is followed by one that begins with a consonant sound, so that 'he walked to work' sounds like /hiwɔːtəwɜːk/. I discuss further examples of what I shall call 'syntactic simplification' in the section on syntax below, but it is important to bear in mind that a cause of syntactic simplification may be phonological.

Another major influence upon the pronunciation of languages is whether they are stress-timed or syllable-timed. Simply put, the difference between them is that, in syllable-timed languages, each syllable takes more or less the same amount of time to produce, while in stress-timed languages, the number of stress points determines how long it will take to say something. Thus in a syllable-timed language like French, the greeting '*Comment-allez vous?*' will tend to apportion equal stress to each syllable. But in a stress-timed language like Australian, the equivalent greeting, 'How are you going?' will stress the 'go' sound of 'going' and the other syllables will sound as though they have been swallowed by the speaker. This means that syllable-timed languages are often easier for learners of those languages to understand than stress-timed languages, because each syllable gets an equal amount of time to be said, while in stress-timed languages, syllables between stress points get shortened and vowels are often sounded as 'schwas' in these contexts. It is important to stress, however, that these differences are not absolute and it is safer to say that some languages are more stress–timed and some more syllable-timed than others. Varieties of British and American English are more stress-timed than syllable-timed, although syllable-timing does occur in special circumstances in British English, for example when people are using baby talk or showing irritation or sarcasm (Crystal, 1995).

The point to be made here is that speakers of syllable-timed languages will develop Englishes that are characterised by syllable-timing. Malaysian and Singaporean Englishes are good examples of this.

I shall conclude this small section on phonology by looking at word stress and the way different varieties place different stress patterns on the same words. Look at these two pronunciations of the word 'photographer': /fəˈtɒgrəfə/ and /ˈfoʊtoʊgræfə/. The first is the word pronounced in RP – the ˈ mark signals that the main stress is on the following syllable – and the second is as it might be pronounced in standard Singaporean. You can see significant differences in the ways this common word is pronounced in these two varieties. In RP the first, third and fourth vowel sounds are shortened to a 'schwa', which is characteristic of stress-timing. The Singaporean version, however, is more syllable-timed with each of the first three vowel sounds receiving the same amount of time and thus giving completely different vowel sounds from the RP version. There is only one vowel sound that is pronounced the same in both versions and that is the final 'schwa'. The point I wish to make is that if two varieties can differ so radically over the pronunciation of a common word like 'photographer', we can see how normal and common variation is across varieties of English. We need to expect variation and not be worried about it.

2.2 **Vocabulary**

A word in one variety of English may have a different meaning in another variety. Different varieties of English also have words that are unique to them. This is hardly surprising, as vocabulary provides ways of talking about things or concepts that are of particular importance to people of a particular culture. As an example of how a variety gives a different or special meaning to a common word, let's take the main meaning of the word 'bush' in British and Australian Englishes. In British English, a bush is a short tree or collection of plants, usually thickly covered with leaves or thorns. While it can also mean this in Australian English, 'bush' in Australian English primarily refers to the countryside as opposed to the towns. It conjures up an image of flat, rather desolate landscapes stretching as far as the eye can see and beyond, a harsh land interspersed with small low-lying bushes and scrubs. Another Australian term for this is 'the outback'. I shall further explore the meaning of 'bush' in Australian English in Part B.

'Alphabet' is another example of how a word can have one meaning in one variety of English but another meaning in another. In British English 'alphabet' refers to a system of writing. Therefore speakers of British English will say that English uses the Latin alphabet but Greek uses the Greek alphabet. In Singaporean English, however, 'alphabet' also means a single letter of the alphabet. So a Singaporean may say 'English has twenty-six alphabets'. In this context it is interesting to remember that the word 'alphabet' derives from the first two letters (if I use British English) or alphabets (if I use Singaporean English) of the Greek alphabet, *alpha* and *beta*.

There are literally hundreds of differences in the meanings of words in British and American English. For example, the different words British and American speakers use to describe parts of their cars could make you think they were talking about completely different things. In American English cars have a trunk at the back and a hood at the front. In British English, they have a boot at the back and a bonnet at the front. American cars have stick shifts, British ones have gear levers. American cars have odometers and British ones speedometers. And despite all this and despite the fact that they drive on different sides of the road, American and British car manufacturers appear quite able to sell cars in each other's countries.

Different varieties of English can also adapt words so that they suit the culture in which they are used. As I shall argue in Part B, Australian culture values informality and this gives rise to the shortening or clipping of common words in Australian English to give them a special Australian or informal flavour. For example, a politician becomes a 'pollie', a journalist a 'journo' and a refugee a 'reffo'.

The vocabularies of varieties of English are enriched by words from local languages. Englishes need these words, as they refer to local cultural practices and traditions. They also describe geographical features and the local flora and fauna. These local words are often then adopted by other varieties of English. In the Australian context, the contribution to Australian English made by Australian Aboriginal languages is immense. Perhaps the three words that most evoke the image of Australia are *kangaroo*, *koala* and *boomerang* and these all come from Aboriginal languages. These words have now become understood by speakers of many other varieties of English.

All varieties of English will have borrowed words from local languages in this way to describe local phenomena. So Malaysian English has *sarong* (a type of wrap-round skirt, but one that is worn by both men and women), *laksa* (a spicy coconut-based noodle soup dish) and *kiasu* (used to describe people who put their own interests ahead of everyone else's).

The adoption of words from one language by another is a common phenomenon. It is not necessary for there to be a local variety of English for this to happen, although when a local variety of English does develop, these words will be part of it. For example, the 'English' words *kimono, judo, sumo, karaoke, sushi, sashimi* and *sake* are all originally Japanese words. Many Japanese words that are currently common in many varieties of English will obviously become part of a Japanese variety of English, as it develops. These will be supplemented by many others.

To summarise, different varieties of English will adopt many different words from local languages to describe local phenomena of one sort or another. They will also give different meanings to familiar words and they will also alter familiar words so that they suit the culture of their speakers. These different usages of vocabulary can cause misunderstanding among people who speak different varieties of English, precisely because they reflect local cultures and contexts. But without them, a variety of English could not survive. Words provide a language or variety with its cultural foundation.

2.3   Morphology and syntax

The way people pronounce their variety of English and the words they use are the two most obvious features of any variety. However, varieties also differ in the way they use grammar. I shall provide many examples of these differences in Part B and here just consider number and tense, and illustrate some differences in the way these are used. The way English marks number and tense is through inflection of one sort or another. That is to say, the form of the word changes to indicate either tense or number. So, in English we usually make a plural of a noun by adding an '-s', so the plural of 'book' becomes 'books'. Tense is a part of the inflectional system of English. The verb 'work' takes the past tense '-ed' inflection to become 'worked'. While tense may appear an extremely complex topic, at its simplest level it refers to the way languages signal time by changing the form of the verb. In some languages, including Chinese, the form of the word does not change and there is no inflection. The form of the word always stays the same. By definition, therefore, such languages do not have a tense system. Instead, they use different ways of signalling time. Often they use adverbs of time such as 'yesterday' or 'next year' to show when the action being described takes place.

In English, inflection can also change the part of speech of a word. For example, the noun 'beauty' becomes the adjective 'beautiful' by adding an ending '-ful'. Similarly, 'beauty' can be changed or inflected to give a verb 'beautify', and adverb 'beautifully'.

While, in general terms, we can say that English has tense and uses inflection, the use of inflection in English has reduced slowly over centuries. For example, the inflectional system of the present tense was more complex than today's. There was a second person singular inflection '-est' and the third person singular inflection was '-eth'. There was also a second person singular pronoun 'thou', so today's 'you make' was 'thou makest'. Both the second person singular pronoun and the inflectional endings '-est' and '-eth' have disappeared from most modern varieties of English. English has therefore slowly simplified its system of inflection over the centuries. This is an example of diachronic change, or change that has taken place over a long period of time, and suggests that a process of syntactic simplification is taking place.

On the other hand, the variety of English spoken in Yorkshire, a county in the northwest of England, still retains the more complex system of inflection and the use of 'thou' as a second person singular pronoun. For example, 'Have you seen him?' becomes 'Hast thou seen him?' Similarly, 'Where'st thou bin?' (Where hast thou been?) is the Yorkshire English version of 'Where've you been?' (Where have you been?).

Another example of this diachronic change of syntactic simplification is that some irregularities slowly get dropped. For example, the regular way of making the simple past of a verb in English is to add the '-ed' inflection. But there are many irregular past tense endings. There is 'ran' not 'runned' and 'sat' not 'sitted', to give just two examples. But, centuries ago, the past tense of 'work' was also irregular. It was 'wrought'. This use still occurs in the phrase 'wrought iron' which simply means 'worked iron'. While many irregular past tense forms still exist, there is evidence that they have slowly been disappearing over time. This will be further explored in Chapter 4.

Changes are still taking place at the moment and these are examples of synchronic change. As a possible example of synchronic change, varieties of English that are developing among speakers whose own languages do not have tense or inflection might develop a simpler system of tense and inflection than traditional Englishes. For example, we might predict that such varieties of English would lose the '-s' present tense third person singular inflection. In other words, in the same way that most varieties of English have dropped the inflections '-est' and '-eth', so these varieties might drop the '-s' third person present tense inflection but in a much shorter period of time. As I mentioned earlier, one cause of this simplification might be phonological. Speakers simply find it hard to pronounce these inflections when they occur as consonant clusters. In Part B, I shall use examples of syntactic change in specific varieties of English to test the prediction that new varieties will introduce synchronic changes relatively quickly and consider whether these synchronic changes mirror and are of the same type as the slower diachronic changes.

There are also differences in the ways tenses are used across varieties. A common difference between American English and British English is that, in certain contexts, American speakers may use the simple past while British speakers will use the present perfect. For example, 'Have you bought that car yet?' is common in Standard British English, but 'Did you buy that car yet?' is acceptable in Standard American English.

A common feature of Indian English is the use of the present continuous or progressive in contexts where British English would use the present simple. So an Indian speaker might say 'I am knowing very well . . .' in a context where a British speaker might say 'I know very well'. This is probably caused by influence from the Indian speaker's first language, as 'the form of the present progressive tense in English is the same as the form of the simple present tense in Punjabi, except for the order' (Jackson, 1981: 201).

2.4 Cultural conventions and schemas

There are a large number of terms that are used to describe the way language is used in real situations. These include 'pragmatic norms', 'rhetorical structures', 'text structures', 'schema', 'scripts', 'discourse', 'cultural conventions', 'cultural norms' and so forth. I shall use the terms 'cultural conventions' and 'schemas'. Cultural conventions are cultural routines. For example, the way people greet and address each other can be considered a cultural convention. These cultural conventions have fairly predictable sequences. That is to say they follow a predictable schema. I shall also use the term 'schema' to refer to the way longer pieces of extended discourse are constructed and sequenced.

The word 'schema' is itself an example of a word being adopted from one language by another with a consequent change of meaning. In its general sense it now means something like diagram or plan. It is also used as a special term in philosophy and psychology. The English scholar Bartlett used it in a special sense to describe the way people remember things:

> Schema refers to an active organisation of past reactions, or of past experiences, which must always be supposed to be operating in any well-adapted organic response. That is, whenever there is any order or regularity of behaviour, a particular response is possible only because it is related to similar responses which have been serially organised, yet, which operate, not simply as individual members coming one after another, but as a unitary mass.
>
> (Bartlett, 1932: 201)

Linguists have built on this meaning and divided schemas into content and formal schemas, where formal schemas are the rhetorical structures of texts (Carrell and Eisterhold, 1988).

There is also a sense of grammatical insecurity or indecision about what the plural of 'schema' is. It is originally a Greek word and, following Greek rules of number, its plural would be *schemata*. However, the number rules for English say add an '-s' to form a plural. So people are unsure whether the plural should be 'schemata' or 'schemas'. In my view, it does not matter a great deal, but in the spirit of the nativisation of Englishes, I shall use 'schemas' as the plural form.

I shall now first consider two examples of cultural conventions, greeting and addressing, and then provide examples of schemas. The ways people greet each other in British, American and Australian English respectively may differ in remarkable ways.

BrE	How are you?	Fine thanks.
AmE	How are you doing?	(Just) great (thanks).
AusE	How are you going?	Good thanks.

While there are many other ways of greeting, especially in informal situations in these three varieties, it is interesting to note the significant differences in these 'standard' greetings and responses. British English contents itself with a simple 'How are you?', while American and Australian Englishes add a verb, 'doing' and 'going' respectively. The standard reply in British English is with the adjective 'fine' plus 'thanks'. Australian also uses an adjective, but a different one, although we might expect an adverb given the inclusion of the verb 'going'. These differences may cause misunderstanding when people move from one culture to another and greetings may not be immediately recognised as such. For example, British people who move to live in Australia can be confused by being asked 'How are you going?' by an Australian, as, in certain contexts, a sensible answer might well be to say 'By bus'.

There are, of course, many other ways of greeting in all three varieties. The type of greeting a person chooses will depend on context including the type of people involved and the relationships between them. I just use this example to underline again how common and normal variation is.

In certain Asian cultures it is customary to greet people by asking the equivalent of 'Where are you going?' or 'Have you eaten?' Perhaps these cultural conventions will be reflected in new varieties of English in Asia to produce 'Have you eaten?' as a normal greeting.

As a second example I shall briefly describe forms of address in Australian academic culture and consider how these might differ from forms of address in American academic culture. Simply put, most Australian students will address their lecturers by their first names. This is true even when a first year (or freshman in American English) addresses a senior academic. It is not considered impolite for students to call his or her lecturers by their first names as long as the lecturers themselves have indicated that this is OK.

In American academic culture, on the other hand, it is normal for students to address academic staff by title and family name. Thus, American students in Australia might feel uncomfortable about addressing their lecturers by their first names even though they knew this was acceptable in Australian culture, as this form of address would violate their own American cultural norms. Li has termed this sense of discomfort felt by a speaker when using language that is appropriate in one language or variety but that violates the rules in the speaker's own language or variety 'pragmatic dissonance' (Li, 2002a: 559ff.).

These two examples show how cultural conventions differ and how these differences are reflected in the respective varieties of English. In Part B, I shall provide more examples of how cultural conventions are reflected in specific varieties of English and how differences in these can lead to misunderstanding or a sense of pragmatic dissonance.

As an example of a schema, look at this excerpt of a conversation that took place between an expatriate police officer and a Chinese police constable. It comes from data collected as part of a survey into the communicative needs of the Hong Kong police in which I was involved in the days when Hong Kong was a British colony. EO is the expatriate (English) officer and CPC the Chinese police constable:

CPC: My mother is not well, sir.
EO: So?
CPC: She has to go into hospital.
EO: Well?
CPC: On Thursday, sir.

The interesting point is that, although the Chinese speaker is speaking excellent English, the English officer appears not to understand him. Leaving aside the distinct possibility that the English officer is being deliberately unhelpful, the reason for the misunderstanding is that the Chinese speaker, while speaking standard English in terms of grammar, is using Chinese cultural norms and these influence the schema he adopts. The reason for his visit to see his boss is to obtain some leave in order to attend to his sick mother. He is therefore making a request, and it is normal in a context such as this for a Chinese to justify and explain the reasons for the request before actually making it. Actually he is probably hoping that his boss will realise what he wants and offer this before he has to ask for it. In British English, however, it would be more usual to start with the request in this context and then give reasons if required. So, the 'English' request schema would give:

CPC: Could I take a day off please?
EO: Why?
CPC: My mother is not well . . .

Indeed this is the pattern that the English officer said he preferred and that he wanted people to use when coming to see him. However, let me stress that I am **not** suggesting that there is only one way of making a request in Chinese and English in this context and that their respective ways of doing it are different. This is simply not the case, as variation is as normal in discourse as it is in accent, vocabulary and grammar. The point I do want to draw attention to is that a speaker's cultural background will influence their variety of English as much as their linguistic background. Varieties of English reflect the cultural conventions and norms of their speakers and these are mirrored in the schemas they use. So a Chinese variety of English might prefer a request schema that placed reasons for a request before the request itself.

The use of schemas that are appropriate in one culture but inappropriate or unusual when transferred into another can lead to misunderstanding. In the example above, the English officer became exasperated because he felt the Chinese speaker couldn't or wouldn't come to the point. He then made a judgment about the speaker's personality and felt that he was too deferential. So the English officer made an incorrect judgment about the Chinese speaker's personality based on the way the Chinese speaker was using English. The Chinese speaker's transfer of a schema that was culturally appropriate to him led to him being incorrectly judged by the English speaker. I shall consider further examples of this in Part B.

Conclusion

In this chapter I have given examples of the ways varieties of English can differ. It is clear that there is wide variation between varieties and, as we saw in Chapter 1, there is also variation within varieties. The most obvious differences between varieties are in pronunciation and vocabulary, but there are also significant differences in syntax and grammar. These differences are obvious and immediately noticeable and I will argue that they are only likely to cause temporary misunderstandings.

More importantly, varieties reflect the cultures of their speakers and this is another cause of difference between varieties, as the ways cultural norms are expressed thus differ across varieties. This is why the way people present information may differ and why they will use different schemas. Differences in schemas are much less obvious than differences in pronunciation, vocabulary and grammar and, as the example above shows, may lead to misunderstanding or impatience. I will argue that variation in schemas may therefore lead to more serious misunderstandings among speakers of different varieties of English than differences in pronunciation, vocabulary and grammar.

In the next chapter I shall discuss and compare different models of World Englishes.

3 Models of World Englishes

In this chapter I shall first describe and discuss the classifications or models of World Englishes that have been proposed by certain scholars. These classifications attempt to explain the differences in the ways English is used in different countries. I shall then summarise the stages through which a new variety may proceed on its way to becoming an established variety. These stages or developmental cycles are frequently linked to classifications and models and it is sometimes hard to separate them. Finally, I shall consider the ideological and political standpoints taken by different scholars, with a particular emphasis on the debate over whether the speakers themselves choose to use English or whether they have that choice thrust upon them.

3.1 Models

Perhaps the most common classification of Englishes, especially in the language teaching world, has been to distinguish between English as a native language (ENL), English as a second language (ESL) and English as a foreign language (EFL).

In this classification, ENL is spoken in countries where English is the primary language of the great majority of the population. Australia, Canada, New Zealand, the United Kingdom and the United States are countries in which English is said to be spoken and used as a native language.

In contrast, ESL is spoken in countries where English is an important and usually official language, but not the main language of the country. These countries are typically ex-colonies of the United Kingdom or the United States. Nigeria, India, Malaysia and the Philippines are examples of countries in which English is said to be spoken and used as a second language.

The final classification of this model is EFL. EFL occurs in countries where English is not actually used or spoken very much in the normal course of daily life. In these countries, English is typically learned at school, but students have little opportunity to use English outside the classroom and therefore little motivation to learn English. China, Indonesia, Japan and many countries in the Middle East are countries in which English is said to operate as an EFL.

This ENL/ESL/EFL distinction has been helpful in certain contexts. There is no doubt, for example, that the motivation to learn English is likely to be far greater in countries where English plays an institutional or official role than in countries where students are unlikely to hear any English outside the classroom or ever need to use it. This classification, however, has shortcomings. One is that the term 'native language' is open to misunderstanding. As speakers in ENL countries are described as native speakers, people feel that the variety used is a standard variety that is spoken by **all** of the people. People then feel that ENL is innately superior to ESL and EFL varieties and that it therefore represents a good model of English for people in ESL and EFL countries to follow. In actual fact, however, many different varieties of English are spoken in ENL countries. The idea that everyone speaks the same 'standard model' is simply incorrect. Second, the suggestion to use ENL as 'the model' ignores the fact that such a model might be inappropriate in ESL countries where the local variety would be a more acceptable model, as there are many fluent speakers and expert users of that particular variety.

A second shortcoming of the classification is that the spread of English also means that it is more difficult to find countries that can be accurately classified as EFL countries. As we shall see, English is playing an increasing role in EFL countries such as China and Japan. The ESL vs EFL distinction appears to be more valid when applied to the contrast between city and countryside. City dwellers in both ESL and EFL countries have far more opportunity and need to use English than their rural counterparts. Furthermore, ESL varieties are said to operate in countries that were once colonies of Britain or America, but, as I shall show below, the type of colony has influenced the current roles of English in such countries.

An alternative and influential classification has been put forward by Kachru (1985). This is the 'three circles' model. You will note from the following quote that Kachru refers to the ESL/EFL classification.

> The current sociolinguistic profile of English may be viewed in terms of three concentric circles . . . The Inner Circle refers to the traditional cultural and linguistic bases of English. The Outer Circle represents the institutionalised non-native varieties (ESL) in the regions that have passed through extended periods of colonisation . . . The Expanding Circle includes the regions where the performance varieties of the language are used essentially in EFL contexts.
>
> (Kachru, 1985: 366–7)

Countries in the Inner Circle include the USA and the UK. Countries in the Outer Circle include Bangladesh, Ghana and the Philippines. Countries listed as being in the Expanding Circle include China, Egypt and Korea.

The great advantages of this model over the ENL/ESL/EFL one are, first, that it makes English plural so that **one** English becomes **many** Englishes. Second, the model does not suggest that one variety is any better, linguistically speaking, than any other. The spread of English has resulted in the development of many Englishes and not the transplanting of one model to other countries: '. . . English now has multicultural identities' (Kachru, 1985: 357).

Kachru first proposed this classification in 1985 and it has occasioned great debate. I shall consider the debate and the implications of the 'three circles' model for language teaching and international communication in more detail in Part C. Here I shall just make two observations about the model. The first observation is about the use of the term 'colony' and the second is about how expanding circle countries are increasing their use of English.

First, as Mufwene (2001) has elegantly argued, the **type** of colony a nation was has influenced the way English developed there, although the developmental processes that each variety went through were similar. Mufwene distinguishes between 'trade colonies', 'exploitation colonies' and 'settlement colonies' (2001: 8–9). Contact in trade colonies started with European traders and local people. This contact typically led to the development of pidgins. The language varieties that the European traders spoke would have been non-standard varieties. As these trade colonies became exploitation colonies, they came under the administrative and political control of the respective European nation. Contact between local and imported languages increased. In the case of many British colonies, for example, the colonisers needed people who could speak English to help administer the colony. They recruited these administrators from three main sources. First, they sent their own people to act in senior positions. Second, they imported administrators from other colonies. Much of the Burmese civil service of the time was staffed by Indian clerks, for example – indeed the Burmese word for chair is '*kalathain*' and this literally means 'foreigner-sit'. Foreigners to the Burmese were Indians. Third, the colonisers trained locals as administrators and this necessitated the establishment of special schools where English became the medium of instruction. In such contexts, the variety of English developed through contact with local and other languages and through contact with non-standard and 'school' varieties of English.

In settlement colonies, on the other hand, there was less need to import administrators from other colonies, as the colonisers provided the great majority of the settlers. These settlers, however, brought with them a wide range of varieties. A difference between the Englishes which developed in settlement as opposed to exploitation colonies is the relatively small influence local languages had on the Englishes of the settlers. This is not to say that there was no contact and no influence. In the settlement colony of Australia, for example, local languages provided a wide range of culturally and geographically specific vocabulary items. The comparative lack of contact with local languages, however, meant that there was relatively little influence on the grammar and schemas of the variety as it developed. Interestingly, as I shall show in Part B, the grammatical and schematic influences of local languages are reflected in the variety spoken by the indigenous people, Australian Aboriginal English.

In short, in exploitation colonies such as India and Malaysia, the influence of local languages and cultures was greater in the development of the local English varieties. In settlement colonies such as Australia and New Zealand, the same influences were seen in the development of the local variety of English, but to a lesser extent. The difference was in the degree of influence rather than in the type of influence.

The second observation about Kachru's 'three circles' model is that it underestimated the roles that English would come to play in Expanding Circle countries, although the term 'expanding circle' suggests that the roles of English would develop in these countries. If we take China as an example of an expanding circle country, the increasing roles of English are remarkable. Here I shall mention just three. First, it is now being used in education. The number of people learning English in China is now greater than the combined populations of the inner circle countries. In other words, there are more people learning English in China than the combined populations of countries such as the United States, the United Kingdom, Canada and Australia. Startling as this figure is, it is not as significant as the role English is beginning to play in formal education. Several Chinese schools and universities now offer courses through the medium of English. In other words, Chinese students are now beginning to be able to study **in** English.

A second area in which English is playing an increasing role within China is as a *lingua franca*. China's increase in international trade and contact means that English is becoming the *lingua franca* of business and trade in China itself. Businessmen from Asia conduct business meetings in China in English. Third, the increased use of computer technology has increased the use of English in computer mediated communication. This is not restricted to international communication. Some Chinese are now choosing to use English when sending emails to each other. I shall argue in Part B that the increased role of English in this Expanding Circle country is leading to the development of a local Chinese variety of English.

To return to the discussion of models, Gupta (1997: 147–58) has proposed a classification system that divides English use into five different categories: 'monolingual ancestral', such as in Britain and the USA; 'monolingual contact', such as in Jamaica; 'monolingual scholastic', such as in India; 'multilingual contact', such as in Singapore; and 'multilingual ancestral', such as in South Africa.

Other scholars, including Görlach and Strevens have suggested other models. These are well summarised in McArthur (1998), where he also describes his own 'Circle Model of World English' (1998: 97). A particularly useful summary of approaches to the study of World Englishes is provided by Bolton (2003: 42–3).

There is a close link between these models of English and the developmental cycles of these Englishes and I now turn to considering these.

3.2   Developmental cycles

As I mentioned in Chapter 1, there is a close relationship between the development of pidgins and creoles and varieties of English. Here I shall focus solely on developmental cycles as applied to varieties of English, although it should be stressed that these cycles are often comparable to pidgin and creole developmental cycles.

Many scholars have suggested the phases or processes through which varieties of English go. I shall not review all of these here, but consider three main proposals and refer to others. The reader will note that scholars agree in many areas and that many of the phases identified by one scholar mirror those of another. There are also a number of different terms that refer to the same idea. For example the terms 'exonormative model', 'transported variety' and 'imported variety' refer to the English spoken by the settlers that arrived in a particular country. It is called 'exonormative' because the model originates from outside the place where it is spoken. This is contrasted with an 'endonormative model', that is, a locally grown variety. 'Transported' or 'imported' varieties obviously refer to the varieties spoken by the settlers, as opposed to the varieties spoken by the locals, which are referred to as 'nativised' or 'indigenised' or 'acculturated'. I have argued in Chapter 1 that all varieties are actually nativised in the sense that they all reflect the local cultures of their speakers. This term is also used, however, to distinguish the local variety from the transported variety. The process through which an imported variety goes on its way to becoming a local variety is variously referred to as 'nativisation', 'indigenisation', or a combination of 'deculturation' (of the imported variety, as it loses its original cultural roots) and 'acculturation' (of the local variety, as it grows new cultural roots).

Kachru has suggested three phases through which 'non-native institutionalised varieties of English seem to pass' (1992b: 56). The first phase is characterised by 'non-recognition' of the local variety. At this stage the speakers of the local variety are prejudiced against it and believe that some imported native speaker variety is superior and should be the model for language learning in schools. They themselves will strive to speak the imported, exonormative variety and sound like native speakers, while looking down upon those who speak only the local variety.

The second phase sees the existence of the local and imported variety existing side by side. The local variety is now used in a wide number of situations and for a wide range of purposes but is still considered inferior to the imported model.

During the third phase, the local variety becomes recognised as the norm and becomes socially accepted. The local variety becomes the model for language learning in schools. In places where the local variety has become accepted, local people who continue to speak the imported variety can be seen as outsiders or as behaving unnaturally in some way.

Moag (1992: 233–52) studied the development of a particular variety – Fijian English – and proposed a 'life cycle of non-native Englishes'. He identified five processes, four of which are undergone by all varieties, and a fifth which may only be experienced by some. The first process he called 'transportation'. This is when English arrives in a place where it has not been spoken before and remains to stay. The second process, 'indigenisation', is a relatively long phase during which the new variety of English starts to reflect the local culture and becomes different from the transported variety. The third process, the 'expansion in use' phase, sees the new variety being used in an increasing number of situations and for more and more purposes. This process is also marked by an increase in variation within the local variety. The local variety becomes the local varieties. The fourth phase is marked by the use of the local variety as a language learning model in school. During this phase, local literature in the new variety will be written. Moag calls this fourth phase 'institutionalisation'. The fifth and final phase sees a decline in use. He suggests that the Philippines and Malaysia are examples of countries where the increased official promotion of a local language – Tagalog in the Philippines and Malay in Malaysia – results in a decline in the use of the local variety of English. He wonders whether this decline in use might lead to the eventual death of English in these countries, but there is no evidence of that happening. In fact, in the Malaysian context, there has recently been an officially approved and promoted increase in the uses of English.

A more recent and detailed theory for the development of new Englishes comes from Schneider (2003a: 233–81). I call it a theory as Schneider hopes, albeit cautiously, that, 'in principle, it should be possible to apply the model to most, ideally all of the Englishes around the globe' (2003a: 256).

He agrees with Mufwene (2001) in arguing that 'postcolonial Englishes follow a fundamentally uniform developmental process' (2003a: 233). He identifies five phases in this developmental cycle. The first phase he calls the 'foundation' phase. This is when English begins to be used in a country where, previously, English was not spoken. This is typically because English speakers settle in the country.

The second phase he calls 'exonormative stabilisation'. This means that the variety spoken is closely modelled on the variety imported by the settlers. Schneider does distinguish, however, between the variety spoken by the settlers – which he calls the STL strand – and the variety spoken by the local or indigenous people – which he calls the IDG strand. Schneider argues that this phase sees the slow movement of the STL variety towards the local variety and the beginning of the expansion of the IDG variety. He argues that 'what happens during this phase may not be unlike the early stages of some routes leading to creolisation' (2003a: 246).

The third phase is the 'nativisation' phase and Schneider considers this to be the most important and dynamic phase. It sees the establishment of a new identity with the coupling of the imported STL and local IDG varieties. This phase 'results in the heaviest effects on the restructuring of the English language itself' (2003a: 248), although the restructuring occurs mostly at the level of vocabulary and grammar.

Phase four is the phase of 'endonormative stabilisation', which is when the new variety becomes gradually accepted as the local norm or model. At this stage the local variety is used in a range of formal situations.

Schneider calls the fifth and final phase 'differentiation'. At this stage the new variety has emerged and this new variety reflects local identity and culture. It is also at this stage that more local varieties develop. For example, Schneider suggests that differences between STL and IDG varieties resurface as markers of ethnic identity.

All three scholars have suggested developmental cycles that have their similarities. These can be seen in Figure 2. Basically, the variety spoken by the settlers becomes changed over time through contact with local languages and cultures. The new indigenous variety is initially considered inferior to the original imported one, but gradually it becomes accepted and the institutionalised. Once it is accepted and institutionalised, it then develops new varieties.

All three scholars are really addressing the processes that occur in postcolonial societies. But it is possible that new varieties are also developing in what Kachru termed 'expanding circle' countries, where, by definition, there has been no significant settlement of English speakers. It would appear that, in certain circumstances, expanding circle countries can develop their own Englishes without going through the first 'transportation' or 'foundation' phases.

Figure 2: Developmental cycles of new varieties of English

Scholar	Phases				
Kachru	1 non-recognition	2 co-existence of local and imported varieties	3 recognition		
Moag	1 transportation	2 indigenisation	3 expansion in use	4 institutionalisation	5 (decline)
Schneider	1 foundation	2 exonormative stabilisation	3 nativisation	4 endonormative stabilisation	5 differentiation

The great majority of non-Chinese English speakers in China, for example, are people from the Asian region for whom English is not a first language but who use English in China as a *lingua franca*. And, while an exonormative variety is promoted as a model by the Ministry of Education, the sheer scale of the English language learning enterprise means that speakers of exonormative inner-circle models are heard only by the tiniest fraction of Chinese learners of English. The overwhelming majority of learners are being taught by Chinese teachers; and those Chinese learners who are interacting in English with non-Chinese are, in the main, interacting with people from other expanding-circle countries. As I shall argue in Part C, the increasingly common phenomenon of local teachers + intranational *lingua franca* use is providing an alternative process for the development of new varieties of English.

A slightly different way of looking at the development of Englishes has been proposed by Widdowson (1997, 2003). While agreeing that 'the very fact that English is an international language means that no nation can have custody over it' (2003: 43), Widdowson makes an important distinction between the spread of English and the distribution of English. He argues that English is not so much *distributed* as a set of established encoded forms, unchanged into different domains of use, but rather that it is *spread,* as a virtual language. He sees the two processes as being quite different. 'Distribution implies adoption and conformity. Spread implies adaptation and non-conformity' (1997: 140). Ghanaian and Nigerian Englishes are examples that have resulted from the spread of English. What Ghanaians and Nigerians speak 'is another English, not a variant but a different language' (1997: 141), and he argues that such varieties 'evolve into autonomous languages ultimately to the point of mutual unintelligibility' (1997: 142). He also argues that their developmental processes are different from the development of regional varieties of English within England which are, he claims, 'variants of the same language, alternative actualisations' (1997: 140). In contrast, varieties found in 'far flung regions . . . have sprung up in a relatively extempore and expedient way in response to the immediate communicative needs of people in different communities with quite different ancestors' (1997: 141).

Widdowson makes a clear distinction between the developmental processes in indigenised Englishes and other Englishes, and his position moves us to a debate on the nature of the new varieties of English and whether they can rightfully be called Englishes or whether they are, as is Widdowson's view, 'autonomous languages'.

Widdowson's position is broadly representative of the views of those who argue that the development of different intranational varieties of English will necessarily result in a range of mutually unintelligible languages, as, for example, French and Italian developed from Latin. Following the distinction between a dialect and a register (Halliday *et al.*, 1964), Widdowson (2003) suggests that nativised local varieties of English can be considered as dialects in that they are primarily concerned with distinct communities. These dialects are 'likely . . . to evolve into separate species of language . . ., gradually becoming mutually unintelligible' (2003: 53). In contrast, Widdowson argues that the varieties of English used for specific purposes such as banking or commerce can be seen more as registers, that is varieties of language that have developed to 'serve uses *for* language rather than users *of* it' (2003: 54) (italics in original). Universally agreed *registers* of English will thus be used for international communication and *dialects* will be used for local communication and the expression of identity. As suggested by the 'identity–communication continuum', however, I do not see the need to draw a distinction in this way. Rather, I agree with Mufwene and Schneider that all varieties of English develop from similar stimuli and through similar processes. All varieties must, on the one hand, reflect the cultural realities of their speakers and, on the other, be adaptable enough to allow international communication. This is as true of Nigerian English(es) as it is of Liverpudlian English.

In Chapter 4 I shall try and show that varieties of British English have developed, following exactly the same type of stimuli as have the new varieties in Ghana, Nigeria or Singapore. An 'English' base has been influenced by contact with several other languages. Kandiah has argued that, in a process he calls 'fulguration', new varieties of English create a new system based on 'elements, structures and rules drawn from both English and from one or more languages used in the environment' (1998: 99). I shall show in Chapter 4 that this is precisely how English developed in England. Whether these varieties are mutually intelligible or not depends more on the motivations of the speaker (the identity–communication continuum) and the listener's familiarity with the variety than it does on the linguistic features of the variety itself. These differ, but they differ from each other in the same ways, and familiarity with them brings quick understanding.

As pointed out by Kachru, Moag and Schneider, once a new variety of English is established, internal or local variation begins to appear. Each variety of English is represented by a continuum of styles. Thus, as we saw earlier, Australian English has been classified into three styles: cultivated, general and broad. Singaporean English has also been classified into three comparable styles: acrolectal, mesolectal and basilectal. The use of style depends on a particular motivation. And, as I argued in Chapter 1, these motivations can be placed along the identity–intelligibility continuum. In contexts where identity is considered important to the speaker, such as in informal situations with peers, s/he is likely to adopt a broader, more colloquial (or more basilectal) style. When the contexts require intelligibility across more than one speech community, however, the identity motivation will take second place to the intelligibility motivation. Speakers, whether they be Nigerian or Liverpudlian, will choose the style to suit the occasion. In other words, all speakers of English are capable of being intelligible (or uinintellgible) to speakers of other varieties if they are so motivated.

Intelligibility is thus not a useful criterion for determining whether a variety has become a different language. As I pointed out in Chapter 1, many varieties of British English can be mutually unintelligible. This is especially the case if the motivation of the speaker is to highlight his or her identity. I shall consider the issue of intelligibility in more depth in Part C but here will quote Smith (1992). Smith has long argued that different varieties do not necessarily equate with unintelligibility. In a well-known study conducted in response to the frequently voiced concern over 'the possibility that speakers of different varieties of English will soon become unintelligible to one another' (1992: 75), he argued that this is a natural phenomenon and nothing to worry about. 'Our speech or writing in English needs to be intelligible only to those with whom we wish to communicate in English' (1992: 75). To this I would add that, following the 'identity–communication continuum', our speech or writing in English can be made intelligible to speakers of other varieties of English.

In the final part of this chapter I shall briefly outline the main arguments for and against the proposition that the spread of English is the result of a deliberate imperialist policy, one that Phillipson in a well-known book of the same title (1992) has termed linguistic imperialism or 'linguicism':

> Linguicism can be intralingual and interlingual. It exists among and between speakers of a language when one dialect is privileged as standard. Linguicism exists between speakers of different languages in processes of resource allocation, vindication or vilification in discourse of one language rather than another – English as the language of modernity and progress, Cantonese as a mere dialect unsuited for a range of literate and societal functions – (. . .)

> (Phillipson, 1997: 239)

This is relevant to the concept of World Englishes, as the linguistic imperialism argument would seem to imply that a native-speaking model of English that reflected an Anglo-cultural framework would supplant not only local varieties of English, but also other local languages.

3.3 English as an International Language or World Englishes?

The political debate over the spread of English centres around two questions: (1) is it due to imperialism or linguicism; or (2) is it due to a genuine desire of people to learn English because it has become so useful and because it can be adapted to suit the cultural norms of the people who speak it? I return to this debate in more depth in Part C and here simply provide an introduction to it. In a way, this is a debate about one English and many

Englishes. Those who see imperialism as the cause argue that it is British and, to an increasingly greater extent, American English, that is being spread across the world. They argue that British and American English necessarily bring with them Anglo-cultural norms and that to learn this English means adopting British and American culture. As Rahman (1999) has argued in the case of Pakistan, English 'acts by distancing people from most indigenous cultural norms' (cited in Phillipson, 2002: 17).

There is little doubt that there are people and institutions who see the spread of English as being both commercially and politically extremely important for their own interests. An example of such an institution could be said to be the British Council. A major task of the British Council is to give access to British culture across the world. What better way to do this than to offer access to British English? Hence British Councils across the world have established English language schools. These schools promote a British or native speaker model and language teaching materials published by British publishing houses. However, it is noteworthy that the British Council sees these schools as operating with an overall purpose of building mutually beneficial relationships between people in the UK and other countries.

There is also little doubt that the British government sees great advantage in the spread of English, especially British English and especially in post-communist countries of Eastern Europe and in countries such as China. The ex-British Prime Minister, Gordon Brown, extolled the virtues of English in a trip to China he made in 2005.

There is also little doubt that certain varieties of English are considered superior in a range of international contexts. Academic publications in the United States and Britain favour articles written in Anglo varieties and which follow Anglo rhetorical styles. This has led to scholars such as Swales (1997), Ammon (2000) and Kandiah (2001) to consider how any possible prejudice against scholars who are either speakers of different varieties of English or who are second language speakers of English can be addressed.

Phillipson's (1992) elegant argument for the linguistic imperialism thesis has won many followers. Needless to say, however, there are many who disagree with his analysis and who argue that, far from being forced upon people unwillingly, English has been actively sought out by people throughout the world (Conrad, 1996; Davies, 1996; Li, 2002b; Brutt-Griffler, 2002). In their view, people are making sensible and pragmatic choices; they are not being coerced into learning English. And, far from English being a purveyor of Anglo-cultural norms, the development of new varieties of English shows how English can be adapted by its speakers to reflect their cultural norms.

Kandiah (2001) sees both motivations in action and feels that there is an inherent contradiction for people in postcolonial countries. On the one hand, people realise they need to learn English as it is the international language. On the other, they fear that the need to use English in so many situations and for so many functions will threaten their own languages, cultures and ways of thinking. Yet, as Kachru and others have argued, local Englishes reflect local cultures and ways of thinking. Second, many non-Anglo or non-Western ways of thinking have received international attention through English. To take just three examples from Chinese culture, traditional Chinese medicine, the writings on the

Art of War by Sun Zi and the tenets of Confucianism are now much better known in the West than in the past, precisely because this Chinese cultural knowledge and these Chinese ways of thinking have been disseminated through English. As Jacques (2005) has argued, with the rise in power of India and China, American and Western values will be contested as never before. It is highly likely that they will be contested through the medium of English.

In closing this chapter, I want to introduce a conundrum that we face in an attempt to standardise and classify World Englishes. We like models and norms. The conundrum that we have to solve is that we are faced with many models all of which are characterised by internal variation. This has been pointed out by Kachru in his call for a 'polymodel' approach to replace a 'monomodel' approach (1992a: 66). A monomodel approach supposes that English is homogenous, a single variety, it is 'English as an international language'. In Kachru's view, this approach ignores the incontrovertible fact that English is actually characterised by variety and variation. A polymodel approach, on the other hand, supposes variability. Kachru lists three types: 'variability related to acquisition; variability related to function; and variability related to the context of situation' (1992a: 66).

By examining the linguistic features of a range of Englishes and the sociocultural contexts in which they operate, I hope to show how the real situation is characterised by variation and variety and that we need to study 'global' English in specific places (Sonntag, 2003). While varieties of English go through similar linguistic and developmental processes, the current status and functions of those Englishes can differ markedly. For example, the roles and functions of English differ markedly today even in Malaysia and Singapore, two countries whose historical backgrounds are so closely related that one was actually part of the other at one stage in the past. I now turn to the description and discussion of individual varieties of English.

Part B: Variation and Varieties

4 Variation and impurity in British English

In Part A I discussed a number of key linguistic and sociolinguistic concepts that will underpin the description of the varieties of English in Part B. I also summarised theories of World Englishes and their development so that these could be used to compare the developmental processes that the varieties of Englishes described in Part B go through. In this chapter I shall give a brief summary of the historical development of English in England and focus on demonstrating and exemplifying its variation and 'impurity'. I shall provide examples of variation over the ages and illustrate how the language has changed over time and give examples of how present-day varieties of English in England differ from each other. In the final part of the chapter I shall outline the history of the development of English in Scotland and give some examples of varieties of Scots English, concentrating on a variety currently spoken in the northeast of Scotland.

4.1 Old English and Middle English

There is no evidence to support the popular myth that English suddenly appeared as a pure language untouched by others. As Crystal has pointed out, 'The notion of purity was as mythical then as it is now' (2004: 19). The truth is that English has been influenced by contact with a range of languages over many hundreds of years. It is a member of the Indo-European language family and a very simplified version of its family tree is given in Figure 3 (overleaf).

The development of the English spoken in England today has had four stages. The dates given below are only approximate dates. While linguistic change is constant, it is also gradual, so it is impossible to say that one version of English suddenly developed into another on a particular date:

Figure 3: The English language family tree

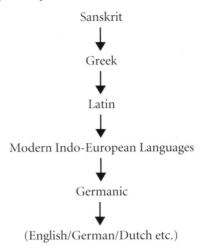

Sanskrit

↓

Greek

↓

Latin

↓

Modern Indo-European Languages

↓

Germanic

↓

(English/German/Dutch etc.)

Stage 1: Old English (OE), from 450 to 1150;
Stage 2: Middle English (ME), from 1150 to 1450;
Stage 3: Early Modern English (EME), from 1450 to 1750; and
Stage 4: Modern English (ModE), from about 1750.

These dates also approximate key events in the history of English. From around the middle of the fifth century AD, tribes from different parts of Europe – the Jutes, Angles and Saxons – arrived in England. They spoke a wide range of Germanic dialects. Four OE dialects have been recognised, namely West Saxon, Kentish, Mercian and Northumbrian, but Crystal argues that 'in reality there must have been many more' (2004: 34). It is important to note that, by the time these Germanic tribes arrived in England, their languages had already had some 400 years of contact with Latin, so the varieties they spoke will have been influenced by this Latin contact.

Variation was evident in the varieties of the dialects spoken by these early settlers to Britain. The following examples of different vocabulary come from Crystal (2004: 47):

ModE	Anglian OE	West Saxon OE
bell	clucge	bell
feed	alan	fedan
loss	los	lor
border	faes	fnaed

The next several hundred years saw the arrival of the Scandinavian tribes, the adoption of Christianity, the Norman invasion of 1066 and Caxton publishing the first book in 1476, after Gutenberg's invention of the printing press in c. 1450.[1] All of these represented major influences on variation and change in English.

One major syntactic change that took place over time and created an important difference between Old English and Modern English is that, compared with Old English, Modern English has relatively few inflections. For example, the inflectional system of nouns in OE had nominative (subject), accusative (object), genitive (possessive), dative (agent) and number inflections. The declension of the OE masculine noun '*stan*' (stone) below is taken from Blake (1996: 65):

Case	Singular	Plural
nominative	stan	stanas
accusative	stan	stanas
genitive	stanes	stana
dative	stane	stanum

Today, we basically retain inflections for number on nouns, usually by adding the suffix '-s', although the Old English suffix of '-en' remains in some 'irregular' plurals, as in 'children' and 'oxen'. Gender and case markings have all but disappeared. The marking of the gender of nouns disappeared by the thirteenth century (Williams, 1975). The accusative and genitive are now restricted to 'whom' and the possessive 's', although there is evidence that the possessive apostrophe is dropping out of use, as is 'whom', except, perhaps, in formal writing.

The inflectional system on verbs was also more complex in OE. In OE, as in ModE, there were two ways of marking past tense, the strong forms and the weak forms. The strong forms marked past tense by changing the internal vowel. Examples of strong forms were:

rīdan – rād (ride/rode)
findan – fand (find/found)
beran – baer (bear/bore)
sprecan – spraec (speak/spoke)

(Blake, 1996: 67–8)

The weak forms marked past tense by adding a suffix. Examples include:

endian – endode – endod (end/ended/ended)
cysson – cyssede (kiss/kissed)
cepan – cepte – ceped (keep/kept/kept)

(Blake, 1996: 69)

Over time, the strong forms have lost out to the weak forms (for example OE 'rap' was the past tense of 'ripan', but this has been replaced today by 'reaped') so that today nearly all new

---

[1] In Europe; the Chinese had invented printing several centuries earlier, during the Southern Song Dynasty (1127–1279).

verbs take '–ed' as their past tense marker (Burchfield, 1985: 43). This is interesting because this trend is also observable in new varieties of English (NVE). In other words, the tendency for new varieties of English to favour regular '-ed' past tense endings simply mirrors a historical pattern. However, as is always the case, it is not quite as neat and simple as that. Many verbs had both weak and strong form past tense endings and in some cases the strong forms have won out. For example, 'raught' was common for the past tense for 'reach' until about 1650 (Lass, 1999: 174), and 'teached' and 'catched' were both possible alternatives for 'taught' and 'caught' until well into the eighteenth century (Lass, 1999: 194). 'Wrought' was the past tense of 'work' and survives today as an adjective, as in 'wrought (i.e. 'worked') iron'.

Nevertheless most verbs moved to the weak class and the inflectional system of the verb became gradually more simplified so that 'many forms of the verb became indistinguishable' (Blake, 1996: 151). In short, the highly inflected English of OE has become, over time, a language with only a few inflections. The reasons for the loss of inflection by the Middle English period is instructive, as it provides a clue as to why new varieties of English are also following this pattern. Fisher (1992) mentions two possible causes, namely phonology and pidginisation. With regard to the pronunciation system or phonology of OE, OE's initial stress was important 'as it must have contributed to the neutralisation of vowel qualities in inflectional endings and their almost total subsequent demise' (1992: 207). Phonology is also a cause of the dropping of certain past tense endings in NVEs, especially when they occur as part of consonant clusters. Thus 'walked' becomes something like 'walk' in certain varieties of spoken English. The second cause Fisher mentions stems from contact with Scandinavian languages after England had been invaded by Vikings. This contact between OE and Scandinavian languages 'led to a process of pidginisation, with a concomitant loss of morphological structure' (1992: 207). This reduction in inflections is given additional impetus after contact with French. It is further evidence that 'traditional' English followed developmental processes that are comparable with the developmental processes of new varieties of English.

A change associated with the simplification of the inflectional system has been the move from a relatively free to a relatively fixed word order. The presence of inflections means that word order can be much more flexible. Burchfield (1985: 157) gives the following example of this. The Modern English sentences 'the king betrayed the queen' and 'the queen betrayed the king' have fundamentally different meanings. In OE, however, the sentences 'sēo cwēn beswāc pone cyning' and 'pone cyning beswāc sēo cwēn' mean the samething ('the queen betrayed the king'), despite their quite different word order, as the subject and object of the sentences are indicated through inflections.

Latin has influenced English at different periods. As pointed out earlier, the Germanic languages that we now call English had had 400 years of contact with Latin before their speakers even arrived in England. The second phase of Latin influence occurred with the adoption of Christianity. This saw Latin words entering the language and these words becoming nativised, so 'papdom' (today 'papacy') developed from 'papa' plus the OE suffix '-dom', which survives today in words such as 'kingdom'.

As Fisher pointed out above, Scandinavian languages also provided a major influence on OE. In addition to influencing the syntax of OE, these languages also supplied many words. A very common word of Norse origin is '*husbonda*', householder or husband. These examples come from Crystal:

Norse	OE	Mod E
log	lagu	law
utlagi	utlaga	outlaw
vrang	wrang	wrong

(Crystal, 2004: 177)

After the influences and consequent changes to English brought about by contact with Latin and Scandinavian languages, a third major influence was felt from 1066 when the Normans invaded from France and conquered England. For around the next 300 years the official language of Britain was French and French words routinely replaced OE words. The examples below are taken from Burchfield:

OE	French
eam	uncle
milts	mercy
sige	victory
stow	place

(Burchfield, 1985: 15)

Thousands of French words entered English during the time of the Normans. Today we use English and French pairs in many expressions, possibly without realising their different origins. The following pairs have the OE word mentioned first and the French one second:

will and testament
keep and maintain
breaking and entering
final and conclusive

(Crystal, 2004: 153)

English also developed different words of similar meanings from different languages as this table of OE, French and Latin words shows. The dates in brackets after each word give an approximate date of their entry into English:

OE	French	Latin
ask (885)	question (1470)	interrogate (1483)
fast (888)	firm (1340)	secure (1533)
rise (1000)	mount (1362)	ascend (1382)

(Crystal, 2004: 188)

These several influences mean that there are words in English that might look the same, but actually have quite different linguistic origins. For example, the 'boil' that you lance comes from Old English but what you do to water in a kettle comes from French.

The French influence was not limited to vocabulary, but was evident in syntax too. French left an indelible mark on Anglo-Saxon by 'drastically simplifying its . . . syntax, modifying its spelling and vastly enlarging and enriching its vocabulary' (Murison, 1979: 6).

4.2 **From Middle English**

The period of Middle English was a period in which variation was at its greatest. It is the dialect phase 'par excellence' of English (Strang, 1970: 224). Consider these alternative spellings of the word 'knight' for example, bearing in mind that 'knight' would have been a key word during this time:

knight, knighte, knyght, knyghte, knith, knizt, knyzt, knyzte, knict, kincth, cnipte, cniht

(Crystal, 2004: 211)

By 1400 the amount of variation presented cumulative difficulty in writing between literate people. Note this occurred with the rise of the importance of English, as English started to gain ascendancy over French as the language of the English court at this time (Richardson, 1984). It was also the time of the so-called Great Vowel Shift, when the pronunciation of vowels altered significantly. The extent of this shift in pronunciation can be seen by comparing how the great English writer Chaucer would have pronounced the following sentence in his lifetime – he died in 1400 – with the way I might pronounce it today:

'way doe sah it's teem to gaw noo' (we do say it's time to go now) /widuseɪɪtstɑɪmtəgoʊnaʊ/

(Crystal, 2004: 252),

Middle English was, above all, a dialect age and 'for a glorious 300 years, people could write as they wanted to, and nobody would say they were wrong' (Crystal, 2004: 195). It was also the time when many of the OE inflections dropped out of common usage, but when the progressive form emerged (*I am going*) along with a range of auxiliaries (*I have seen*, *does she know*, *I didn't go*, *they can ask*) (Crystal, 2004: 250).

Not everyone was happy with this variation and linguistic prejudices were voiced. York, a city in the north of England, was the earliest town to be publicly berated by a Southerner for its 'bad' accent. Ranulph Higden writes in the 1350s:

'all the speech of the Northumbrians, especially at York, is so harsh, piercing and grating, and formless, that we Southern men can hardly understand such speech'

(cited in Crystal, 2004: 216)

The period 1475–76 was a further period of great change. The introduction of printing into England by Caxton in 1476 meant that reading and writing became popular and not pastimes restricted to the educated elite. But even after Caxton there remained a great deal of variation. The Renaissance brought many new words from Latin and Greek and this started to upset people. Sir John Cheke, writing in 1557, is often quoted as an example of someone who felt that the language was sliding into anarchy:

'I am of the opinion that our own tung should be written cleane and pure, unmixt and unmangled with borrowings of other tunges.'

(cited in Crystal 2004:292)

Underlining the dangers of pedantry, 'opinion', 'pure', 'unmixed' and 'unmangled' are themselves words of French or Latin origin.

That variation and change have always been a natural and normal phenomenon is underlined by this quotation from Burchfield:

The patterns of accidence and syntax of a language wax and wane from generation to generation, and seem always to meet the daily needs of the tribes, families, or groups using them.

(Burchfield, 1985: 32)

4.3   Examples of change (1476–1776)

Unless otherwise indicated, the following examples come from Burchfield (1985). It should be noted that many varieties of English have retained some of these features.

(i)   The initial /fn/ of OE becomes /sn/ so 'fnesen' becomes 'sneeze'.

(ii)   The /t/ in words like 'listen', 'castle' and 'whistle' has become silent, but it remains optional in words like 'chestnut' and 'often'. The /r/ before a consonant in final position has also become silent in the many non-rhotic varieties of English in words such as 'beard', 'scared' and 'part'.

(iii)   Most nouns lose their '-en' plural inflection. Instead plural is marked by '-s'.

(iv)   The changes associated with the second person pronouns give a good example of how significant the changes were:

OE

thou (singular nominative), thee (accusative)
ye (plural nominative), you (accusative)

When talking to people, 'thou' (sing) and 'you' (pl) were used.

13th C

'you' had become singular.

16th C

'thou' and 'you' were playing the tu–vous role, where 'tu' indicates friendship and intimacy and 'vous' social distance and formality, as well as singular and plural.

17th C

'thou' disappears from standard English.

(Crystal, 2004: 307ff.)

(v)   The third person present simple inflection changes. In 1620, *Mayflower* settlers to the United States all said 'he runs, he lives', but their parents probably said 'he runneth, he liveth'.

(vi)   Up to 1776, negation continued to be cumulative and not self-cancelling as this 1576 example shows: 'they should not need no more to feare him than his shadowe' (Burchfield, 1985: 32).

These examples of continual change show that Caxton and printing did not produce a 'standard' language. Further evidence of this can be gleaned from the views of people at the time. In 1605, a Richard Verstegan said that when people from different parts of England met, 'they are not able to understand what the others say, notwithstanding they call it English that they speak' (Crystal, 2004: 346).

It is perhaps not surprising then that, at the time when people were increasingly beginning to show concern about the wide range in variation, we see the appearance of the first dictionaries and grammars. Below is a list of the most important of these, together with their dates of publication.

- The first English grammar was William Bullokar's *Pamphlet for Grammar*, published in 1586.
- The first English dictionary was *A Table Alphabetical* by Robert Cawdrey, published in 1604.
- 1674 saw the publication of the first dialect dictionary. This was John Ray's *A Collection of English Words, not Generally Used, with their Signification and Original.*
- The Irish satirist Johnathan Swift, author of *Gulliver's Travels*, was keen to establish a standard and in 1712 he published his *Proposal for Correcting, Improving and Ascertaining the English Tongue.*
- Samuel Johnson's dictionary was published in 1755. In the preface he wrote that he found our speech 'copious without order, and energetick without rules . . . there was perplexity to be disentangled, and confusion to be regulated . . .' (cited in Crystal, 2004: 365). In the context of language teaching, given the amount of time English language teachers spend on drilling the difference between countable and uncountable nouns in English, it is instructive to note that Johnson's dictionary treats 'information' as a countable noun, as he gives the plural form as 'informations'.
- John Walker published his *Critical Pronunciation Dictionary* in 1791. In it he was critical of a habit that will be familiar to many people today:

'A still worse habit . . . prevails, chiefly among the people of London, that of sinking the h at the beginning of words where it ought to be sounded, and of sounding it, either where it is not seen, or where it ought to be sunk'

(cited in Crystal, 2004: 411)

He is complaining that some people do not pronounce the 'h' sounds in certain words, so 'heart' becomes 'eart', but do sound them in others where they do not occur, so 'arm' becomes 'harm'. The fact that people still do this shows that prescriptive rules tend to be unsuccessful.

- Lindley Murray's English grammar was published in 1795 and became the most famous prescriptive grammar of its day. Nevertheless, the poet Keats wrote in a letter in 1819, 'I should not of written' (Crystal, 2004: 464). This is the type of 'error' that upsets today's prescriptivists, but is one that is becoming increasingly common and occurs in the dialogues of contemporary novels. It is possible that this replacement of 'have' by 'of' will become accepted in the relatively near future.

One might have expected that the publication of all these manuals would have led to some form of stability and a decrease in variation and change. However, change continued and below I list some examples of change in British English that have taken place since 1776, the date of American independence. Unless otherwise indicated, the following examples come from Burchfield (1985: 40ff). Note that we are not dealing with American English here; that will be the topic of the next chapter.

4.4 Examples of change (since 1776)

As with the examples of earlier changes, it should be noted that many varieties of English have retained some of these features:

(i) /n/ – /ng/ so 'huntin' becomes 'hunting', although 'huntin' remains common.
(ii) Initial /h/ in words of French origin was silent until about 1830 and then we get 'herb'/'hospital'/'hotel'.
(iii) 'Lost'/'cloth'/'cross' (/ɔː/ etc.,) becomes /ɒ/ etc.
(iv) Four-syllable words have two main models, as in the words '**ma**trimony' and 'mo**no**tony' and this is unstable in some words. For example, there is '**con**troversy' over the pronunciation of 'con**tro**versy'.
(v) New verb forms and the use of the passive develop. These were not available before 1800. For example, we first see forms such as: '*we were having*', '*he is having to give up . . .*', '*he has been known to . . .*'.

From these examples and the account above, it is clear that the development of English is characterised by variation and change. Changes routinely occurred in pronunciation, vocabulary and syntax, and a major cause of these changes was contact with other languages. From considering change over time, some examples of linguistic differences between varieties spoken in England today are provided in the next section.

4.5 Variation in contemporary England

While there is some debate over the number of major varieties of English spoken in England today, there is no debate that varieties continue to exist. Ellis (1890) identified six major dialects, which he then subdivided into forty-two districts (Ihalainen, 1994). Ihalainen (1994: 252ff.) also shows that Viereck, writing in 1986, identifies seven major dialect areas of England, namely the north, the northwest, the county of Lincolnshire, East Anglia, the Midlands, the extreme southeast and the southwest. Trudgill distinguishes between traditional (rural) dialects and modern (urban) dialects and lists 13 of the former and 12 of the latter (Ihalainen, 1994: 252–9).

There is not space here to consider many distinctive features of so many varieties, but 'the northern subject rule' (Ihalainen, 1994: 221) is of particular interest to people involved in the study of World Englishes. This rule says that plural present tense verbs take '-s' unless they are immediately preceded by a personal pronoun subject. The examples Ihalainen gives are: 'they peel them and boils them', and 'birds sings'. He contrasts this rule with southern usage where '-s' is affixed after a personal pronoun subject to give 'they peels and boils them'. He also gives a fascinating list of the ways different varieties mark the present tense. These include:

> *The North* (following the subject rule provided above):
> 'He makes them / they make them / farmers makes them.'
> *Northwest Midlands:*
> 'He makes them / they maken them / farmers maken them.'
> *East Anglia:*
> 'He make them / they make them / farmers make them.'
> *The South:*
> 'He makes them / they makes them / farmers makes them.'

(Ihalainen, 1994: 228)

English teachers may be startled (or possibly relieved) to see this wide variation in the marking of the present tense. Many may regret that the East Anglian variety of English did not become the standard one. Examples of further variation from other British varieties are provided by Burchfield (1994a: 9). These include the double modal in Scots, 'he'll can get it', and the 'do + be' construction of Irish English, 'these pancakes do be gorgeous'. Some of these features will be seen in other varieties of English, including American. Two features of Welsh English that appear in some of the English varieties of East Asia are the 'isn't it' all-purpose tag question and a preference for topic–comment sentence constructions as in 'coal, they're getting out mostly'.

I now turn to consider the development of varieties of English in Scotland and provide examples from one such variety, the Buchan Doric, spoken in the northeast around the city of Aberdeen.

4.6   Scottish English and variation in Scotland

Scots developed from the variety spoken in the north of England (Northumbria) from the seventh century (McArthur, 1998). The north of Northumbria eventually became part of Scotland, while the south remained part of England and the varieties diverged.

The 'golden age' of Scots is considered to be the century between 1460 and 1560. It was a full national language and 'as distinct from English as Portuguese is from Spanish . . .' (Murison, 1979: 9). As McClure puts it 'the flourishing cultural life of a small but confident kingdom was reflected in an exuberant development of Scots' (1994: 31). This was the final period of the alliance with France against England, a period during which Scots gained French words that English did not have, including the word for the quintessentially Scottish New Year's Eve celebration, 'hogmanay'.

Thus, while the Scots variety was influenced by the same languages as its southern counterparts (Latin, Scandinavian and French), it was influenced by them to different degrees. Apart from the additional influence French had until the Reformation of 1560, the influence of Scandinavian languages on Scots has been greater than it has on other varieties of English. For example the Scandinavian word *quine* refers to girls in general in certain varieties of Scottish English, but has the specific meaning of 'queen' in other varieties of English. From 1560, the increasing political power of England over Scotland led to the southern varieties of English reasserting great influence on Scots. The Union of 1707 saw the Scottish legislature move to London and English became the official language, both spoken and written (Murison, 1979). The increased influence of English is viewed with distaste by many. Standard English is not only a *lingua franca*, it is 'the chief influence at present disrupting the status and make-up of regional dialects . . .' (McIntosh, 1952: 31). However, all is not lost. In the words of one scholar, despite the Anglicisation of Scottish speech over recent centuries, there is still 'a vast amount of Scots material current in everyday spoken usage . . . as well as in our literary and oral tradition generally' (Aitken, 1979: 116).

Readers will note that Scots is described as a variety of English, but this begs the question: is Scots a variety of English or is it a separate language? Here it will be treated as a variety of English, although some will argue that its political status demands that it be called a language in its own right. However, this is a political not a linguistic argument and here we are dealing with linguistic criteria for the classification of languages, so we shall call it a variety or, more correctly, a range of varieties.

There are several varieties of Modern English spoken in England today, but how many varieties of Scottish English are there? Kay (1988) identifies seven dialects of Scots, namely Southern, South, West and East Central, Northern, Highland and Insular. The examples below are from the Northern dialect, which is also called the Doric or Buchan Doric. The Buchan Doric is spoken around and north of Aberdeen in the northeast of Scotland. According to Fenton, 'The speech of the Northeast is one of the best preserved in Scotland, still flexible enough to adapt to modern times' (2005: 1). The Doric is still widely used and, importantly, written. For example, *The Leopard* magazine, which is edited and published in northeast Scotland, regularly carries articles about the Doric and articles that are written in it. It also includes a cartoon, 'Councillor Swick', that is written in the Doric.

[Note that *swick* means 'swindle'.]

Swick: Clear the table, Mary. Let the dog see the rabbit. OK, boys, careful with it. Put it down there beside the wife. I'm much obliged to you both. I would offer you a beer but I

know (*ken*) you're driving, Dave, and it wouldn't be fair to you if I gave (*gied*) one to Ronnie.

Mary: What's (*fit's*) the idea? We've got a TV already. And it can't stay (*bide*) there. It's just something more for me to dust. Where (*far*) did it come from (*fae*)?

Swick: You're looking at the future there, Mary. That is my new PC. Well, it's not exactly new. It was surplus to requirements in the Council's finance department, because the boys there were getting fed up with the old one (*wi the auld een*) – well, it could only play solitaire, and they wanted more variety, you see (*ken*)? Well, they got a new state of the art, all singing, all dancing model now (*noo*). At this very moment, to while away the boring hours (*oors*) in the cashroom, they are surfing the net, looking for a game of pontoon with somebody on Christmas Island.

Swick: But getting back to this little baby, darling. Using this PC you could send an email to your little brother Henry in his posh office in New York and you could get a reply from (*fae*) him by tea-time.

Mary: I don't want (*I'm nae wintin*) a reply from him by tea-time. See this. To heck with your PC – I've got a PC (post card) of my own and I'm writing it to Henry now. Look, it's a lovely view of the Bridge (*Brig*) of Dee (a river), with all the traffic going (*gan*) over it, and Boots and Currys (both well-known shops) in the foreground. It's really attractive. This is my year to send a PC to Henry and I'll get one back from him next year. That's the best kind of communication. After all the years that Henry's been in America, we're still very close.

Mary: You see, you can have too much communication – the more you have, the more chance (*chunce*) there is of having (*haein*) rows. So, as far as I'm concerned, you can keep your personal computer, you can keep your email.

Swick: Know what (*ken fit*) you are, Mary? You're a dinosaur. Look let's get this thing plugged in and I'll give you a demonstration. I just hope it works all right (*aa richt*). I hope it wasn't damaged when (*fan*) it fell off the back of the lorry (*larry*).

Yet, the Doric is much more than a cartoon language. In the February 2005 edition of *The Leopard*, the following articles contained substantial sections written in Doric:

'Spik o The Place' (Speak of the Place) by Norman Harper
'Toonser' (The Townsman) by Bill Mackie
'Buchan Wirds and Wyes O' Daein' (Buchan Words and Ways of Doing) by Sandy Fenton.

Below I give some further examples of the Doric. This one is taken from *Buchan Claik*, a glossary of Doric words and phrases compiled by Peter Buchan and David Toulmin (1989). This excerpt provides a context to describe the meaning of the word '*marless*', a non-matching pair (as of shoes and socks):

The farmer's son who had to go to school wearing his mother's shoes while his own were being repaired, remarked,

'Ye've nivver haen tae dee that, hiv ye? Ging tae the skweel wi yer mither's sheen on? I wis near greeting aboot it in front o aa the ither loons, and then I saw anither lad wi his mither's sheen on, and then I didna feel sae bad. At least my mither's sheen werna marless'.

(Buchan and Toulmin, 1989: 87)

The pronunciation of this variety is obviously distinctive. In addition there is significant variation in vocabulary. The above extract could be 'translated' as:

You've never had to do that, have you? Go to school with your mother's shoes on? I was close to crying about it in front of all the other boys, and then I saw another lad with his mother's shoes on, and then I did not feel so bad. At least my mother's shoes were a matching pair (were not matchless).

A common grammatical feature of this and other varieties of Scottish English is the '-it' suffix as a past tense ending. The example below comes from Fenton (2005: 23) and the past tense suffixes are highlighted in bold. Notice also the use of the past simple here in the first sentence, where in 'standard' British English the present perfect would be used. Note also the use of /f/ for /w/ in 'wh'-words:

'I aye lik**it** tae rake aboot ither fook's places. It's just winnerfae fit ye can learn. Eence fin I wis hame frae Cambridge I bik**it** over tae see a freen o mine . . .'

> *I have always liked* to look around other people's places. It's just wonderful what you can learn. Once when I was home from Cambridge *I biked* over to see a friend of mine. . .

And the memorable opening line of a short story by Kynoch (1997: 12):

> 'Nyaakit as when the howdie skelp**it** his doup . . .'
>
> Naked as when the midwife slapped his bottom. . .

This short story describes a boyhood incident in the life of a local millionaire, called Geordie Peerie. He grew up in a poor home that had only two rooms. If people wanted to wash, they had to use the sink. Geordie has just started to wash. The rest of the opening paragraph continues:

> '. . . Geordie hid ae leg in ower the sink an ae fit in the nammel basin, fin, o a suddenty, there wis a chappin at the door. Fit a fleg a got. Niver myn, he thocht, he widna hae tae ging tae the door. His mither wis ben the hoose. She wid awa tae the door; an wi him in the state he wis in, she widna tak onybody in. He haird her opening the door. "Och, it's yersel, Mr McKillop." (The meenister!) "Come awa in!"'
>
> Geordie had a leg in over the sink and a foot in the enamel basin, when, suddenly, there was a knocking at the door. What a fright he got. But never mind, he thought, he would not have to go to the door. His mother was inside the house. She would go (away) to the door; and with him in the state he was in, she would not let anybody in. He heard her opening the door. "Oh, it's you, Mr McKillop." (The Presbyterian Minister!) "Come in!"

The whole story is in the Appendix and is also recorded on the accompanying CD along with a poem written in the Doric. (For a selection of written and spoken Doric texts, see McClure, 2002.)

Despite their rich history and cultural basis, varieties of Scottish English are still looked down upon by some people, often by the speakers of those varieties themselves. Speakers of other varieties of English in many parts of the world will, I suspect, be only too familiar with the prejudices voiced by the people quoted here. I hope they may take some comfort in the knowledge that prejudice is expressed against old varieties of English as well as new ones. As Kay points out, 'The myth of Scots as a debased form of English often prevails' (1988: 22) and that therefore,

> One of the most debilitating phenomena of Scottish society is the false notion that to get on you have to get out.

> (Kay, 1988: 14)

In other words, you have to learn standard English at the expense of your own variety. People report that children were 'skelpit', or hit, if they used their home language to the teacher, as this was considered a sign of insolence, in spite of the fact that they started school with no other language. Kay even suggests that this led to Scots children deciding education was not for them, 'the omnipotent standard of having one correct way of speaking colours our society's attitude and results in false value judgements about people' (Kay,

1988: 16). Kay also reports a specific instance of prejudice against the Doric itself. It is important to note that prejudice often comes from speakers of the variety:

> 'Five of our former pupils have lost their places in offices, under a youth training scheme, because they either could not or would not attempt to speak standard English on the phone. If you allow the use of Doric by your pupils in your (class) room, you could be a contributor to what can only be described as a sorry state of affairs.'
>
> (Kay, 1988: 17)

Kay sums up the difficulty of maintaining one's own variety by quoting the Scottish poet Hugh MacDiarmid:

> 'Tae be yersel and tae mak that worth bein
> Nae harder job tae mortals has been gien.'
>
> (Kay, 1988: 20)

> To be yourself and make that worth being
> No harder job to mortals has been given.

4.7 Conclusion

This has been the briefest of introductions to variations occurring in British English since AD 500. My main aim in this chapter has been to show that both variation and change have been common and normal in the development of English in England. I have also shown that there continue to be many different varieties of English spoken in both England and Scotland and have given some examples from these. I hope that these show that the variations that occur in other varieties of English are not at all strange, nor are they reflective of deviation or error. In closing, it is helpful to consider these quotes from Burchfield:

> Stability of meaning is rare in any language.
>
> (1985: 114)

> No construction is everlastingly stable, no cherished rule remains unbroken.
>
> (1985: 157–8)

> At any given period linguistic conservatives regard selected parts of the pronunciation system as necessary ingredients of social superiority or acceptability . . . other social groups . . . because of a different line of inheritance display different, and therefore potentially threatening, modes of speech. In the slow turning of the centuries the rivalry of such competing systems produces an alternation of socially triumphant variants.
>
> (1985: 139)

In short, all language is characterised by variation and change. No language is pure. Varieties will develop to serve the needs of their speakers no matter how many rules or obstacles prescriptive grammarians or linguistic bureaucrats will put in their way. Rather than worrying about variation and change, we should rejoice in the cultural and linguistic diversity they represent. I hope to celebrate that diversity in the remaining chapters of Part B.

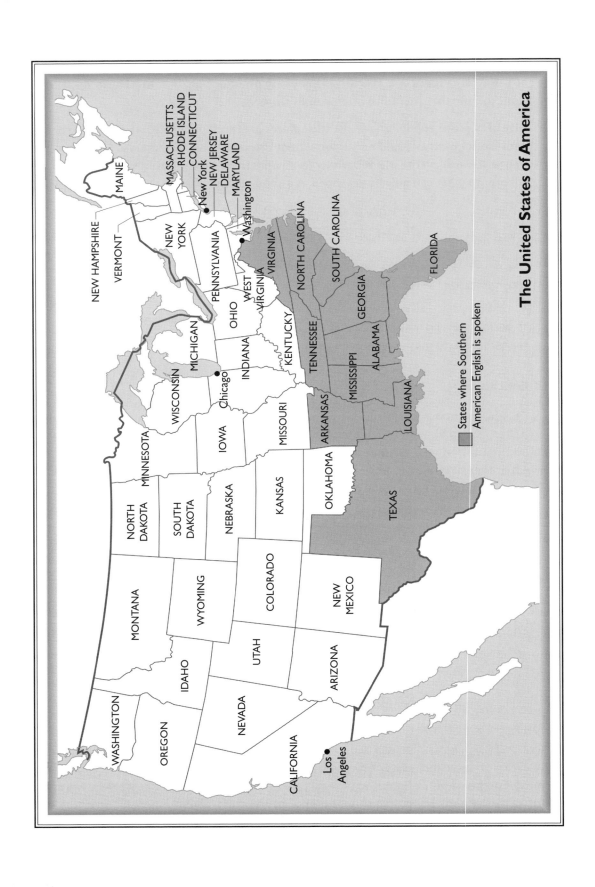

The United States of America

States where Southern American English is spoken

MAINE
NEW HAMPSHIRE
VERMONT
MASSACHUSETTS
RHODE ISLAND
CONNECTICUT
NEW YORK
NEW JERSEY
DELAWARE
MARYLAND
New York
Washington
PENNSYLVANIA
WEST VIRGINIA
VIRGINIA
NORTH CAROLINA
SOUTH CAROLINA
FLORIDA
GEORGIA
ALABAMA
OHIO
INDIANA
MICHIGAN
KENTUCKY
TENNESSEE
MISSISSIPPI
Chicago
WISCONSIN
IOWA
MISSOURI
ARKANSAS
LOUISIANA
MINNESOTA
NORTH DAKOTA
SOUTH DAKOTA
NEBRASKA
KANSAS
OKLAHOMA
TEXAS
NEW MEXICO
COLORADO
WYOMING
MONTANA
UTAH
IDAHO
ARIZONA
NEVADA
WASHINGTON
OREGON
CALIFORNIA
Los Angeles

5 The powerful variety: American English

5.1 The development of American English

American English is, without doubt, the most influential and powerful variety of English in the world today. There are many reasons for this. First, the United States is, at present, the most powerful nation on earth and such power always brings with it influence. Indeed, the distinction between a dialect and a language has frequently been made by reference to power. As has been said, 'A language is a dialect with an army'. Second, America's political influence is extended through American popular culture, in particular through the international reach of American films (movies, of course) and music. As Kahane has pointed out, 'The internationally dominant position of a culture results in a forceful expansion of its language . . . . the expansion of language contributes . . . to the prestige of the culture behind it' (Kahane, 1992: 232). Third, the international prominence of American English is closely associated with the extraordinarily quick development of communications technology. Microsoft is owned by an American, Bill Gates. This means a computer's default setting for language is American English, although of course this can be changed to suit one's own circumstances. In short, the increased influence of American English is caused by political power and the resultant diffusion of American culture and media, technological advance and the rapid development of communications technology.

But while American English is now the most influential variety of English, it was not always so. In this chapter I shall outline the development of American English and focus on two key issues. The first is that, in the beginning, the variety was derided by many. As will become increasingly clear through the course of this book, this is a fate that befalls almost all new varieties of English in the early stages of their development. The second focus of the chapter will now be familiar to readers, as the naturalness of variation is a primary focus of the book. It should be no surprise then to learn that American English is characterised by variety. There are too many varieties of American English to be able to describe here and so I shall focus on just two: African American Vernacular English (AAVE) and white Southern American English (SAE). First, however I shall briefly consider the development of American English, attitudes to it and ways in which the idealised standard variety, here called General American, differs from 'standard' British English.

The first official English-speaking group to visit the Americas arrived in 1497 under the leadership of John Cabot (Dillard, 1992: 1), but perhaps the best-known English-speaking immigrants to America were the English Puritans who arrived on the *Mayflower*, in 1621. There followed several waves of migration to America. While many of these migrants were from Britain, it must not be forgotten that many were also from other countries in Europe and many were imported as slaves from African countries during the period of the infamous slave trade. This meant that America provided a contact point for English and many other languages, both European and African. Dillard (1992) points out that, in 1644, 18 different languages were spoken on Manhattan Island (now part of New York) alone. Two further factors made the linguistic situation even more complex. The first was that the migrants from Britain brought with them many different varieties of British English and, as we saw in the previous chapter, these varied significantly from each other and included the varieties of the poorly educated. By and large, it is not the powerful and rich who migrate, it is the oppressed and the poor who do. The second factor was that the indigenous American population spoke several different American languages. The presence of so many languages gave rise to American Indian Pidgin English (AIPE) and AIPE was an important *lingua franca* in the days of early settlement and also during the move west across the United States. Dillard gives an 1886 example of this type of frontier pidgin:

> 'Wild turkey hard to kill. Indian break some stick, turkey stop one second, say maybe Injin, Injin be good hunter he got shot. White-tailed deer, he hear some little noise way off – say Injin – W-u-zz he gone, Injin no get one shot.'
>
> (Dillard, 1992: 145)

It was not this type of pidgin, however, that people were referring to when deriding the new English of America, but rather the varieties spoken by the settlers, as the comments below illustrate. Samuel Johnson, the author of *Johnson's Dictionary* mentioned in the previous chapter, described the 'American dialect' as 'a tract of corruption' (Burchfield, 1985: 36). A few years later, a Scot, John Witherspoon, who had arrived in America in 1769 to become the President of Princeton University, thundered in despair:

> 'I have heard in this country in the senate, at the bar, and from the pulpit . . . errors in grammar, improprieties and vulgarisms which hardly any person of the same class in point of rank and literature would have fallen into in Great Britain'.
>
> (Mencken, 1965: 5)

Mencken (1965: 32) also quotes a more recent example of prejudice against American English. An English politician in 1930, emerging from having seen an American film, complained, 'The words and accent were perfectly disgusting, and there can be no doubt that such films are an evil influence on our language'. There can be no doubt, by 'our language' the English politician was referring to British English. Such prejudices remain today.

When America achieved independence from Britain in 1776, an American academic, Noah Webster, saw that political independence provided an opportunity for linguistic independence and compiled the famous 'Webster's' dictionary. Among other things, he attempted to rationalise English and to make it more systematic. He proposed new spellings, some of which have now become standard American spellings. Examples included the dropping of what he felt were unnecessary vowels to give 'flavor', 'armor', 'smolder', 'anemic', 'catalog' and 'program' as opposed to the British 'flavour', 'armour', 'smoulder', 'anaemic', 'catalogue' and 'programme', spellings influenced by contact with European languages. Webster certainly made the stomach complaint 'diarrhoea', if not easier to cure, at least easier to spell, 'diarrhea'. However, he was not entirely successful in these attempts, as spellings with 'unnecessary' vowels such as 'feather' and 'definite' stubbornly remained (Crystal, 2004: 423). Webster's attempt to establish independence for American English was not welcomed by all Americans, and he was attacked by many. One wrote, sarcastically, 'If the Connecticut lexicographer considers the retaining of the English language as a badge of slavery, let him not give us a Babylonish dialect in its stead, but adopt, at once, the language of the aborigines' (Mencken, 1965: 12).

Along with Webster, Mencken, from whose work many of the above quotes are taken, is perhaps the name most associated with the promotion of the American language. As he pointed out, American English has long since become accepted by its speakers because the American people have 'shown an increasing inclination to throw off their old subservience to English precept and example' (1965: vi). Mencken himself admits that in the early editions of his work, *The American Language*, he felt that it would increasingly diverge from British English. By 1965, he had changed his mind. In the edition of the book that year he proposed that, far from diverging from British English, American English had 'begun to drag English with it' (1965: vi). In other words, he argued that American English was now influencing British English. This was causing the varieties to converge rather than diverge because of increasing American influence and the sheer numbers of those who speak American varieties of English, compared with those who speak British varieties of English. In statements that are remarkably prejudiced for a linguist, Mencken leaves the reader in little doubt as to which variety he feels is the superior. 'The absurdities of standard English (i.e. RP and Oxford English) are denounced by every English philologian' and 'the American believes, and on very plausible grounds, that American is better on all counts – clearer, more rational, and above all, more charming' (1965: 608–9).

Kahane (1992: 213) suggests four influences that caused American English to break from British English:

1. A decline in Anglophilia – in other words a decline in respect for 'things' English.
2. The standardisation of informal speech – this is essentially the consequence of adopting democratic principles and a general levelling of society.
3. The levelling of social dialects – in other words, no single dialect was associated with prestige.
4. The integration of foreign elements – in particular, influence from the languages of African and European immigrants.

America has certainly seen a levelling of social class, especially when compared to Britain, and, in the early days of settlement, a particular dialect was not necessarily associated with prestige. It will be demonstrated later that this does not mean that prejudice against accent and variety is absent in contemporary America.

Kahane's second and third influences can be seen as a consequence of democratisation. Democratisation often pushes the vernacular or low form of a variety into becoming the standard accepted form. This shift towards the acceptance of the vernacular explains why, in England today, RP is now only spoken by about 3 per cent of people, while other varieties have become more popular.

What are some of the differences between the standard British and American dialects? As with all varieties, the most noticeable difference between them is in their different pronunciations. One difference is that the /j/ glide after certain consonants does not occur in American English. Thus a 'duke' is a /djuːk/ in conservative RP, but is a /duːk/ in American English, although /dʒuːk / is also common in Britain. Stress patterns on words also differ. A British 'la**bo**ratory' has four syllables with the main stress on the second, an American 'laboratory' has five syllables with more or less equal stress on each. 'Extra**or**dinary' has four syllables with the main stress on the second syllable in British English, but six syllables and main stresses on the first and third syllables in American English. 'Fertile' is /ˈfɜːtaɪl/ in British English and /ˈfɜːtəl/ in American. Similarly, a 'missile' is a /ˈmɪsaɪl/ in British and a /ˈmɪsəl/ in American. The American pronunciations are not necessarily newer than the British ones. For example, the American pronunciations of 'fertile' and 'missile' retain the original English pronunciations of these two words.

There are also many differences in vocabulary. To return to and extend the examples given in Chapter 2, when the British and Americans talk about cars and driving, you would think they were talking about completely different things. In England, cars have bonnets, boots, gear levers, number plates, tyres and windscreens. In America, they have hoods, trunks, stick shifts, license plates, tires and windshields. In England, drivers stop at pedestrian or zebra crossings and at traffic lights. They go round roundabouts and avoid driving on the pavement. They drive on motorways and ring roads, they pull off at junctions and pull up on the hard shoulder. In America, drivers stop at crosswalks and stop lights. They go round traffic circles and avoid driving on the sidewalk. They drive on interstates and beltways and exit at exits and pull off at pull offs.

There are also grammatical differences. In certain contexts, an American can use the past simple tense when a British speaker would use the present perfect. For example, 'Did you buy your car yet?' is possible in American English but, in British English, a speaker would say 'Have you bought your car yet?'

Differences also exist in the way people speak to each other. For example, when greeting and leave taking the British may say 'How are you?' and 'Goodbye', while Americans may say 'How are you doing?' and 'Have a nice day'.

5.2 Variation in American Englishes

Although there are differences between the standard languages, the variation increases further when regional and social varieties are considered. Mencken called his book *The American Language* but there are, in fact, a number of varieties of American English that differ markedly from one another. The manner in which they differ has been the subject of much controversy. In particular the differences between African American Vernacular English test (AAVEs) and White American English Vernacular(s) (WAEVs) have been explained by two competing theories. The first theory is the colonial lag theory. This argues that WAEVs developed by preserving or introducing features from varieties of British English. The colonial lag theory, however, is now largely discredited (Dillard, 1992; Mufwene, 2001). Dillard explains the initial popularity of the colonial lag theory, at least among some White Americans, by suggesting that 'there was perhaps a need, no longer felt, to legitimise American English by proving that we used little or nothing that had not been previously used in England' (1992: 228). The second theory is the language contact theory. This argues that AAVEs differ from WAEVs because they developed from the contact of English with other languages, primarily African languages. Today the language contact theory is the more accepted theory and Mufwene (2001) persuasively argues that what he calls African American English test (AAEs) and WAEVs developed as a result of language contact and that the differences between them can be explained by a number of variables, including the different typological features of African and European languages. For example, he suggests that the tonal nature of many African languages may have influenced the rhythms and intonation patterns of AAEs, and that the different linguistic features of African and European languages allowed different features to be selected into AAEs and WAEVs respectively. In short, Mufwene's position is that 'virtually the same language contact equation and the same selection principles applied in the formation of AAEs and WAEVs' (1991: 103). Dillard draws a similar conclusion saying that language contact theory is the theory most supported by the data (1992: 228).

In the context of AAVE and Southern American English, the two varieties which will be considered in some detail later in the chapter, Mufwene makes a similar point. In pointing out that both varieties have clearly influenced each other, he notes that the similarities between them can be explained by some 200 years of common history and regular interaction between the speakers. The differences resulted from 'the widespread institutionalisation of segregation in the late nineteenth century' (2003: 64).

American varieties of English have been subject to further, more recent stimuli. Three specific forces for change can be identified, namely accelerating metropolitanisation, increasing migration, both domestic and foreign, and expanding ethnic diversity (Tillery, Bailey and Wikle, 2004: 228). The figures provided by the authors are startling (2004: 229ff.): In 1860, 80 per cent of the American population lived in rural communities. Now 80 per cent live in 280 metropolitan areas. Today there is evidence of the divergence between rural and metropolitan varieties in many states. 'Urbanisation has been the catalyst for widespread change in Southern American English over the last 125 years' (2004: 244). The authors further report that, between World War I and 1970, 15 million white southerners and 5 million black southerners moved to the North. This flow has now reversed with many people heading for the southern sunbelt. Major cities throughout the country are also affected. The population growth of the major cities of Los Angeles, Houston, Dallas, San Diego, Miami and New York City is entirely accounted for by foreign immigration. This means that much, and in some cases the majority, of the population are not native to the community. This, in turn, means that the varieties of English spoken in these communities are likely to undergo significant change. Urban varieties 'show "observable" language change in progress', while rural varieties, especially those spoken in relatively isolated areas, are likely to be more stable (Dubois and Horvath, 2003: 202).

In the early years of colonial settlement, diversity was characteristic. Each settlement developed different varieties, and for an excellent account of this the reader is referred to Dillard (1992). There are now four major dialect regions in the United States, namely the Inland North, the South, the West and the Midland (Labov, Ash and Boberg, 2005). There are also other dialect areas. For example, a city such as New York itself houses a range of dialects including Brooklynese and Black American. Labov *et al.* also show that many cities have developed their own dialects – Philadelphia, Pittsburgh, Columbus, Cincinatti, Indianapolis, St Louis and Kansas City all have distinct dialectal features. As indicated earlier, I am unable here to describe all these, but will provide examples from two varieties of American English: African American Vernacular English (AAVE), the variety spoken, as its name suggests, by many Black Americans, especially those living in cities, and Southern American English (SAE), the variety spoken by many White Americans across the South of the country.

Before proceeding, it is important to note that a variety of different acronyms and terms are used to describe certain varieties of American English. For example, the variety spoken by Black Americans has been variously described as Black English Vernacular (BEV), African English Vernacular (AEV), African American English (AAE), African American Vernacular English (AAVE) and Ebonics. 'Ebonics' was a term originally created to indicate that Black American English was actually a variety of *African* languages rather than a variety of *English* (Green, 2002), but this analysis is not widely accepted (cf. Mufwene, 2001). I shall refer to this variety as AAVE, unless citing an author who uses a different label. Similarly, 'standard' American has been referred to as Standard American English (SAE), White American English Vernaculars(s) (WAEV), General American (GA) and Mainstream US English (MUSE). I shall refer to this variety as GA, unless citing an author who uses a different label. In this chapter I use SAE to refer to Southern American English as spoken by the white population.

5.3   African American Vernacular English (AAVE)

It was suggested above that, in the early days, no one American accent or variety was considered to be more prestigious than another, but that this has changed in more recent times. A prime example of a current American variety that attracts negative prejudice is AAVE. Lippi-Green (1997) argues that a speaker of AAVE is likely to be pigeon-holed as being capable of only certain types of work. For example, an AAVE speaker can be successful in the sports and entertainment industries but not in others. She quotes a school administrator betraying this prejudice:

> 'An African-American accent would be more acceptable in a physical education teacher for example than it would in a teacher of speech.'

(1997: 122)

As is common among speakers of certain varieties around the world, speakers of the particular variety are among those most prejudiced against it.

> 'It cannot be denied that some of the most scornful and negative criticism of AAVE speakers comes from other African Americans.'

(1997: 200)

These prejudices came to the fore in the controversy that erupted over the decision by Oakland, California, to classify AAVE or Ebonics as the second official language in schools there. The following two reports encapsulate the opposing views. The first appeared in the *International Herald Tribune* of 24–25 December 1996 and the second is in a letter to the *New York Times* of 26 December by a John Templeton. Both are here adapted and reprinted from McArthur:

> 'The Reverend Jesse Jackson said Sunday that the school board in Oakland, California, was both foolish and insulting to black students throughout the United States when it declared that many of its black students speak a language distinct from traditional English . . . . "It's teaching down to our children" . . . Mr Jackson said the Oakland school board had become a laughingstock, and he urged its members to reverse their decision.'

> 'Those like the Rev Jesse Jackson who seek the quick headline will find themselves out of step with the legitimate demands for cutting edge education.'

(McArthur, 1998: 218)

The question of whether to and/or how to legitimise the home varieties or languages of children in the school has, of course, been a matter of debate and controversy for centuries. The previous chapter noted that the use of the Doric was banned in Scottish schools and I'm sure many readers whose first language happens not to be the mainstream school language will identify with the debate. Lippi-Green argues that everyone should have the right to be heard in their variety and that this is as much a right as being treated equally on the basis of religion and colour (1997: 241). I consider this issue in some detail in Part C when I consider which model of English should be taught in which contexts.

Clearly, questions of identity and power along with cultural and stylistic issues are at least as important as linguistic ones in any discussion of AAVE. AAVE can be seen as symbolic of black resistance to the cultural mainstream. Kretzschmar quotes McDavid:

> 'As urbanisation and its consequent segregation led to the development of new speech communities, the evolution of [African American English] came to be closely bound to the establishment of cultural identity and bonds of solidarity. If some educators regard it as dysfunctional in an academic context, its speakers clearly regard it as an asset within their culture.'

(Kretzschmar, 1997: 315)

It is in this context of cultural identity that the Black American writer and poet June Jordan has compiled a list of guidelines for the writing of Black English that includes 19 'rules'. I include these below. She developed these from the writing of her students and included them in her collection of essays *On Call* (Jordan, 1985: 131–2):

1. Minimal number of words for every idea.
2. Clarity.
3. Eliminate the use of the verb 'to be' whenever possible.
4. Use 'be' or 'been' only when you want to describe a chronic, ongoing state of things.
5. Zero copula (eliminate the verb 'to be' whenever it would combine with other verbs).
6. Eliminate 'do'.
7. Try to formulate really positive ideas by using emphatic negative structures.
8. Use double or triple negatives for dramatic emphasis.
9. Never use the -ed suffix to indicate the past tense of a verb (if this is used in 'standard' English).
10. Only use the third person singular, present, indicative.
11. Observe a minimal inflection of verbs.
12. Never use an apostrophe ('s) construction. (The possessive case scarcely ever appears in Black English.)
13. If the modifier indicates plurality, then the noun remains in the singular case.
14. Listen for or invent special Black English forms of the past tense ('losted' etc.).
15. Do not hesitate to play with words, even invent them.
16. Stay in the present tense unless you want to underscore the past tense.
17. Never use the suffix -ly form of an adverb.
18. Never use the indefinite article 'an'.
19. Invariant syntax: it is possible to formulate an imperative, interrogative, and declarative with the same syntax.

While these guidelines are aimed at allowing Black writers to capture a distinctive Black identity as writers, it is important to note that many of the rules seem to capture the rules of the historical development of English, many of which will be illustrated in these chapters, especially with regard to the overall simplification of the inflectional system. This simplification of the inflectional system is part of the natural development of Englishes and is thus a common feature of many varieties of English.

Before looking at specific examples of AAVE, some words of caution are important here. While many scholars suggest that there are striking similarities between varieties of AAVE and that it has developed 'as a sort of national dialect that transcends regional Anglo dialects' (Tillery, Bailey and Wikle, 2004: 243), there is some social and regional variation (Lippi-Green, 1997). 'Regionality, rurality and cultural identity are all significant in assessing the past and present development of AAVE' (Wolfram, 2003: 126). As with all other varieties of English, AAVE has changed over time. Thus, in the context of inflection simplification, for example, Poplack and Tagliamonte (1991) have convincingly demonstrated that present tense '-s' inflection to mark third person singular was once an integral part of Black English grammar. It was variable, but it was not random and was likely to have been a prestige marker. Yet Cukor-Avila has shown that the use of the verbal '-s' inflection was once unsystematic in the 'typical' speech of black inhabitants in Springville, Texas, in the period between 1920 and 1940. She gives the following example (2003: 98). The instances of '-s' usage and non-usage are bolded.

> 'S: What's her, what's her name that coo**ks** them? She a real young girl. She bri**ng** 'em in every mornin'. An' they, an' they sel**ls** 'em, an' they sel**ls** 'em for that girl there in that store.'

This example also illustrates features of AAVE that are still in use. For example, there is no need for the copula 'is' in 'she a real young girl', and note the deletion of the /d/ in the consonant cluster 'and'.

The use of present tense '-s' provides an interesting synopsis of language change, as Cukor-Avila has shown (1997). In her study of the speech community in Springville, Texas, she shows that the gradual loss of this verbal '-s' marker occurred over three stages. It is now used only 17 per cent of the time by the post-1970 generation, and the more urban influence there is, the less the frequency of verbal '-s' use. What is of particular interest, however, is the linguistic environment in which '-s' was used and the order in which these uses have disappeared among the AAVE speakers of Springville. As Cukor-Avila notes, '. . . it initially disappears from the first singular, next in the third plural, and lastly in the third singular' (1997: 304). In other words, this '-s' inflection occurred in instances of present tense first singular ('I cooks for him') and with the present tense third plural ('they fools with 'em'). This use of plural '-s' also occurs in the speech of white Southerners as will be shown below. Cukor-Avila also provides an example of it occurring in first plural ('we does all that stuff') (1997: 297–8). These uses bring to mind the variation in the use of this '-s' inflection noted in contemporary dialects of English in England in the preceding chapter. Increasingly, however, urban AAVE speakers appear to be following Jordan's eleventh 'rule', which is to observe minimal inflection.

Jordan's fourth 'rule' says that 'be' should only be used to describe a chronic, ongoing state of things. In her detailed and thorough description of AAVE, Green (2002) supports this in showing that the verbal marker 'be' signals habitual occurrence. Green also reports that multiple negation is possible, as expressed in Jordan's 'rule' no. 8. The following example demonstrates the use of habitual 'be' and multiple negation in the same sentence:

> 'If you don't do nothing but farm work, your social security don't be nothing.'
> If you only do farm work, then your social security isn't usually very much.

(Green, 2002: 77)

Other examples show this habitual use of 'be':

> 'They be waking up too early' (they usually wake up too early) and
> 'Those shoes be too expensive' (those shoes are usually too expensive)

(Green, 2002: 25)

While the use of 'be' as a copula is rare compared with its use in General American, it often occurs with the first person singular pronoun ('I'm') and the neutral third person singular pronoun ('it's'). Its use is obligatory in the past tense 'was', but 'was' is used for both singular and plural subjects (Green, 2002: 38).

Occasionally 'be' can also be used with an '-s' inflection, and Green argues that this verbal '-s' inflection is possibly a redundant habitual marker, as in the example:

'Well, that's the way it bes' (Well, that's the way it usually is)

(Green, 2002: 101)

Bernstein (2003: 117) notes this use in the speech of white Southerners, as in 'sometimes it bes like that', and argues that this derives from Scots–Irish influence.

What is certain is that AAVE possesses a complex and systematic grammar, which differs from General American in significant ways, but which shares some features with other varieties of English. It also possesses distinct lexical items and phonological features. Many of the lexical items come, as would be expected, from other languages, particularly African ones. For example:

Item	Meaning	Language
tote	carry	Bantu (tota)
goober	peanut	Bantu (nguba)
gumbo	spicy stew	Bantu
bogus	fake	Hausa (boko)
dig	like, appreciate	Wolof (deg)

AAVE also creates a distinctive vocabulary by according different meanings to words commonly found in GA. Here I just provide two examples (Green, 2002: 22–3). The first demonstrates the use of the verb 'mash' to mean 'press', as in 'mash the accelerator' to mean press the accelerator as hard as possible. This use now occurs in other varieties. For example, 'mash the pedal' to mean 'drive as fast as you can' has become part of colloquial Australian English. The second lexical example concerns the use of the verb 'stay'. This has a range of meanings. It can mean 'live', as in 'I stay in Robertson Road'. This meaning also occurs in Singaporean English, among others. But in AAVE it can also carry a habitual meaning, as in 'he stay in the air' and 'he stay hungry', which mean 'he is always flying' and 'he is always hungry'.

A third source of AAVE vocabulary comes from slang and creativity. For example, Green lists the following different terms for money:

greens, bills, dividends, benjis, cabbage, cheese, cream, duckets, franklins, paper, scrila, bucks, dead presidents, dime, knot and dough

(Green, 2002: 29–30)

These three sources of vocabulary – namely borrowing from other languages, extending or limiting meanings of known words and creativity – are common sources for vocabulary in all varieties of English.

AAVE also has a wide range of distinctive phonological features. These include the non-use of consonant clusters, especially in final position. An example of this was provided earlier with the use of 'an' for 'and'. Other examples include 'wes' for 'west' and 'boyfren' for 'boyfriend'. As is the case with many varieties, the sounds /θ/ and /ð/ do not occur so that 'the', 'this' and 'that' become 'de' and 'dis' and 'dat', and 'nothing' and 'south' are sounded 'nufing' and 'souf'.

5.4 Southern American English (SAE)

Southern American English has occasioned more debate and research than probably any other variety. Several hundred works on the phonology of Southern English have been published (Thomas, 2003) and Southern English is 'a laboratory on the workings of language . . .' (Thomas, 2003: 166).

The South is an area that is not easy to define, either geographically or culturally. It comprises the states of Virginia, North Carolina, South Carolina, Tennessee, Georgia, Florida, Alabama, Mississippi, Arkansas, Texas and Louisiana (Wolfram, 2003). It is not surprising, given this geographical spread, that SAE cannot be considered a single variety. Algeo (2003) notes four major hierarchical levels of SAE: coastal; interior; delta; and south midland. These four levels can themselves be further classified to give a total of 18 sub-varieties. Here, I shall describe features of SAE that can be considered common to most, if not all, of these sub-varieties.

SAE has developed in response to three major influences. The first is an 'English core', the second and third are Scots–Irish and African languages respectively (Algeo, 2003: 9–12).

The phonological feature most associated with Southern English is the so-called 'southern drawl'. This is realised by the prolongation of certain vowel sounds and the 'breaking of vowels and diphthongs into triphthongs' (Thomas, 2003: 156). For example, 'there' can be pronounced /ðajæ/ and 'bad' /bæeɛd/ (2003: 157). Upgliding diphthongs occur in 'pass', 'bath' and 'after' to give the vowel sound /æɛ/ or /æy/ (2003: 163).

Another distinctive characteristic of Southern English is the merging of the vowel sounds /ɪ/ and /e/ as in the words 'pin' and 'pen' (Bailey, 1997: 255). This distinctive southern drawl excites prejudice in some people, as illustrated in the following quotes, taken from Lippi-Green (1997). The first demonstrates the speaker's surprise that someone who spoke with a southern drawl might be intelligent and the second, first quoted in Chapter 1, that a highly educated person – a one-time President of the United States – could speak with a southern drawl:

'. . . Beneath that deceptive North Carolina drawl, there's a crisp intelligence.'

'Governor Clinton, you attended Oxford University in England and Yale Law School in the Ivy League, two of the finest institutions of learning in the world. So how come you still talk like a hillbilly?'

(Lippi-Green, 1997: 210–12)

These quotes show that people who speak with the southern drawl may be considered ill-educated. The quotes were about men's speech, however. The third quote below is from a woman, herself a speaker of the southern drawl, expressing frustration that her accent means that listeners do not take her seriously:

'Instead of listening to what you're saying, they're passing the phone around the office saying, "Listen to this little honey from South Carolina."'

Interestingly, the speaker who exemplifies General American on the CD is from the State of Maine in the northeast of the States and she also cites a similar prejudice as the motivation that led her to lose her original Maine accent. The different type of prejudice to the southern drawl if the speaker is a woman is also evident in the next quote. The speaker is a woman who sells mailing lists over the phone. She is describing the effect her southern drawl has on men:

'It's hilarious how these businessmen turn to gravy when they hear it. I get some of the most callous, and I start talkin' to them in a mellow southern drawl, I slow their heart rate down and I can sell them a list in a heartbeat.'

(Johnstone, 2003: 203)

As we can see from this quote, attitudes towards the southern drawl and 'style' are not always negative. Southerners are thought to have 'elaborate civility' (Johnstone, 2003: 192) and to be more polite, more eloquent and less direct than their northern compatriots.

To turn to the syntax of SAE, below is a list of distinctive features of Southern English syntax noted in the speech of Texan Southern English speakers. These examples are drawn from Bailey (1997: 259–60). Once again the rich variation within and across varieties of English is apparent:

Feature	Example
a-verb-*ing*	he left a-running
plural verb-*s*	folks sits there
perfective 'done'	she's done left
you-all, yall	we saw yall
fixin' to	I'm fixin' to eat
multiple modals	we might can make it
past simple 'dove'	they dove in
past simple 'drug'	he drug it

Of these features, three are considered to be 'among the most salient features of southern grammar' (Bernstein, 2003: 117). They are 'you-all' or 'yall', multiple modals and 'fixin' to', of which 'no feature has been more closely associated with southern speech than the use of yall' (Bernstein, 2003: 107). Bernstein argues that its popularity stems partly from a need in English to find a plural pronoun for 'you'. She reports that, in the northern states, the term 'you guys' is fulfilling this role, and can be used to refer to women as well as men. As an example of a multiple modal, Bernstein gives 'might could' which means something like 'maybe I could' and is used by Southerners 'to express a degree of uncertainty and politeness (2003: 109). Its origin is Scots (see Chapter 4).

The third feature 'fixin' to' means 'about to' as in 'I was just fixin' to leave' (2003: 114). The action has to be imminent so that it would be inappropriate in the sentence 'I was fixin' to travel to Canada in ten years' time'.

A sample of the accent associated with Southern American English is on the CD along with samples of General American and AAVE. The tapescripts and notes appear in the Appendix.

Conclusion

In this chapter I have provided a brief insight into the variation between selected American varieties and into the linguistic complexity of the United States. I shall conclude by emphasising that the increasing metropolitanisation of America is causing significant and rapid change to varieties of American English. Cities are developing distinctive varieties, but the phenomenon of increasing migration and immigration to the cities makes for an extremely complex situation. This may mean that the notion of a variety of General American is becoming ever more an idealisation than a reality. Kretzschmar has proposed that, far from being an easily identifiable model, the American national standard is a variety 'with a minimum of features connected with any one regional or social group' (1997: 319) and that it is this that will compete with English RP in the international marketplace. In the following chapters and in Part C, I shall argue that, in certain contexts, local and regional varieties of English have at least an equal right to compete with British and American standards in the international marketplace for English.

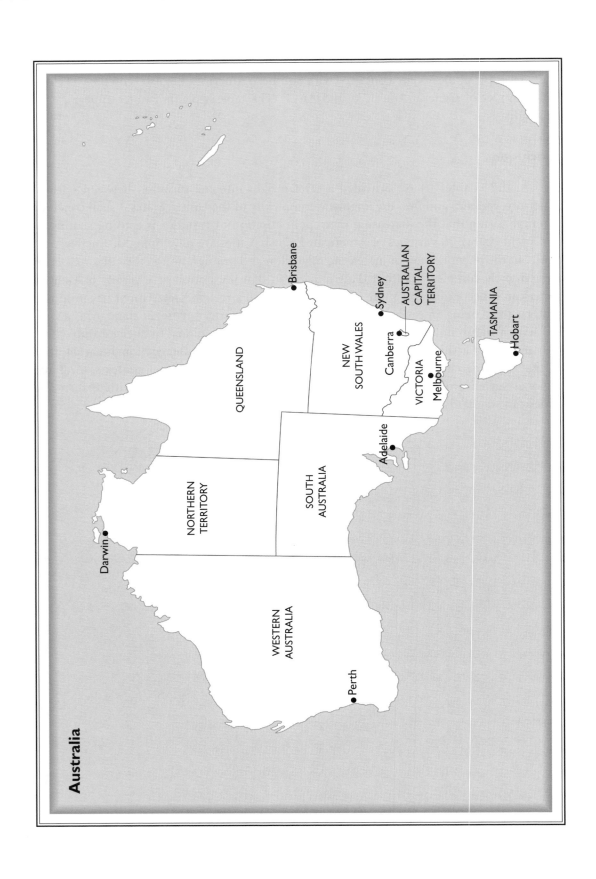

Australia

6 **A younger 'cousin' and indigenous identity**

In this chapter Australian varieties of Standard English are described and considered. Standard Australian English (SAE) – not to be confused with the Southern American English of the previous chapter – itself comprises a continuum of varieties. I shall briefly consider its history, and then describe a selection of the distinctive features of Australian English at the levels of pronunciation, vocabulary and syntax, and look at the ways in which these differ from Standard British English. I shall also examine how Australian identity and cultural values are reflected in Australian speech styles and pragmatic norms. I shall then follow a similar process in describing Australian Aboriginal English (AAE) but use SAE as a point of comparison. In the discussion on Australian Aboriginal English, some of its features will be described and then its role as a language of communication and as a *lingua franca* will be compared with its role as a marker of Aboriginal identity.

As variation in English is both natural and normal, people are commonly able to speak a continuum of varieties. Furthermore, while some of the differences between varieties are unique to a particular variety, many other differences can be found in more than one variety. The choice of which variety to speak is usually determined by the audience the speakers are communicating with, and the extent to which the speakers wish to promote or play down their identity. In this context, I also discuss the 'identity–communication continuum' introduced in Chapter 1.

6.1 **SAE: History and prejudices**

Although the variety of Australian English has been developing for more than 200 years, it is only relatively recently that Australian English has been regarded as an acceptable standard variety. In 1920, the Director of Education in New South Wales was urging teachers to stop the use of Australian English in the classroom. In a telling note on the relationship between language and identity, he said:

'It is sad to reflect that other people are able to recognise Australians by their speech.'

(Delbridge, 1999: 260)

Concerns that Australian English was somehow inferior were voiced frequently and over a long period of time. Görlach quotes an 1829 source, when Australia comprised a number of British colonies:

'Bearing in mind that our lowest class brought with it a peculiar language and is constantly supplied with fresh corruption, you will understand why pure English is not, and is not likely to become, the language of the colony.'

(Görlach, 1991: 147)

These prejudices were not confined to people from the mother country, England. An American linguist, William Churchill, wrote in 1911:

'. . . the fact remains that the common speech of the Commonwealth of Australia represents the most brutal maltreatment that has ever been inflicted upon the mother tongue of the great English speaking nations.'

(Görlach, 1991: 147)

These comments recall the prejudices voiced against regional varieties of English in England, Scotland and the United States and they serve as a reminder that all varieties of English, whether they be native speaker or non-native speaker, are subject to prejudice, often from the speakers of the varieties themselves. It was only as recently as 1940 that Australian English had a champion (Delbridge, 1999): Arthur Mitchell, an Australian university lecturer. Returning home after having studied linguistics in London, Mitchell started to promote the notion that Australian English should be adopted as a national standard, arguing that Australian pronunciation should not be regarded as a corrupt derivation but as an acceptable norm. But his views received a hostile reception and only when Mitchell became Chairman of the Australian Broadcasting Commission (ABC) in 1952 did the ABC start to accept Australian English. Later, Delbridge worked with Mitchell on the national survey into Australian pronunciation, which resulted in the description of the pronunciation of Australian English along a broad–general–cultivated continuum. This research led to three major publications that helped Australian English become established as a standard (Delbridge, 1999):

A Dictionary of Australian Colloquialisms (John Wilkes, 1978);
The Macquarie Dictionary (Arthur Delbridge et al., 1981); and
The Australian National Dictionary (William Ransom, 1988).

Note how recent these publications are – it was more than 200 years after the British first arrived in Australia that The Macquarie Dictionary was published.

What features of Australian English are distinctive and different? As with all varieties, the most obvious differences lie in the area of pronunciation and vocabulary, although there are some grammatical and cultural differences as well.

6.2 Pronunciation

Australian English has been described along a continuum that ranges from 'broad' to 'general' to 'cultivated'. This is similar to the ways that linguists have characterised other varieties. For example, as will be discussed in Chapter 9, Platt and Weber (1980) have classified Singaporean English as ranging along a continuum from basilectal, mesolectal and acrolectal, or low, middle and high levels.

Particularly in broad Australian, the pronunciation of the diphthongs is distinctive (Bernard, 1988). For example, one well-noted feature of Australian English pronunciation is that many Australians, especially when speaking broad or general Australian, do not make a great distinction between the diphthongs /ai/ and /ei/. This is most commonly mimicked and mocked by speakers of other varieties who like to greet Australians with the typical Australian greeting /gudai mait/ ('Good day mate'). This reduction of two diphthong sounds into one can lead to occasional misunderstandings between speakers of different varieties. For example, when I first arrived in Australia, I was mistakenly taken by a taxi driver to Main Street rather than Mine Street, which is where I had actually asked to be taken. Both 'main' and 'mine' are pronounced in a similar way in broad varieties of Australian English.

Another feature of Australian English is the frequent presence of an epenthetic 'schwa' vowel sound before final nasals in words such as 'film' and 'known', to give 'filem' and 'knowen'. This feature also occurs in other varieties, in Irish English, for example.

A further distinctive feature of Australian pronunciation is the use of a rising intonation. This has been called 'Australian questioning intonation' or AQI (Guy and Vonwiller, 1989). The term is a little confusing, as the use of this rising AQI does not signal a question. Instead, it is often used with statements and functions in the same way as tag questions and expressions such as 'OK?' It thus expresses a speaker's request for confirmation that the listener is attending to and understanding and/or that he or she can continue with the speaking turn. Guy and Vonwiller give this example. The speaker is a teenage girl. The italics indicate where AQI is used.

(1) 'Oh, occasionally Mrs L_ used to blow up* kids when they hadn't done anything. And once, a girl and I were walking down the stairs, and she touched a doorknob or something, 'cause she didn't realise what was *wrong with it*. And it fell *off* and she got the cane for *breaking it*. And I know very well *she hadn't broken it*. And I tried to tell the teacher. The teacher was really mean you know.'

(1989: 22ff.)

*to blow up – a colloquial expression, to get very angry with or to tell off

The example below of a young man describing where he lives was recorded from the radio.[1]

(2) 'Little place called Cranbrook, about 80 ks *north of Albany*'

The use of AQI can cause misunderstanding among speakers of different varieties of English, as this example will show. When I was living in Singapore and before I had become familiar with Australian speech styles, I was introduced to an Australian man. He put his

---

[1] The recordings in this chapter were all taken from broadcasts by the Australian Broadcasting Commission (ABC) on 7 March 2003.

hand out and said, using AQI, *David Peebles*. I took his use of AQI to signal a question, so I assumed he was checking to see if I was called David Peebles. So I replied, 'No, I'm Andy Kirkpatrick'. He looked surprised and corrected me saying, 'No, I'm David Peebles'. He was, of course, simply introducing himself.

An Australian commentator's recent view of the use of the rising inflection associated with AQI provides evidence that some Australians remain prejudiced against Australian English:

> 'Elocution would be worth the trouble if it did nothing more than exterminate the rising inflection. Unknown in this country until the 1970s, great numbers of Australians these days turn all their sentences into questions with this fiendish contrivance.'

(Watson, 2003: 157)

6.3 Vocabulary

All varieties of English contain vocabulary items that are unique to their variety. The speakers of these varieties need to find ways of describing a range of phenomena and concepts that exist only in their own natural environment or culture. The local variety of English is therefore likely to borrow words from indigenous languages, as they will already have words for the phenomena that English is now required to describe or to refer to. Although these are commonly words for plants and animals, they can also refer to cultural concepts. Australian English has borrowed hundreds, if not thousands, of words from local Aboriginal languages. Probably the three words that are most commonly associated with Australia are 'kangaroo', 'koala' and 'boomerang'. These are all Aboriginal words. 'Kangaroo' comes from the Guugu Yimidhirr language of Northern Queensland. Both 'koala' and 'boomerang' come from the Dharuk language, originally spoken around the Sydney area. Dixon, Ramson and Thomas (1990) have collected Australian Aboriginal words in English and explained their origin and meaning. Some of their examples include:

Corroboree: a dance ceremony (from Dharuk)
Galah: a parrot, also used metaphorically for a stupid person (from Yuwaalaray)
Humpy: a temporary dwelling (from Yagara)
Koori: an Aboriginal person (from Awabakal)
Yabbie: a type of crayfish (from Wemba-wemba)

A second way in which a variety develops new words is to take words that exist in English but to use them in a different way in order to reflect the uniqueness of the local culture. In the case of Australian English the word 'bush' is an extremely good example of this. 'Bush' is a very important concept to Australians and is part of people's psyche. 'The bush' refers to pretty well all Australia, except for the towns. 'To go bush' means to go into the countryside or even disappear into it in order to lose contact with urban civilisation. Butler (2002) demonstrates its comparative importance to Australian culture by listing the number of entries under the word 'bush' in three major dictionaries, *The Macquarie Dictionary* (Australian), *The Random House Dictionary* (American) and *The New Oxford Dictionary* (British). *The Macquarie* has 97 listings, *the Random House* 54 and *the New Oxford* a mere 37, many of which are actually examples of Australian English.

Australian composites with 'bush' include 'bush ballad' (a ballad that tells about life in the bush), 'bush carpenter' (a rough, amateur carpenter), 'bushcraft' (the ability to live in the bush), 'bushranger' (a bandit or outlaw), 'bush tucker' (simple, country food) and 'bushwhacker' (someone who lives in the bush). The importance of this concept of bush is well captured in an excerpt from an interview with the Australian folk singer John Williamson. This is on the accompanying CD and the tapescript is in the Appendix.

Here are two examples recorded from the radio of the word 'bush' being used in its unique Australian sense:

(3) 'Lived in the bush, worked in the bush, wrote about the bush.'
(4) I: . . . How are you Craig? What What's your story?
    C: I come from Cooma, a truck driver ah during the week and got a bit of a block up the back of Adaminaby.
    I: Bit of a block?
    C: Yeah, bit of a bush block.

C is explaining that he has a piece of land in the countryside just outside the town of Adaminaby.

Below are examples of two words, 'huge' and 'top', being used in a special Australian sense. In describing a country show, on radio, the speaker says:

(5) 'We had a huge day yesterday.'

This does not mean it was very big, but means that the show was a great success.

In the next example, the interviewer is admiring the hat of the person he is talking to. He is not describing a particular type of hat. Notice also the common colloquial use in broad Australian of the word 'buggered' to mean ruined or falling apart:

(6) I: That's a top hat, that one.
    M: Ah, it's about buggered now.
    I: That's why I say it's a top one, it's great.
    M: Yeah, they just get comfortable and you've got to throw 'em away.

These examples and further excerpts from the conversations are provided on the accompanying CD. The full tapescripts are in the Appendix.

In its adoption of new vocabulary items from local languages and its adaptation of the meanings of words that are common in other varieties of English to suit a local context, Australian English is operating in the same way as all varieties do. Each variety of English will contain vocabulary items that either are unique to that variety and which have often been borrowed from local indigenous languages, or are English words that contain special meanings when used in that variety.

The way speakers use vocabulary items can also tell us something about their cultural values. When speaking the broad and general varieties of Australian English, many speakers like to shorten nouns and add diminutive suffixes to them. This clipping is a sign of informality, a key Australian cultural value. Examples of nouns that are shortened or clipped in this way include:

arvo: afternoon
Aussie: an Australian
barbie: barbecue
cozzie: swimming costume
journo: journalist
pollie: politician

This also commonly happens with people's first names. Barry will almost certainly be called 'Bazza' by his friends. This process is also applied to surnames and family names (Poynton, 1989), so someone with the family name Simpson may be called 'Simmo' by their friends. The names of sports stars also often undergo this process, so that Damien Martyn becomes 'Marto', David Campese becomes 'Campo', John Newcombe becomes 'Newk' and Alex Jesaulenko becomes 'Jezza'.

6.4   Syntax

Görlach (1991) mentions two distinctive features of Australian grammar. One is the use of the third person female pronoun in circumstances where speakers of other varieties might use the impersonal pronoun. For example, Australians may say 'she'll be right' meaning 'it'll be (all) right'. Here is an example of this use recorded from the radio:

(7) A: . . . and thank Sophie
     B: yeah she'll be right
     A: she'll be right . . . good on ya

Here 'she'll be right' does not refer to Sophie but the speakers are merely reassuring one another that everything will be all right.

The second feature Görlach mentions is the use of 'but' as a sentence ending in speech. The example he provides is 'I'll finish her this arvo, but' (1991: 161). The function of this 'but' is hard to define, but it seems to act as an informal marker of emphasis. It is more commonly used in the eastern states of Australia, where it is also often preceded by 'though', so we might hear 'She'll be right though but', which means that the speaker is emphasising that everything will be all right.

The following examples of Australian English come from the radio. It is common, especially in the broad and general varieties of Australian English, to use the adjective 'good' in places where speakers of Standard British English would use the adverb 'well':

(8) 'He does not play as good as before.'

The example (9) below was uttered by a happy football supporter while he was watching his team. It illustrates a distinctive use of the 'third conditional'. Speakers of other varieties, including Standard British would use the past perfect in the 'if' clause of this conditional sentence. 'If you had said to me that . . . , I'd have (I would have) . . .'

(9) 'If you <u>had have said to me</u> (AQI) that by the twenty second minute mark we'd be up by two goals, I'd have laughed at you, fair dinkum.'

This 'had have' use is becoming common among speakers of general and broad Australian English. Other recently heard examples include: '*If Fevola had have run* a further few metres', 'He could have slipped it across *if he had have made the tackle*', '*If you had have said . . .*', '*If he had have been*, he would have . . .' and '*If he hadn't have gone* there . . .' It is, of course, possible that this use of 'have' is, in fact, the speaker saying 'of'. Because the pronunciation in context of 'have' and 'of' can be the same, speakers mishear 'have' as 'of', as the poet Keats did (see Chapter 4). In this case, however, it looks like a 'new' third conditional form, as it is hard to know where else the construction 'had have' could have come from. The football supporter above also uses the quintessential Australian phrase 'fair dinkum'. This means something like 'no joking'. Some people have suggested that it came into Australian English from the Chinese goldminers who were working in Australia in the middle of the nineteenth century and that it comes from the Chinese word for gold 'jin'. 'Fair dinkum' originally meant 'real gold', they claim. Sadly for romantics who love this kind of exotic explanation for the meaning of words, ' "dinkum" meaning "work" and "fair dinkum" meaning "fair play" were both used in some English dialects in the nineteenth century' (Ransom, 1987: 38).

Another common grammatical feature of Australian English is the use of 'what' in a relative clause in circumstances where it is not required in certain other varieties. This use is also common in cultivated Australian English, as in this example from John Howard, who became the Prime Minister of Australia in 1997:

(10) 'Prices are lower than *what* they have been.'

A second example of this use of 'what' also provides a common example of the use of 'less' when speakers of Standard British English would probably use 'fewer'. Again, however, this use of 'less' is becoming increasingly common in many varieties of English:

(11) 'The chief is saying that we may have to run on *less resources* than *what* we have before.'

The use of 'less resources' in the above example raises a key question for classroom teachers of English. When can we say that something is a mistake and thus correct it, and when can we say that this is an acceptable feature of the variety? This, I think, is a hard question to answer and will be discussed further in Part C. The usual answer is to say that it is acceptable usage when it becomes systematic. But how do we know when a usage becomes systematic? After all, we have seen that it was some 200 years before even the vocabulary of SAE became codified in *The Macquarie Dictionary*. And even here we must remember that presence in the dictionary does not mean a word's use is systematic across the variety, only that it occurs. The dynamic nature of language also means that usage changes, so that we would expect each new edition of any dictionary of any language or variety to contain examples of new usage. We must also remember that even fluent speakers frequently make mistakes, especially when they are speaking spontaneously. Thus, when someone says 'it's just the tip of the icing', speakers of the variety notice that this is odd, even if they don't immediately see that it is a mistake caused by the speaker blending the two common expressions 'it's just the tip of the iceberg' and 'it's the icing on the cake'.

The above examples from phonology, vocabulary and grammar all serve to remind us that variation within and between varieties is normal and standard. Both native and non-native varieties all behave in the same way. As we shall see later, this has extremely important implications for language teaching and learning.

6.5 SAE cultural conventions and pragmatic norms

Probably the most difficult cultural convention for foreigners and speakers of other varieties of English to get used to concerns Australian terms of address. Australians tend to address each other by their first name, although there are exceptions to this rule which are considered below. The age, gender or status of the people is not the most important consideration. So, it is not considered impolite for university students to call their lecturers by their first names as long as the lecturers themselves have indicated that this is acceptable. In the same way, lecturers will commonly call their students by their first names.

Students from other cultures can find this a very difficult thing to do. In response to the request from their lecturer, 'Please call me Bill', many students may feel very uncomfortable. As Li, who is himself a university professor at the City University in Hong Kong, has said:

> For many Asian learners who are accustomed to patterns of interaction characterised by deference and respect, such an invitation may not be readily accepted without the ESL learner undergoing some identity crisis.
>
> (Li, 2002a: 580)

When speaking about the way he himself operates in cross-cultural settings, Li says that he finds it difficult to address a teacher-turned-colleague by his or her first name:

> In my own case, having been exposed to both Chinese and Western norms which may be broadly characterised by opposing ideological positions on two ends of a continuum – hierarchical vs egalitarian – I often have to undergo a mental struggle in the intercultural workplace before settling on a particular choice . . . . I constantly feel that following one set of norms entails violating another.
>
> (Li, 2002a: 581)

In the context of naming and address conventions at university, however, this is not simply an 'Asian' vs 'Western' divide. American students studying in Australia report the same sense of discomfort in addressing their lecturers by their first names. In the United States, students, even postgraduate students, routinely address their lecturers by their title and their last name. So, it will be 'Professor Wilson' or 'Doctor Wilson', not 'Bill' or 'Jane', as in Australia.

Why do foreign students feel so uncomfortable at addressing their lecturers by their first name? There may be several reasons, but the main one is that students misinterpret the use of the first name by automatically comparing it to the ways of naming in their own cultures, where calling people by their first name signals closeness and equal status. It is important to point out, then, that addressing someone by their first name in Australian culture does not necessarily signal closeness or equal status. What it does signal is the value Australians attach to informality and this is expressed in the common use of first names. This means, therefore, that in formal settings, Australians may use titles and family names as terms of address.

Linked to terms of address are ways of greeting and it should be no surprise to learn that Australian ways of greeting differ from those in other varieties of English. If you have taught or learned English from a textbook, you have probably taught or been taught a greeting convention something like this:

A: Hello, how are you?
B: I'm fine thank you. And you?
A: Fine thanks.

In the previous chapter, I suggested that in the United States 'How are you doing?' is a likely common greeting. Australians, on the other hand, may say:

A: Good day, how are you going, mate?
B: Good thanks.

Note, therefore, that Australians are more likely to say 'How are you going?' rather than simply saying 'How are you?' In the same way that 'How are you?' is not a question about your health but a greeting, so 'How are you going?' is not a question about your means of transport. So, while 'by bus' would be a perfectly grammatically correct response, it would be pragmatically incorrect. Note also the Australian preference for using the adjective 'good', used here both before 'day' and in the reply. Finally, the use of the word 'mate' is extremely common in Australian English. It can be used between people, especially men, even if they are strangers.

Needless to say, there is variation in greeting too. Here are greetings recorded off the radio:

(12) 'How's things Bruce?'

Note also the use of the singular copula verb 'is' with the plural noun ('things'), a common feature of many varieties of English.

(13) 'Good day, this is XXX, hello.'

(14) A: Good morning XXX

    B: Good morning XXX

    A: How are ya?

    B: Oh, good.

The examples above all remind us that there are important cultural distinctions between English native speaker societies and that these cultural differences are reflected in the different speech styles of different native speaker varieties of English. Once again we have evidence that variation is natural and normal. All varieties will differ at all the different levels, at the levels of phonology, lexis, syntax and discourse. Cultural differences will also be reflected in different cultural and pragmatic norms.

6.6 Roles and status

English is the national language of Australia and plays a role in every walk of life. But the roles for the broad and cultivated varieties can differ. We noted above how long it took for Australian English to be accepted within Australia. In particular, it was not until the middle of the twentieth century and nearly 200 years after the English arrived in Australia that the Australian Broadcasting Commission accepted Australian English. Today, broadcasters who speak the cultivated variety will be heard on programmes talking about 'serious' matters. For example, most newsreaders and hosts of current affairs and highbrow arts programmes are likely to speak the cultivated variety. In contrast, however, sports commentators, especially if they report quintessentially Australian sports such as Australian rules football, will use the broad or general variety.

The majority of Australian English speakers can use all three varieties. 'Most Australians have the ability to upgrade at will some distance in the spectrum in the direction of cultivated when it seems appropriate under certain social conditions' (Bernard, 1988: 22). The context will determine which variety to use. In general terms we can say that the more people want to express their Australian identity, the more likely they are to use a broad or informal variety. This is a perfectly normal and natural strategy and one that is used by speakers of all varieties. However, there is a general feeling (see Görlach, 1991: 161) that Australians are moving towards a more frequent use of the general pronunciation at the expense of both the broad and cultivated.

I now turn to a discussion of these themes in the context of Australian Aboriginal English (AAE) with a particular focus on comparing AAE's role as an intra-Aboriginal *lingua franca*, and thus as a language of Aboriginal identity, and its role as a *lingua franca* between Aboriginal and what I shall call migrant (i.e. all other) Australians, and thus as a language of communication. As discussed in Chapter 1, this tension between identity and communication is always evident when considering the roles of varieties of English. To what extent is English needed for communication? To what extent is English needed to express identity and to talk about and explain cultural values? To what extent is English needed to construct knowledge in a culturally appropriate and distinctive way?

6.7   **Australian Aboriginal English: Background**

It has been estimated that, when the British, that is Captain Cook and his fleet, arrived in Australia in 1770, there were some 250 Aboriginal languages (Dixon, 1993). Dixon stresses that these were languages and not dialects. He distinguishes language from dialect on the criterion of mutual intelligibility. Mutually intelligible 'languages' would thus be classified as dialects, according to Dixon. In other words, Aboriginal Australia was a richly multilingual and multicultural society possessing 250 mutually unintelligible languages. It is this very richness, however, which has contributed to the current relative linguistic poverty. Many Aboriginal languages had a small number of speakers and have since died out. Dixon estimates that, today, no more than 20 are currently being learned by Aboriginal children, although Mackay (1996) estimates that about a third of the original 250 are still spoken today, albeit with many having a very small number of speakers. A key cause of this linguistic death was the arrival of English. The multilingual nature of Aboriginal society meant that a single Aboriginal language was unlikely to assume the role of the language of communication among all Aboriginal Australians. Ironically, this role has been assumed by English in the form of AAE. AAE has become the *lingua franca* between Aboriginal groups themselves. In this intra-Aboriginal *lingua franca* role, English has been extremely successful. Harkins (2000) notes that Aboriginal English is now the primary form of communication for Australian Aboriginals.

The role that AAE plays as a *lingua franca* among Aboriginal people means that AAE must also provide its speakers with Aboriginal identity. It can be predicted, therefore, that Aboriginal English will be characterised by the transfer of pragmatic and cultural norms from Aboriginal languages and, as shown below, this expectation is met.

What is Australian Aboriginal English? Harkins provides this definition:

> AAE is an indigenised variety of English in the sense that it was adopted, however involuntarily, by an indigenous population for whom it is now the primary language of internal and wider communication, and has undergone changes at all levels of language structure to become a distinct dialect with a unique set of linguistic features.
>
> (Harkins, 2000: 61)

And while Aboriginal English is still in contact with diverse Aboriginal languages, including creoles, 'the degree of homogeneity across the several varieties that have been most thoroughly described is quite remarkable' (2000: 61). This relative homogeneity is also commented on by Malcolm *et al.*, who find 'confirmation of remarkable similarities in Aboriginal English across Australia' (1999: 7), and that 'Aboriginal English has become a very significant marker of identity for indigenous Australians' (1999: 8).

6.8   **Syntax of AAE**

Many of the syntactic features of AAE have been transferred from Aboriginal languages. Nevertheless, it is interesting to note that many of these features occur in other varieties of English. Harkins (2000) gives the following examples; I have provided a 'standard' alternative in brackets after each:

- double subjects:
  (15) 'My mother, she came from down there.' (My mother came from down there.)

- multiple negative marking:
  (16) 'They didn' give us nothing.' (They did not give us anything.)

- noun phrase ellipsis:
  (17) 'We went with Christine, with bus, to get alla wild bananas, and come back Tricking Yard . . .'
  (We went with Christine by bus to get bananas and we came back to the Tricking Yard . . .)

The transfer of grammatical features from Aboriginal languages into AAE has also been demonstrated by Koch (2000). In a study of the influence of the Australian Aboriginal language Kaytetye on a variety of AAE known as Central Australian Aboriginal English (CAAE), Koch (2000) has shown that many of the differences between CAAE and SAE are due to the influence of grammatical meanings that are encoded in the indigenous languages of Central Australia. For example, the use in CAAE of a marker '-gether' indicates kinship terms such as 'father and child'. In CAAE, therefore, 'father-gether' means father and child, 'mother-gether' means mother and child, 'brother-gether' means elder and younger brother or sister and 'sister-gether' means elder sister and younger brother or sister (Koch, 2000: 44).

Koch provides many other examples and (18) below shows the use of the CAAE preposition 'belonginto'. Note that the verb ending '-em' in 'callem' is a transitivity marker, also transferred from Kaytetye:

(18) 'Mangwe. That's proper Kaytetye, mangwe. That pussycat **belonginto** — name **belonginto** you fella. We callem mangwe.'

Mangwe is the proper Kaytetye word. The word pussycat is your (i.e. English speaker's) word. We call it mangwe.

(Koch, 2000: 47)

There is no doubt, then, that Aboriginal English is characterised by the transfer of linguistic features from Aboriginal languages. The transfer of pragmatic norms can also be identified.

6.9 AAE cultural conventions and pragmatic norms

An early pioneer into research into pragmatic transfer has been Eades (1991). While it is true to say that Aboriginal society remains multicultural and multilingual, there are a number of shared cultural traits that identify Aboriginal cultures. In her study on the communicative strategies of Aboriginal English, Eades shows that many of these strategies can be traced to the communicative strategies of Aboriginal languages. These include what Eades calls an indirectness in Aboriginal English where Aboriginal people avoid making direct requests and prefer to ask a type of 'trigger' question in order to obtain information. For example, a typical Aboriginal way of asking for a ride into town is to say 'You going to town?' or 'What time are you leaving?' (1991: 88). Related to this is a typical Aboriginal response to direct questions. Speakers of Aboriginal English may not respond at all to a direct request, but provide what has been called the 'yes of gratuitous concurrence' (Eades, 1991: 92). This is used as a strategy for accommodating the directness of interacting with white, or migrant, Australians. This 'yes' lets the speaker know that the listener is attending to what is being said, but it does not mean that the speaker agrees with what is being said, and, in this way appears very similar to the Japanese use of '*hai*' and back channels or '*aizuchi*' (Lo Castro, 1987).

The normal way of eliciting substantial information is to present information, and there is no obligation to respond to either direct or indirect requests for information. If the other person does choose to respond, it may be minutes, hours or even days before the desired information is supplied. All this leads to communicative clashes in settings such as schoolrooms and courts of law. A specific example of this is provided by Cooke (1995) in his report on an inquest that was investigating the shooting of an Aboriginal man. There was an interpreter in the court whose task it was to translate what the Aboriginal witness said.

He points out that 'It became clear . . . that, while counsel showed themselves to be masters of the language games of court, some were quite inept at basic communication with Aboriginal people' (1995: 59). Most importantly, the speech style associated with cross-examination with its reliance on direct questions that follow on one after the other in rapid succession coupled with the counsel's right to interrupt the witness 'tends to be considered highly offensive and inflammatory in any Aboriginal social context' (1995: 87).

Cooke provides some examples of where Aboriginal speech styles are transferred into English and how these created misunderstanding. The following excerpt provides a nice example:

(19) Counsel: But the old man didn't go into the boat, did he?
Aboriginal witness: Yes.
Counsel: I beg your pardon?
Witness: Yes.
Interpreter: He's affiming that he did not go into the boat.

Here the English-speaking counsel is obviously expecting the reply 'no' rather than 'yes'. What the Aboriginal speaker is doing is transferring an Aboriginal speech style into English. In Aboriginal languages, the reply 'yes' would mean 'yes, you are right. The old man did not get into the boat'. In Standard English, however, 'yes' means 'yes, the old man did go into the boat'.

It was also apparent that the complexity and importance of Aboriginal kinship relationships were not fully understood or appreciated, as this extract from the trial shows:

(20) Counsel: What relation was he to you?
      (The Aboriginal witness told the interpreter '*maralkur*'.)
      Interpreter: The word is *maralkur* but I have to interpret that word, as there's no direct translation. Are you ready for the translation?
      Coroner: Yes.
      Interpreter: Maternal grandmother's brother's son.
      Coroner: There's a name for that isn't there? I haven't worked it out yet.

(Cooke, 1995)

A further example of an Aboriginal cultural norm concerns a tolerance for silence, and its reflection in the speech styles in AAE. In Aboriginal culture, Harkins writes: 'Silence is often a sign of comfortable deepening of communication, of preparation for a seriously considered response' (2000: 74). Silence is also the appropriate response when one does not have the authority to speak about a matter and it is accepted 'as a valid response to a question or attempt to elicit information' (2000: 74). Silence is thus tolerated in Aboriginal culture. While it may seem odd to include 'silence' in a discussion of the speech styles, its tolerance in Aboriginal English serves to show how different cultures are reflected in different ways in different varieties of English.

AAE continues to thrive as the *lingua franca* of a growing Aboriginal population. The linguistic features reflect social and cultural meanings and themes for the speakers in ways that make this unique English functional for them as both product and instrument of cultural survival. In order to be accepted by the Aboriginal community as a marker of Aboriginal identity, it is essential that AAE reflects the cultural and pragmatic norms of Aboriginal languages. Only in this way can it ever possibly become an accepted *lingua franca* for Aboriginal Australia. To quote Darlene Oxenham in Collard *et al.*: 'So it's a cultural marker but also a political statement. This is who we are. This is our language' (2000: 96).

Two major functions of language are communication and identity. To refer back to the 'identity–communication continuum' described in Chapter 1. Australian Aboriginal English (AAE) and the broad variety of Standard Australian English (SAE) can be placed at the identity end of the continuum, the general variety of SAE can be placed somewhere in the middle and the cultivated variety of SAE at the communication end. In the context of

Figure 4: The identity–communication continuum

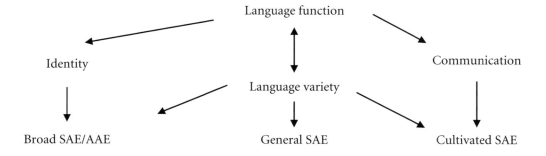

World Englishes and the teaching of English, we need to decide where on this continuum we want our classroom model to be. How important is it for 'our' English to be an identity marker and how important is it to help us communicate internationally? Discussing these questions will help us determine which variety of which model we might then choose.

6.10 **Conclusion**

In this chapter I have looked at varieties of English in Australia and have described features of various varieties of Standard Australian English and compared them with other varieties. I have also described features of Australian Aboriginal English and compared those with SAE. Again this illustrates how normal and natural variation is. Varieties of English are influenced by indigenous languages in a number of ways and are able to reflect the different cultural and pragmatic norms of their speakers. Some varieties of English may be more focused on identity, while others may be more focused on communication. In the next chapter I look further at how varieties of English fulfil the functions of language. In particular, I shall consider how Indian and Sri Lankan English not only fulfil the pragmatic functions of language, but consider the extent to which they are able to fulfil the mathetic functions of language. In contrast to the pragmatic uses of language that demand responses and represent a way of participating in a situation, the mathetic uses of language do not demand a response but represent a way of learning and arise out of the personal and heuristic functions of language (Halliday, 1978: 54–6).

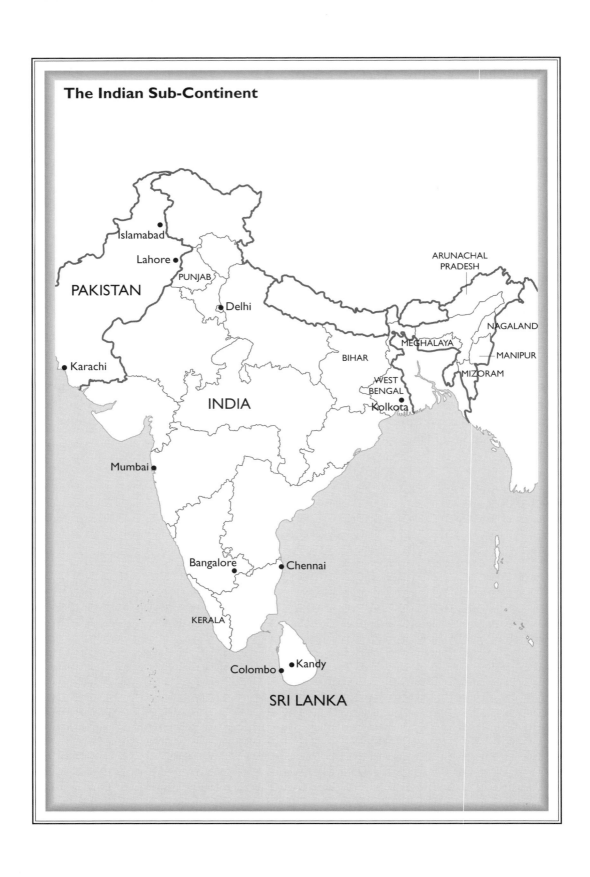

The Indian Sub-Continent

PAKISTAN

- Islamabad
- Lahore

PUNJAB

- Delhi

- Karachi

INDIA

ARUNACHAL PRADESH

NAGALAND

MEGHALAYA

MANIPUR

BIHAR

MIZORAM

WEST BENGAL

- Kolkota

- Mumbai

- Bangalore
- Chennai

KERALA

- Colombo
- Kandy

SRI LANKA

7 Englishes of the subcontinent

7.1 A network of varieties

The following seven extracts (A–G) are examples of just some of the many different varieties of English spoken in South Asia, ranging from an informal 'pidgin-like' oral variety to a formal literary variety. A Sri Lankan poem is also included later. Apart from the poem, I have presented the texts together at the beginning of the chapter to give the reader a feel for this rich variation, but I repeat each one in turn when I discuss them. I also explain the Indian language words italicised in these texts.

A 'Hellow sir! Some rickshaw, some bazaar market, some two rupees, some go and come back. Some silk, some sari, some Ganges. I rickshaw driver. Somebody some friend coming here Varanasi I help you.'

(rickshaw driver touting for business; Mehrotra, 2000: 49)

B 'Happy that British time that very happy madam. Now no (laughter) . . . on that time very nice. British time. Money is controlled time. Now rice is at a 1 kilo – 2.50. That time get 1 rupee 8 kilo. British time . . . lot of money that is all cheaper. Take eh ones any clothes take 10 rupees you get 1 shirt 1 pant. Now 1 shirt 1 pant you take 100 rupees – no.'

(sample of 'Butler' English; Hosali, 2005: 36)

C 'Two rival groups are out to have fun . . . you know generally indulge in *dhamal* and pass time. So, what do they do? Pick on a *bechaara bakra* who has entered college.'

(from a teenage journal; D'Souza, 2001: 152)

D 'And if he says *ki* I want the *matlab* dowry sort of thing.'

(from a conversation; Valentine, 1991: 331)

E 'She bent her head to receive her mother-in-law's blessing. *"Sat Sri Akal"*.
"Sat Sri Akal," replied Sabhrai lightly touching Champak's shoulder.
"Sat Sri Akal," said Sher Singh.
"Live in plenty, live a long age," replied Sabhrai taking her son's hand and kissing it.
"Sleep well".'

(from I Shall Not Hear the Nightingale by Khushwant Singh, quoted in Kachru, 1991a: 301)

F 'Years ago, a slender sapling from a foreign field was grafted by "pale hands" on the mighty and many-branched Indian banyan tree. It has kept growing vigorously and now an organic part of its parent tree, it has spread its own probing roots into the brown soil below. Its young leaves rustle energetically in the strong winds that blow from the western horizon, but the sunshine that warms it and the rain that cools it are from Indian skies; and it continues to draw its vital sap from "this earth, this realm," this India.'

(Naik and Narayan, 2004: 253)

Now follows a discussion of each example.

> A 'Hellow sir! Some rickshaw, some bazaar market, some two rupees, some go and come back. Some silk, some sari, some Ganges. I rickshaw driver. Somebody some friend coming here Varanasi I help you.'
>
> (rickshaw driver touting for business; Mehrotra, 2000: 49)

'A' is a sample of what Mehrotra has classified as Pidgin Indian English. He makes this classification based on criteria including that it is a sample of a reduced and simplified language, that it is no one's mother tongue, that its use is restricted to a trade or occupation and that it is shaped by more than one language. Of these criteria the fact that it is no one's mother tongue does not distinguish it from any other variety, and being 'reduced and simplified' is, as discussed in Chapter 1, a criticism often made about new or dialectal varieties of English and one that is often based on prejudice rather than linguistic evidence. As for being shaped by more than one language, I have argued in Chapter 4 and elsewhere in this book that traditional English itself has been shaped by more than one language. Its use only for trade purposes means that it could be classified as a register, except that the speaker is only able to speak this variety, and the term 'register' usually refers to a variety spoken in a certain profession such as the legal or medical profession and its users are assumed to be able to speak a range of other varieties of the language. But however it is classified, it clearly represents an informal variety spoken by a poorly educated person.

> B 'Happy that British time that very happy madam. Now no (laughter) . . . on that time very nice. British time. Money is controlled time. Now rice is at a 1 kilo – 2.50. That time get 1 rupee 8 kilo. British time . . . lot of money that is all cheaper. Take eh ones any clothes take 10 rupees you get 1 shirt 1 pant. Now 1 shirt 1 pant you take 100 rupees – no'.
>
> (sample of 'Butler' English; Hosali, 2005: 36)

The variety exemplified in 'B' above is commonly referred to as 'Butler' English (Hosali, 2005), and originates from the 'variety spoken by native servants when communicating with their English speaking masters' (Hosali, 2005: 34). It is still spoken today by domestic and other servants (hotel and club staff, for example) and is classified as 'pidgin-like' by Hosali.

> C 'Two rival groups are out to have fun . . . you know generally indulge in *dhamal* and pass time. So, what do they do? Pick on a *bechaara bakra* who has entered college.'
>
> (from a teenage journal; D'Souza, 2001: 152)

'C' is taken from a teenage journal and shows the presence of local language, in this case Hindi, which gives it its 'Indian' flavour. *Dhamal* is a Sanskrit word that traditionally meant a type of Sufi trance dance and now just means a type of dance. *Bechaara bakra* means 'a poor goat' in Hindi (D'Souza, 2001: 152).

> D 'And if he says *ki* I want the *matlab* dowry sort of thing.'
>
> (from a conversation; Valentine, 1991: 331)

'D' also shows the use of Hindi words, but in this conversation the Hindi words that have been transferred into English are discourse markers rather than cognates. *Ki* is a complementiser and, in this context, *matlab* is acting as a pause or hesitation marker (Valentine, 1991).

> E 'She bent her head to receive her mother-in-law's blessing. *"Sat Sri Akal"*.
>
> *"Sat Sri Akal,"* replied Sabhrai lightly touching Champak's shoulder.
>
> *"Sat Sri Akal,"* said Sher Singh.
>
> "Live in plenty, live a long age," replied Sabhrai taking her son's hand and kissing it. "Sleep well".'
>
> (from I Shall Not Hear the Nightingale by Khushwant Singh, quoted in Kachru, 1991a: 301)

Text 'E' is an excerpt from the novel *I Shall Not Hear The Nightingale* by the Sikh author Khushwant Singh. The 'Indianness' of this extract stems from the author's use of traditional Sikh greetings. 'Sat Sri Akal' (which means 'God is truth') is a formulaic greeting or farewell. In her analysis of this piece, Kachru (1991a) points out that the exchange suggests that the mother-in-law is cool towards her daughter-in-law precisely because they exchange only these formulaic greetings. This piece reflects local cultures – a 'foreign' reader unfamiliar with Indian cultures would probably not receive this message of coolness between the two women.

A foreigner might, however, perceive the coolness evident in this second extract from Khushwant Singh's writings (Kachru, 1991a: 302):

> '"This is only your kindness. I will do the best I can," said Buta Singh.
>
> The visitors also got up and slipped their feet back into their shoes. "When shall we present ourselves?"
>
> "Come and see me sometime tomorrow – at the law courts."
>
> "Sardar Sahib," spoke another. "We have pinned all our hopes on you. You do this for us and we will sing your praise the rest of our lives."
>
> "We will remain ever grateful," exclaimed the others.
>
> *"Accaji Namastey* . . . some water or something?" asked Buta Singh mechanically and, without waiting for a reply, dismissed them: *"Namastey."*
>
> "This is like our own home. We would ask for anything we want. *Sat Sri Akal.*"'

As Kachru (1991a) explains, the participants are of equal rank, although Buta Singh has power over the others here in that they are asking him for a favour. As is correct in pluralistic India, the Sikh participant uses the Hindi farewell (*Accaji Namastey*) while the Hindi participants use the Sikh farewell (*Sat Sri Akal*). As with Text 'E' above, however, this correct use of formulaic greetings actually suggests a coolness between the parties, as does the use of the superficially warm but formulaic expressions of warmth and closeness ('This is like our own home. We would ask for anything we want.') While this cultural reading might be missed by a foreign reader, the coolness is more transparent in the mechanical way that Buta Singh offers his guests a glass of water and then promptly dismisses them without allowing them the chance to accept. Both these excerpts from Kushwant Singh's writings are obviously 'Indian' and reflect Indian cultural norms.

> F 'Years ago, a slender sapling from a foreign field was grafted by "pale hands" on the mighty and many-branched Indian banyan tree. It has kept growing vigorously and now an organic part of its parent tree, it has spread its own probing roots into the brown soil below. Its young leaves rustle energetically in the strong winds that blow from the western horizon, but the sunshine that warms it and the rain that cools it are from Indian skies; and it continues to draw its vital sap from "this earth, this realm," this India.'
>
> (Naik and Narayan 2004: 253)

Excerpt 'F' is the final passage of Naik and Narayan's book on Indian English literature (2004). This type of style can be considered Indian, a style that might be described as ornate or flowery. Its extended use of metaphor and its 'bookishness' (Kachru, 1983: 41) give it this flavour. As illustrated in the two further examples from their book below, the authors also make frequent use of what Kachru has termed 'phrase-mongering' – his examples include the phrase 'Himalayan blunder' (1983: 40). In the example below, the authors are summing up the current political situation in India and use the splendidly portentous phrase, 'thunderous Jeremiad':

> Nevertheless, the overall situation in India today does not warrant a thunderous Jeremiad.
>
> (2004: 15)

In the second example, the authors are defending the writer who chooses to write in Indian English. It is replete with 'phrase-mongering':

> The regional writer need not debunk his Indian English brother as a rootless wretch, a bastard booby, fattened British butter or a 'bat on the banyan bough'.
>
> (2004: 253)

The final text, 'G', is a poem called *The Cobra:*

> G Your great hood was like a flag
>   hung up there
>   in the village.
>   Endlessly the people came to Weragoda –
>   watched you (your eyes like braziers),
>   standing somewhat afar.
>   They stood before you in obeisance. Death,
>   the powers of the *paramitas*, took you to heaven
>   however.

The sky, vertical, is where you are now
shadowing the sun, curling round and round my mind.
They whisper death-stories –
but it was only my woman Dunkiriniya,
the very lamp of my heart,
that died.

This poem is by one of Sri Lanka's finest poets, Lakdasa Wikkramasinha, and it is one of the poems that you can hear read by the Sri Lankan scholar Thiru Kandiah on the accompanying CD. *Paramitas* are the disciplines Buddhists are expected to observe on their way to Nirvana. Wikkramasinha died tragically young and despite writing all his six volumes of poetry in English apparently hated himself for writing in English. In this and the following chapters of this part of the book, the ability of indigenous varieties of English to reflect and represent the cultures of the authors writing in English will be a frequent topic of discussion. I think it is fair to say that, overall, the majority of such writers feel that English can be adapted to reflect their own cultures, but there are some who are vehemently adamant that it cannot and others who, accepting that English can be nativised, are angry that they feel they have to write in English rather than in a local language. Wikkramasinha is perhaps the angriest of them all, as this excerpt from his artistic manifesto shows:

'I have come to realise that I am writing the language of the most despicable and loathsome people on earth: I have no wish to extend its life and range, enrich its totality. To write in English is a form of cultural treason. I have had for the future to think of a way of circumventing this treason. I propose to do this by making my writing entirely immoralist and destructive'.

(cited in Canagarajah, 1994: 375)

These views and those expressed in Excerpt 'F' could hardly be more different.

7.2 **Background**

The excerpts of different varieties of South Asian English quoted above serve to support the truism that South Asian English in general and Indian English in particular is a 'network of varieties', that include regional and occupational varieties as well as standard Indian English (Hosali, 2005: 34). One reason for this 'network of varieties' is that the linguistic situation in India is extraordinarily complex. Mehrotra (1998) describes India as a baffling mosaic of multilingualism. He reports that the 1961 census of India identified 1652 mother tongues, 67 of which are used as media of instruction in schools (Biswas, 2004). The Indian constitution lists the following 18 languages as the major languages of India: Assamese, Bengali, Gujerati, Hindi, Kannada, Kashmiri, Konkani, Malayalam, Manipuri, Marathi, Nepali, Oriya, Panjabi, Sanskrit, Sindhi, Tamil, Telugu and Urdu.

Hindi is the official language, yet the constitution is actually written in English, and English is classified as an 'associate official language'. But, as the excerpts above illustrate, English is also used in a wide range of domains, ranging from informal through to formal. It is used by people of all classes, from the poorly educated to the middle and upper class elites, although it must be stressed that the majority of the population of more than one billion do not speak it at all. English in India operates thus in public and private domains and its functions include instrumental, regulative, interpersonal and ideational (Kandiah, 1991). To explain how it is that English has maintained this position in India, a brief summary of the history of English in India is needed.

The date commonly given to mark the coming of English to India is 31 December 1600. This was the date on which Queen Elizabeth I of England gave a monopoly on trade with India to a group of English merchants (Ferguson, 1996). The missionaries soon followed, especially after 1659, when they were allowed to use the ships of the East India Company (Kachru, 1983). However, their work was restricted until the beginning of the nineteenth century when a resolution was passed in the British House of Commons in 1813 that resolved to promote 'useful knowledge' and 'religious and moral improvement' among the 'native inhabitants of India' (Kachru, 1983: 20).

Shortly later, the famous Macaulay Minute of 1835 was passed. Macaulay's objective was to form a 'class who may be interpreters between us and the millions we govern – a class of persons, Indian in blood and colour, but English in taste, in opinion, in morals and in intellect' (Kachru, 1983: 22). This Minute officially institutionalised English in India (Kachru, 1996) and led to the establishment of the English-medium universities of Mumbay, Calcutta and Madras. The link between government and trade can be seen here, as these were the cities where the British East India Company had established key presences (Mehrotra, 1998).

At the time, however, the policy of favouring English and using it in education was not universally popular. Two groups appeared that became known as the 'Anglicists' (those who favoured the promotion of English, especially in education) and the 'Orientalists' (those who favoured the promotion of local languages). A similar debate between comparable groups can be seen in many places today and will be discussed in later chapters. The debate in India between these two groups has remained constant and heated over the centuries, but, by and large, the Anglicists have tended to retain the upper hand, as can be seen in the Official Languages Act of 1967. This legalised the use of English and established it as an associate official language to be used with Hindi 'for all official purposes of the Union, for Parliament and for communications between the Union and the States' (Ferguson, 1996: 31).

In order to enhance 'national unity and facile [sic] intra-state, inter-state and international communication' the government has adopted the 'three language formula' (Biswas, 2004: 107). This formula requires that children in Hindi-speaking areas should learn Hindi, English and one other Indian language at school, while children in non-Hindi-speaking areas should learn their mother tongue, Hindi and English. In practice, however, this formula has not been uniformly successful. States have been given the freedom to introduce the third language at any time and this has meant that the results are extremely mixed. It is probably true to say that the Indian film industry, 'Bollywood', is as instrumental in making Hindi known to people outside Hindi-speaking areas as schools. Otherwise, English is preferred to Hindi among speakers of the Dravidian languages of the south. Hindi is spoken only in the north and is a member of a different language family. Not surprisingly perhaps, Hindi-speaking states are sometimes uncommitted to the teaching of a second Indian language with the result that many Hindi speakers speak only Hindi and English with any degree of fluency (Saghal, 1991).

States also have the power to decide which language(s) will be official languages and which will be studied as first, second or third languages. Thus English is the first, official language of Nagaland and an associate official language of Manipur, Meghalaya and Mizoram (Naik and Narayan, 2004). It is studied as a first language in Arunachal Prasad and Mizoram, as a second language in Kerala and West Bengal and as a third language in Bihar and Punjab (Biswas, 2004).

A major reason why English has retained its position is that it is the only language in India that is spoken or used across the entire country and it is therefore an obvious choice as a neutral link language or *lingua franca*. D'Souza goes as far to say that English is, 'perhaps, along with Hindi, the only true Indian language' (2001: 150).

7.3 Sri Lanka

The situation in Sri Lanka, the island nation off the south of India, presents similarities and differences. One similarity is that it was the missionaries who started the teaching of English. It was not until the 1830s that the government started to promote education in English (Kachru, 1983), with the Colebrook-Cameron Commission recommending that 'education should be held out to the natives so that they may in time qualify themselves for holding some of the higher appointments' (Raheem and Ratwatte, 2004: 93). In 1832, some 640 private and 236 missionary schools were using English as a medium of instruction, while only the 97 state schools were teaching in the mother tongue. The culmination of British educational policy came with the establishment of the English-medium University of Ceylon in 1942 (Fernando, 1996). By the time of Ceylon's independence and renaming as Sri Lanka in 1948, however, the situation had radically changed, as only 7 per cent of the total school population were in private or missionary schools and 93 per cent were in state schools using a mother tongue as a medium of instruction (Raheem and Ratwatte, 2004).

A major difference between India and Sri Lanka helps explain this. Sri Lanka is far less complex linguistically than India, as there are only two major languages spoken there: the language of the majority, Sinhala, and the language of the minority, Tamil. The majority are thus able to define the national identity of Sri Lanka through the use of Sinhala and the religion of the majority of Sinhalese, Buddhism (Kandiah, 1991). Thus, shortly after the establishment of Sri Lankan independence in 1948, a Sinhala-only policy was introduced and this led to the rise of a new national bourgeoisie occupying positions that had previously been held by the English-speaking elite (Raheem and Ratwatte, 2004). It has been claimed that this new Sinhala-speaking elite had no desire to promote English, as the promotion of English might lead to a new English-speaking elite that could threaten their own status (Kandiah, 1991).

Nevertheless, as Raheem and Ratwatte (2004) point out, English retained its position in certain domains of Sri Lankan life. It continued to be the medium of instruction in university faculties of science, medicine and engineering. Its international importance meant that certain government ministries, Trade and Tourism, for example, elected to retain English.

It also operates as a *lingua franca* or bridge language between the Sinhala majority and the Tamil minority, for, while some Tamil speakers know Sinhala, few Sinhala speakers know Tamil. Its role as a link language was officially recognised in 1987, and in 1995 it was proclaimed a national language. It has since been introduced from grades 1 to 3 in schools, 'not as a subject but in the form of bilingual teaching where primary teachers are encouraged to use vocabulary items from English and the mother tongue' (Raheem and Ratwatte, 2004: 103). However, at the time of writing, given limited resources, there are insufficient primary teachers with enough knowledge of English to implement this policy in more than a piecemeal way. But it is important to note that, the views of Wikkramasinha notwithstanding, the younger generation of Sri Lankans are more likely to see English as a language of modern life, technology and youth culture, than as a language of colonial control. Code mixing is common and a Sri Lankan variety of English is emerging, which has led scholars such as Parakrama (1995) and Canagarajah (2000) to urge for the acceptance of a wider range of norms than those traditionally associated with the educated elite. In the next part of the chapter a selection of the linguistic features of Indian and Sri Lankan Englishes will be described.

7.4   Linguistic features of South Asian Englishes

7.4.1   Phonology

As was noted above, Indian English operates across a wide range of domains, regions and functions. The phonological examples below represent the pronunciation of Standard Indian English, although, given the number of languages spoken in India, there are obviously regional variations in its pronunciation. Indian English (IE) is rhotic, that is to say /r/ is pronounced in post-vocalic environments, so that the 'r' in 'part' and in 'poor' will be sounded.

Please note that, while I use RP sounds as a point of comparison, this is the only reason for using them. All new varieties of English need to be described in their own right. The sounds of the new varieties are the correct sounds for those varieties. The IE sounds here are taken from Nihalani *et al.* (2004).

The RP diphthongs in 'coat' and 'day' are pronounced as monophthongs in IE to give /koːt/ and /deː/ respectively and the RP central vowels /ɜː/, /ə/ and /ʌ/ are all pronounced /ə/ in IE. The RP vowel sounds in 'cot' and 'caught' are pronounced /kɒt/ and /kɒːt/ respectively in IE.

As far as consonant sounds are concerned, in some varieties of standard IE, both /v/ and /w/ can be pronounced /ʋ/. Both /t/ and /d/ can be pronounced as retroflex sounds and /θ/ and /ð/ as plosives.

7.4.2 Lexis

In an experiment to discover whether words or expressions of Indian English were understood by speakers of British English, Mehrotra (2003) chose 20 such words. A selection of ten of these is included below. The relevant words and expressions are italicised and their actual meanings are given at the end of the chapter. Some of these words derive from local languages and others display a different semantic range in Indian English.

1. Her *face-cut* is very impressive.
2. The students want some *important* questions from their teacher.
3. I came here in a *tempo*.
4. He speaks *chaste* Hindi.
5. Fifty students have applied for *freeship* this year.
6. The sportsmen are given 5% *weightage*.
7. Mr Bajej is the *whole sole* in this factory.
8. This is a *match box*.
9. Please finish the *beer bottle* and then we can go.
10. I hope he will *do the needful* for us.

Influence of the local languages also leads to what Kachru (1983: 38) has called 'hybridisation', whereby a local word and an English word combine to form a word or expression of Indian English. Examples Kachru gives include 'lathi charge' ('lathi' means baton) and 'tiffin carrier' ('tiffin' means lunch or meal and has now become part of many varieties of English, as indeed have countless other Indian words, 'bungalow', 'mango', 'pyjamas', 'junk', 'curry' and 'verandah' to name just a few). Suffixes from local languages can also be attached to English words to give 'policewala', 'goondaism' and 'patelship', for example. Direct translations from local languages create new words and collocations so that from Hindi we get 'on this her flower-bed, her seven children were born' (marriage bed) and from the Sri Lankan language Sinhala we get 'to buy and give' and to 'break rest'.

In Excerpt 'E' above, the Sikh term for greeting was used. Similar terms can be translated (Kachru, 1983: 132) so that other greetings in Indian English can be 'bow my forehead' and 'bless my hovel with the good dust of your feet', while forms of address include 'cherisher of the poor' and 'mother of my daughter'. This use of translation goes well beyond greetings and address. 'Thou shalt write from an inkwell of gold' and 'you goose-faced minion' provide an example of flattery and cursing respectively.

Excerpt 'C' above provides further examples of the transfer of Hindi words and phrases into English and Excerpt 'D' of the transfer of Hindi discourse markers. Valentine also illustrates the transfer of the Hindi tags 'no' and 'nuh' into English, as in these two examples:

> 'If the child shows little interest in something there is a lot of encouragement from the home, from the institution, from the government, no?'

> 'I think you're to that view, nuh?'

(Valentine, 1991: 332).

7.4.3 Syntax

Kachru (1983) identifies three features of Indian English that are shared with many other varieties. The first is the distinctive use or non-use of articles, the second is the reduplication of words and the third is 'yes–no confusion' – also seen in Australian Aborigine English – as in the exchange below:

> A: You have no objection?
> B: Yes. (I have no objection)

(1983: 13)

Further features Indian English shares with other varieties include interrogative word order in indirect questions as in 'tell me where can you meet us' and the use of invariant tag questions as in 'you know it isn't it?', 'he is coming isn't it?', and 'you went there yesterday isn't it?' (Srivastava and Sharma, 1991: 197–9).

In the next chapter a more complete list of syntactic features that are shared by many varieties of English is given and possible explanations for these similarities are considered in Part C of the book.

Perhaps the syntactic feature most associated with Indian English is the use of the present continuous in contexts where other varieties would use the simple present. This use is particularly remarkable with verbs of sense and knowing and stative verbs, as these do not take the present continuous in the same contexts. Examples of Indian English use include:

> 'They were knowing the names.'
> 'Shammi must be knowing my sister.'
> 'We are having our house in Thana.'
> 'You must be having a lot of friends of your own age.'
> 'And what ideas are you having about the descriptive paper?'
> 'You're not being audible.'
> 'There is a matter being before the supreme court now.'

(examples all drawn from the ICE corpus of Indian English, de Ersson, 2005)

This use of the present continuous is usually explained as being caused by direct transfer from Indian languages (Jackson, 1981). It is also important to stress that what Indians are marking here is not so much the progressive as the continuative, so that the sentence 'I am knowing him for 20 years', not only means that I have known him for 20 years, but that I shall continue to know him in the future.

7.4.4 **Cultural conventions**

Culturally distinctive uses of greetings, farewells, curses and flattery have been exemplified above, so I will not repeat them here. In a series of studies on request strategies in Indian English, Sridhar (1991) draws the following conclusions:

1. Indian English speakers use direct questions and 'desiderative' statements (I want/I need etc.) more frequently than speakers of British English and use indirect questions less frequently.

2. The request strategies of Indian English speakers are transferred from local languages.

3. A British form in an Indian context may carry a different meaning. For example, the use of 'will you' might be seen as abrupt or even rude in a British context but not so in an Indian one.

4. There is variety among the request strategies of Indian English speakers.

The findings from this type of research are of particular significance when it comes to the teaching of English, for it would clearly be unwise to teach British request strategies in Indian contexts, as these might well be culturally inappropriate. Questions of this type will be considered in detail in Part C of the book, but it is worth underlining here Kandiah's belief (1991) that members of local speech communities should be the ones who define the norms for those communities. Many speakers of Indian and Sri Lankan English use English habitually and for a wide variety of functions. They are therefore native speakers of their variety and it is they who should have the right to decide what is correct and what is not. This plea is echoed by D'Souza, when she says 'it is for the community to argue about and decide on (standards), rather than have them imposed from outside' (2001: 158).

The 'Indianness' of Indian English is further explored below in the context of creative writing.

7.5 **Indian literature in English**

As previously mentioned, the contrasting views presented in Excerpt 'F' above and by the Sri Lankan poet Wikkramasinha represent two extremes. While Wikkramasinha's views find some support, as can be seen from the quotes provided below, the majority of South Asian writers agree that English is now a language of South Asia and that it can be adapted to suit Indian cultures and tastes.

The author Raja Rao, writing in the foreword to his seminal and iconic piece *Kanthapura* published in 1963, said, 'English is not really an alien language to us . . . our method of expression has to be a dialect which will some day prove to be as distinctive and colourful as the Irish or the American' (cited in Crystal, 1997: 135). Rao continued, 'We shall have English with us and amongst us, and not as our guest or friend, but as one of our own, of our castes, our creed, our sect and of our tradition' (quoted in Srivastava and Sharma,

1991: 190), and he warns, 'We cannot write like the English. We should not. We can only write as Indians' (1991: 205).

Ruchira Mukerjee, author of *Toad in my Garden* (Picador: 1998), suggests that Rao's prediction has been fulfilled:

> 'There are many people writing in English in India and at last people are beginning to think in English. Many are writing with a great flow and flair, which proves that English is no more a foreign language but a part of our psyche.'
>
> (cited in D'Souza, 2001: 148)

In a way that foreshadows the views of the Nigerian novelist Wole Soyinka and which will be considered in the next chapter, D'Souza herself argues that English has been Indianised by being 'borrowed, transcreated, recreated, stretched, extended, contorted perhaps' (2001: 150).

The well-known Indian novelist Anita Desai agrees. Indian life is an amalgam of many languages, cultures and civilisations that form 'one very compactly woven whole' (1996: 221). She has found English 'flexible, elastic, resilient, capable of taking on whatever tones, rhythms and colours I choose' (1996: 222).

Similar views can be heard in Pakistan. The novelist Sidhwa writes:

> English . . . is no longer the monopoly of the British. We the excolonised have subjugated the language, beaten it on its head and made it ours.
>
> (Sidhwa, 1996: 231)

Importantly, Sidhwa is careful to distinguish between British writers of South Asian origin who have lived most of their lives in Britain and who represent a new breed of *British* writer, and people like herself, novelists 'who use English as a Pakistani vernacular' (1996: 239):

> We have to stretch the language to adapt it to alien thoughts and values which have no precedent of expression in English, subject the language to a pressure that distorts, or if you like, enlarges its scope and changes its shape . . .
>
> (1996: 240)

The above authors all agree that English can be adapted to suit and reflect Indian culture. As South Asians, they can write in English to express South Asian experience. They extol the creative and flexible qualities of English. A different tone can, however, be discerned in the writings of another Sri Lankan poet, Yasmine Gooneratne, a selection of whose poems are read by Thiru Kandiah on the accompanying CD. Gooneratne feels:

> 'There is still a deep-seated resentment in countries such as India, Pakistan and Sri Lanka, perhaps in Africa, too, but certainly in regions that possess an ancient and written literature, and a creative literary tradition of their own – against English, which was the principal tool used by their nineteenth century rulers in the process of their deracination.'
>
> (cited in Bailey, 1996: 40)

It is perhaps significant that the two people to express strong antagonism towards the use of English are both from Sri Lanka, a place where English has had a very different history from its history in India. It is important to consider the possibility that, while writers can adapt English to reflect their own cultural backgrounds, many may, at the same time, feel a resentment that they feel obliged to use English as a medium in which to write, and through which they need to gain or disseminate learning.

This resentment can become particularly evident in the field of academic writing, where the empirical–scientific knowledge paradigm and the need for 'Anglo' rhetorical styles can greatly disadvantage those unfamiliar with both. In the context of Sri Lanka, Fernando (1996) points out that Sri Lankan dialectic developed to serve a metaphysical–religious knowledge paradigm. Traditionally, Sri Lankans valued metaphysical and religious knowledge, closely associated with Buddhism, as there was a need to seek spiritual truths to help people cope with the transient nature of life. This has been replaced by what she calls a Western need to seek empirical truths to improve people's material wellbeing (1996: 209) and that this requires a scientific–technological paradigm. Traditional wisdom, it has been claimed, is now no longer valued on the one hand and, on the other, provides no models in terms of the scientific–technological paradigm (see also Canagarajah, 2005). As a result, Sri Lankan university students and academics have to learn and depend on Western models in order to gain 'knowledge'. Kachru makes a comparable point in relation to the Indian tradition. Hindi inherited the Sanskrit tradition and 'all the literary conceits and poetic conventions of Sanskrit are found in Hindi too' (1991b: 230). Hindi also adopted, through its Urdu 'cousin', Perso–Arabic traditions. However, there is no tradition of rhetoric in Hindi or any other modern Indian language, if rhetoric is defined as 'conventions of writing effectively for various purposes' (1991b: 230). As the Sanskrit tradition suggests that Indians think in non-linear patterns and in a 'circle or spiral of continuously developing potentialities' (1991b: 231), the implication is that Indian students and academics have to learn an Anglo-American style of rhetoric and thinking.

This, according to Fernando, disadvantages Indians and Sri Lankans in two major ways. First, their own traditional knowledge paradigms have become devalued. Second, they have to master a new knowledge paradigm and its attendant rhetorical style in order to obtain currently valued knowledge. This in turn means that the flow and dissemination of knowledge can potentially become dangerously one-way, moving from the 'Anglo' centre to the periphery. While acknowledging the inherent danger and injustice in this, it is possible that, in the same way that English has been adapted to reflect local cultural experience, it can be similarly shaped to disseminate local and traditional knowledge back to the Anglo centre and thus encourage a multidirectional flow of knowledge. The extraordinary increase in interest in the United States and elsewhere in the traditional Indian practice of yoga and in the traditional Sri Lankan practice of ayurvedic medicine may give some cause for optimism that traditional knowledge will not be lost, but rather spread to a wider audience. The related question of whether that knowledge necessarily becomes altered when reframed in English needs to be researched.

7.6 **Conclusion**

This chapter has demonstrated the extraordinary range of varieties and functions of Indian English. A brief comparison between the history of English in India and Sri Lanka has been made. Given the range and functions of English, particularly in India, it can be sensibly argued that many speakers of Indian and Sri Lankan English are native speakers of those varieties and that they should therefore determine the norms of those varieties.

Furthermore the rich output of Indian English literature – Naik and Narayan (2004) review the works of no fewer than 56 authors who have published in the two decades between 1980 and 2000 – is firm evidence that English has become a South Asian language. The next chapter considers similar questions in the African context.

Meanings of Indian English words and expressions from page 93:

1. Her *face-cut* is very impressive. (profile)
2. The students want some *important* questions from their teacher. (relevant, questions likely to come up in the exam)
3. I came here in a *tempo*. (a 3-wheeled vehicle)
4. He speaks *chaste* Hindi. (pure)
5. Fifty students have applied for *freeship* this year. (tuition-free place)
6. The sportsmen are given 5% *weightage*. (weighting, in other words people good at sports might get an extra 5% on their exam results)
7. Mr Bajej is the *whole sole* in this factory. (the boss, the man in charge)
8. This is a *match box*. (an empty box)
9. Please finish the *beer bottle* and then we can go. (bottle of beer)
10. I hope he will *do the needful* for us. (do what is necessary)

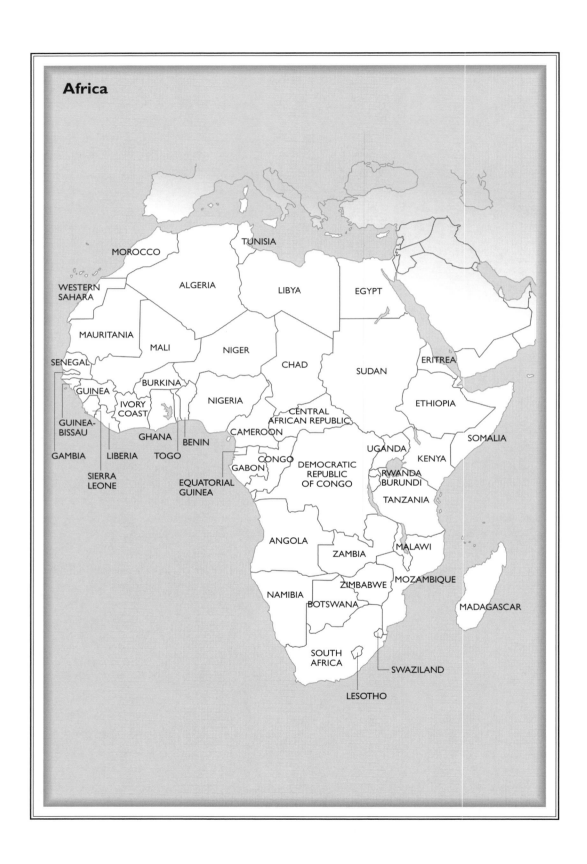

Africa

8 **Voices from Africa**

Africa is a richly diverse continent that is made up of 54 different nation states. It is one of the most multilingual regions in the world with speakers of more than 1,300 languages. Sub-Saharan Africa is one of the world's most complex linguistic areas (Wolf, 2001: 7) and African nations are typically highly multilingual. To take the countries that will be considered in this chapter as examples, more than 300 languages are spoken in Nigeria and there are 11 *official* languages in South Africa. Some 50 languages are spoken in Ghana and the linguistic complexity of Cameroon is heightened, as two European languages, French and English, are both co-official languages. It is essential to bear this linguistic complexity and diversity in mind in a discussion of English in Africa. Each nation presents its own unique sociolinguistic environment. Schmied underlines this complexity, 'The position of the English language in the different African nation-states is complex and varies considerably' (Schmied, 1991: 33).

Nevertheless, the Englishes of the countries of sub-Saharan Africa are often classified into three distinct groups: East African English, spoken in Kenya and Tanzania, for example; Southern African English, spoken in South Africa, Zimbabwe and Botswana, for example; and West African English, spoken in Cameroon, Ghana and Nigeria, for example. As this chapter will illustrate, the roles and varieties of English in these countries differ greatly, despite a number of linguistic similarities. It is also important to stress that, while English is spoken in many African countries, only an educated minority speak and use English. The great majority of Africans speak African languages and, if they speak English, it is as a form of pidgin English. The educated minority are likely to speak at least three languages: a European *lingua franca*, primarily English or French; an African *lingua franca*; and a local African language. The respective roles of a European *lingua franca*, an African *lingua franca* and local languages is a question of great debate in most African countries.

The focus of this chapter will be on the Englishes of Nigeria and South Africa, with examples of other African Englishes provided for comparison. In addition to the linguistic features of these Englishes, the role of English in these countries, especially in regard to education, will also be discussed. Underlying the whole discussion will be the question of whether African Englishes can successfully reflect and represent African cultures while at the same time remaining viable as media for international communication.

8.1   Englishes in Nigeria

Nigeria is one of six West African states that have English as an official language. The others are Cameroon, Ghana, Liberia, the Republic of the Gambia and Sierra Leone. This can be explained by the colonial history of these countries and the previous role of English there as a colonial language. As has been the case in many parts of the world, when these countries attained independence, they elected not to dispense with the language of the colonial powers. English has been the most enduring legacy of British colonial power in Africa and one major reason for this is that it operates as an internally neutral *lingua franca* in these multilingual countries. In Nigeria's case, this was important. While several hundred indigenous languages are spoken in Nigeria, there are three local languages that have a very large number of speakers. These are Hausa, Igbo and Yoruba, all of which are spoken by about 20 per cent of the large population of some 110 million people. While these three languages serve as *lingua francas*, they are regionally distributed, with Hausa being spoken in the north, Igbo in the east and Yoruba in the west. On independence in 1960, in an attempt to avoid privileging any of these regions, the Nigerian capital was built at Abuja, precisely because it was not in a place where any of the three major local languages were spoken.

The history of English in Nigeria differs between the north and the south, partly because colonial administration came late to Nigeria. Although the British set up a trading post in Lagos in 1860, Nigeria did not officially become a colony until 1914. The colonial administration set up schools in the north and brought in English teachers from England who were speakers of RP. In contrast, the English teachers in the south had traditionally been missionaries and their main concern was the teaching of the gospel rather than of Standard English (Schmied, 1991). This has led to differences in the Englishes of North and South Nigeria and in attitudes towards different varieties of English. The Lagos elite in the west still prefers RP while others promote standard Nigerian English – although much debate continues over this, as will be illustrated below.

In fact, four varieties of Nigerian English have been identified (Bamgbose, 1982: 100–101) and these can be classified along the now familiar identity–communication continuum, with V1 and V2 at the identity end and V3 and V4 at the communication end. The varieties are:

Variety 1: This is a pidgin English and marked by a wholesale transfer of phonological / syntactic and lexical features from local languages. This is considered neither socially acceptable nor internationally intelligible, but it is worth noting that 40 per cent of the population of about 110 million use some form of pidgin English.

Variety 2: The syntax is similar to standard English (usually this means British English) but it remains strongly marked by phonological and lexical peculiarities. It is socially acceptable but has low international intelligibility. Variety 2 is spoken by 75 per cent of those who do speak English.

Variety 3: This is close to standard British English but with some distinct phonetic/lexical features. This is seen as socially acceptable and internationally intelligible. This variety is spoken only by 10 per cent of the population, but is probably what most people mean when they refer to standard Nigerian English. This is the variety most commonly taught in schools. Bamgbose argues, 'the features [of Variety 3] cut across different first-language backgrounds and no amount of drilling or stigmatisation is going to lead to their abandonment' (1982: 105).

Variety 4: This variety is modelled on standard British English and still favoured by the elite. There is, however, some dispute over the social acceptability of this variety. Banjo claims that this variety is 'socially unacceptable' and 'spoken only by a handful of Nigerians born or brought up in England' (cited in Bamgbose, 1982: 101), while Todd and Hancock (1986: 305) claim that RP remains a prestigious accent. Jowitt (1994) supports Todd and Hancock over this issue in saying that the promoters of RP and a British standard have been more influential than promoters of a local standard.

As in many places, the debate over the existence and acceptability of a local, indigenised English has been fervent. Schmied (1991: 175) quotes Jibril's (1987) summary of the debate. I give an edited version here:

> Perhaps the most controversial issue in English Language Studies in Nigeria is that of Nigerian English. Scholars such as Banjo, Adetugbo, Adesanoye and Odumuh affirm the existence of Nigerian English . . . Nigerian English has developed distinct phonetic, phonological, lexical and syntactic characteristics which are quite stable and which cannot be regarded as deviations from a native norm which Nigerians do not, in any case, aspire to approximate . . .

More recently, Bamgbose has suggested that, while Nigerian English had British origins, 'it has now assumed Nigerian garb and acquired some American influences (1996: 370). However, other scholars, such as Oji, urge that 'The death knell of Nigerian English should be sounded loud and clear as it has never existed, does not exist now . . .' (cited in Schmied, 1991: 175).

Despite Oji's protestations, it is difficult to argue that Nigerian English does not exist. Todd and Hancock (1986: 305) follow Bamgbose in suggesting that English in Nigeria is a cluster of subvarieties that include:

(i)   Pidgin English
(ii)   Mother-tongue-influenced English
(iii) The Indian-influenced English of many teachers and traders
(iv)   Standard Nigerian English
(v)   Expatriate mother-tongue English

What are some of the characteristic linguistic features of Nigerian English? Below, examples from phonology, lexis, syntax and 'culture' are given. It should be noted that Nigerian language experts see an urgent need to codify Nigerian English (Bamgbose, 1996) and that these examples are subject to change. A more complete list of features that are common to many varieties of English in Africa is given in Section 8.5.1 below.

8.2 Linguistic features

8.2.1 Phonological features

As is the case with almost all African varieties of English, Nigerian English is non-rhotic in that post-vocalic /r/ is not sounded. Nigerian English does not make a meaning distinction with vowel length, so that minimal pairs such as /ɪ/ and /iː/ are not discriminated. Certain diphthongs (as in the RP sounds 'bay' and 'go') are pronounced as monophthongs. Consonant clusters are not sounded and either one consonant is dropped or an epenthetic vowel is inserted between the consonants of the cluster to give 'lis' for 'list' and 'arrang-i-ment' for 'arrangement' respectively (Todd and Hancock, 1986: 306).

8.2.2 Lexical features

Bamiro (1994: 51–64) gives the following examples of words that have developed special meanings in Nigerian English. The prevalence of certain makes of car is reflected in the language. A 'Belgian' refers to a second-hand car, as these are most often imported from Belgium. The presence of Citroën and Volkswagen cars has led to the creative and witty coining of the new words 'footroën' and 'footwagen'. 'They had to do part of the journey by footroën' simply means they had to walk some of the way. Other coinages include 'ricobay hair' (a popular Nigerian hairstyle), 'white-white' (the white shirts worn by schoolchildren) and 'watchnight', which means something like staying up through the night to celebrate New Year's Eve or some other festival.

Ellipsis is common so that 'he is a mental' means 'he is a mental patient'. 'Next Saturday is environmental' means 'next Saturday is Environmental Day', and 'my brother is an army' means that he is a soldier. The word class can also change so that 'my friend would like to become a navy' means 'my friend would like to become a naval officer'.

'Clipping', common also in Australian English, is frequent. 'Perms' in the following example is a short or clipped form of 'permutations': 'We would not have wasted our time running after perms'.

Translation equivalents abound. 'To paste' means to 'brush one's teeth with toothpaste' as does 'to wash mouth'. So a mother might say to her child 'go and paste right now' or exclaim 'he has not even washed his mouth'. Other examples of loan translations that Bamiro provides include 'long throat' to mean a greedy or avaricious person, 'wrapper' to mean a wrap-round skirt, as in 'she rinsed her wrapper', and to 'buy the market' to mean 'buy goods', as in 'these menials began to buy the market'.

A nice example of how local culture and traditions can create new words is illustrated by the words 'enstool' and 'enskin'. These clearly derive from the word 'enthrone', but as some tribes install their chief on a stool and others clothe him in an animal skin, the words 'enstool' and 'enskin' have been created. These words also occur in Ghanaian English (Ahulu, 1994).

Direct borrowings from local languages also appear as lexical items in Nigerian English. To give just two examples, 'wahala' (trouble) and 'wayo' (tricks) come from Yoruba and Hausa respectively.

To move briefly from Nigeria to another West African country, the lexis of Cameroon English (CE) is of particular interest to students of World Englishes because of the co-existence of CE with French, as well as local languages. Wolf (2001: 250ff.) gives these examples of how the spelling and meaning of CE words are influenced by French. Note, for example, how standard English 'gue' becomes 'que' in words like 'fatigue' and 'argue' in CE.

Cameroon English	French	Standard English
acadmique	académique	
adjustement	ajustement	
fatique		fatigue
arque		argue
scolarise	scolariser	(to provide with schooling)

Wolf also gives examples of idiomatic borrowings from French, so that 'chaud(e)', literally 'hot', means a lover, and 'cops', which is derived from 'copain' (friend) means a friend.

8.2.3 Syntax

Many of the syntactic features of Nigerian English can be found in other varieties of African English and, as a collection of these common features is provided later in the chapter, here I simply include some examples of Nigerian Pidgin English (NPE) along with their translations into a more standard variety. It should be stressed that these do not represent examples of standard Nigerian English, although some of the phonological features of this can be detected:

'Wen yo mama rich hie yestade, a de chop' (When your mother arrived, I was eating)
'A si am las mont, I stil de krai' (I saw him last month. He was still crying)
'Monkey de work, baboon dey chop' (Monkeys work, baboons eat)

(http://members.aol.com/AfriPalava2/Pidgin.html)

The following NPE jingle, kindly provided by the Nigerian scholar and poet Tope Omoniyi, refers to banking fraud in Nigeria. You can hear Omoniyi reading a selection of his own poems on the accompanying CD. The standard version is also by Omoniyi.

'Katakata dey inside we country	There's disruption in our country
419 bank fraud	Advance free fraud
Import racket o	Smuggling
All this yanmayanma tin	All these ignoble practices
Dey spoil our name o	Stain our name
Document falsification	Document falsification
Wuruwuru to di answer	Non-transparent processes

Import mago mago	Import fraud
no bi to dey make awufu money	It's not getting easy money
Na im be prosperity	That makes prosperity
O ya make we clean am o	OK, let's clean up our act
O ya make e beta'	OK, let things improve

8.2.4 Cultural conventions

A common example of how cultural norms influence lexical choices involves kinship terms. A Nigerian might address his brother as 'son of my mother'. In Nigerian English the term for an older male sibling is 'senior brother', not the 'elder brother' of British English. This is a very important distinction, as elder brothers in Nigerian cultures have far greater responsibility for and power over their younger siblings than in British culture. So should Nigerian children be taught to say that 'elder brother' is correct, while 'senior brother' is incorrect? Clearly not, as 'senior brother' is the more culturally appropriate term. Cultures differ and, in this instance, the role of brothers differs across cultures and this is reflected in the kinship terms for them. Thus 'elder brother' is the appropriate term in English culture, but 'senior brother' is the appropriate term in Nigerian culture.

Methods of greeting are also culturally determined. Dare (1999) points out that people in Yoruba culture greet each other effusively and warmly and greetings differ according to context and the status, relationship and profession of the people involved. He wishes to see this 'Yorubaness' retained in Nigerian English, especially when the English is being used as a *lingua franca* between fellow Africans.

8.3　Englishes in South Africa

English has had a longer official link with South Africa than with Nigeria. The British occupied 'Cape Colony' in 1795. Lord Somerset, the Governor of the colony, recruited large numbers of schoolmasters from Britain to ensure that English established a firm hold there (Lass, 2002). This was part of an official policy of Anglicisation that sought to replace the language of the previous colonisers, Dutch, with English in all spheres of public life (Kamwangamalu, 2002). It mandated the use of English in all official documents. Not surprisingly, this policy upset the Dutch settlers and lingering resentment against the downgrading of Dutch was one of the reasons for the Boer wars of 1899–1902, won by the British.

In 1910, the Union of South Africa was established and English and Dutch (replaced by the name of Afrikaans in 1925) were made official languages, although English remained more important, especially in education (Kamwangamalu, 2002). However, things changed in 1948, the year that saw the start of the Afrikanerisation of South Africa. Perhaps the most significant policy to ensure this was the infamous 1953 Bantu Education Act which marked an attempt by the apartheid government to reassert the importance of Afrikaans in public life (Kamwangamalu, 2002). It entrenched mother-tongue instruction for blacks in the early years of education and greatly increased the role of Afrikaans in secondary schools. Blacks saw the policy as an attempt to create a semi-literate workforce and reinforce apartheid, and so opposed it vehemently (de Klerk and Gough, 2002). Their opposition to the policy led to the Soweto uprising of 1976, after which schools were allowed to choose their own medium of instruction after the first four years of primary school. English re-emerged as the overwhelming choice (de Klerk and Gough, 2002). It is important to note, therefore, that English is, perhaps surprisingly, seen as a language of liberation by many black South Africans while Afrikaans is seen as the language of colonial oppression and apartheid.

The Republic of South Africa was established in 1961 and Afrikaans and English remained the only two official languages. The situation remained unchanged until the establishment of the new South Africa in 1994 under the inaugural presidency of Nelson Mandela. The 1994 constitution granted official status to 11 languages, English and Afrikaans along with nine African languages (Ndbele, Pedi, Sotho, Swati, Tsonga, Tswana, Venda, Xhosa and Zulu).

In common with other African countries, several varieties of English are spoken in South Africa. A major difference, however, is that English is the first language of some 3.5 million people out of a total population of about 41 million. The L1 speakers are made up of 1.7 million whites, 1 million Indians and more than half a million people of mixed race. These L1 speakers speak different varieties of English, however, and among the varieties spoken in South Africa are White South African English (WSAE), Indian South African English (ISAE) and Coloured (or mixed-race) South African English (CSAE). In common with all regional varieties of English, these comprise a sociolinguistic continuum from standardised to vernacular. WSAE has been described as operating on a continuum of 'conservative–respectable–extreme' mirroring the terms 'cultivated–general–broad' given to the Australian continuum that was considered in Chapter 6. Lass is uncomfortable with the South African terms which he continues to use for convenience sake 'if with a slight shudder' (2002: 110) and classifies them in the following way:

Conservative: used by the 'first families', the upper and middle classes and 'serious' news readers. This variety reflects RP influence.

Respectable: this is the local standard and used by lecturers, teachers and professionals.

Extreme: this is used by people of lower economic status and has much in common with second-language Afrikaans English.

On the accompanying CD there is a recording of a speaker of WSAE.

8.4 Linguistic features of ISAE

Mesthrie (2002: 339–55) provides a description of Indian South African English (ISAE). This is of particular interest, as it is a variety that has shifted over time from being a second language to a first language. The first Indian migrants to South Africa arrived in 1860 and very few of them knew any English at all. Over time, however, English gradually became an L1 so that by the 1960s and 1970s, 'English became the first language of a majority of Indian schoolchildren' (2002: 340). ISAE has remained a distinct variety for several reasons. First, the apartheid policy that lasted from 1948 until the early 1990s kept Indian children away from L1 speakers of English descent. Second, ISAE, while sharing some similarities with Indian English, is also distinct from it, primarily because it operates across the sociolinguistic continuum so that it has a very colloquial form as well as a more educated form. Mesthrie describes this continuum using the terms 'acrolect', 'mesolect' and 'basilect' and shows that educated speakers can switch between these as and when appropriate. He quotes a husband, himself an English teacher, answering his wife's question about whether he has bought some cheese in a basilectal or perhaps mesolectal variety. His answer displays topicalisation and a use of 'lot' for 'a lot of':

Wife: You bought cheese, Farouk?
Husband: No, but a lot butter I bought.

(2002: 343)

Other examples typical of the basilectal variety that he gives (2002: 343–54) include:

'He came there isn't?' ('isn't' as invariant tag question. Note the lack of 'it' in this invariant tag. Many varieties use 'isn't it' as an invariant tag in these contexts.)

'I finish eat' (I've finished eating)

'Do you know what is roti?' and 'I don't know when is plane going to land?' (unchanged word order in indirect questions)

'He's got too much of money'

'I like children must learn our mother tongue' (I'd like our children to . . .)

'Though I visit very often to Durban, but I don't like it.' (parallel conjunctions)

'But it'll come, but too late.' (the use of 'double conjunctions' to add emphasis)

The use of distinctive aspect markers 'an' stay' and 'an' left'. For example:

'We'll fright an' stay.' (We used to be afraid for a long while.)

'We whacked him an' left him'. (We beat him up completely.)

Mesthrie concludes by saying that the differences ISAE exhibit 'are much greater than those exhibited by other new Englishes' (2002: 354). However, while the use of the aspect markers 'an' stay' and 'an' left' indeed appear distinct, the other features can be found in the informal dialects of other varieties, where 'unusual' ways of marking aspect can also be found. In any event, none of the examples he gives of ISAE appears as distinctive as certain older varieties of English such as the Doric that was described in Chapter 4.

8.5   Linguistic features of BSAE and African Englishes

The most widely spoken variety of English in South African is, as one would expect, Black South African English (BSAE). Seven million blacks 'have a command of English as another language' (de Klerk and Gough, 2002: 356) and, according to de Klerk and Gough, BSAE is increasingly viewed as a variety in its own right and its prestige is rising. They are keen to point out that, despite this, BSAE currently offers no automatic access to power, although they feel that 'the prospects are very good for greater acceptance of variability in educational contexts and in business' (2002: 371).

The linguistic features of BSAE are in many respects similar to those of other African Englishes. There is no distinction between certain short and long vowel sounds, between /ɪ/ and /iː/, for example. It is non-rhotic and leans towards syllable- rather than stress-timing. More distinctively, the vowel sounds in the words 'strut', 'bath' and 'palm' are all pronounced as /a/ and those in 'trap', 'dress' and 'nurse' as /e/.

De Klerk and Gough (2002: 362–3) provide a list of 23 distinctive grammatical features but, as these are similar to features of other varieties of African English, I shall not list them here (a list is provided in 8.5.1 below). Also in common with other varieties of English, local languages provide a large number of words. In discourse, there is a preference for indirectness and the preservation of face. Chick (2002) suggests that this has influenced the speaking styles of white South Africans. As an example he notes that there has been an increase in compliment deflection in the new South Africa and explains this by saying that whites wish to avoid 'the implication associated with the acceptance of compliments, namely that they are superior to their interlocutors' (2002: 265), but he cautions that blacks remain far more likely to ignore or reinterpret compliments than either whites or Indians.

In a country that has eleven official languages code-mixing is common. This example from Gough (n.d.) mixes three languages: Zulu is given in normal type, English in italics and Afrikaans in bold:

'*I-Chiefs* isidle nge-*referee's optional time, otherwise* ngabe ihambe **sleg. Maar** *why* benga **stopi** *this system* ye-*injury time*?'

Chiefs (a local soccer team) have won owing to the referee's optional time, otherwise they could have lost. But why is this system of injury time not phased out?

Code-mixing is common in all multilingual societies and is considered in more detail in Chapter 9.

To conclude this section I give Schmied's list of general tendencies in African Englishes (1991: 58ff.). Some of these features have been described above as features of Nigerian or South African English.

8.5.1 Common linguistic features of African Englishes
Pronunciation

(i)   Fricatives tend to be avoided.
(ii) Length differences in vowels are levelled and not used to distinguish meaning.
(iii) The central vowels /ʌ/, /əː/ and /ə/ as in 'but', 'bird' and 'about' become more open as in /ɔ/, /ə/, and /a/.

(iv)   Diphthongs tend to become monophthongs, so that /eɪ/ and /əʊ/ become /e/ and /o/ respectively.

(v)   Consonant clusters either drop consonants or insert vowels to split them.

Grammar

(i)   Inflectional endings are not always added to the verb but general, regular and unmarked forms are used instead.

(ii)   Complex tenses, such as the past perfect and certain conditionals, tend to be avoided.

(iii) The use of verb+*ing* constructions is extended to all verbs to give examples such as 'I am having your book' and 'I was not liking the food in the hotel'.

(iv)   Phrasal and prepositional verbs are used differently, for example, 'I will pick you at 8 o'clock tonight'.

(v)   Verb complementation varies freely to give phrases such as 'allow him go' and 'they made him to clean the whole yard'.

(vi)   Noun phrases are not always marked for number and case or are treated differently, to give 'informations', 'a cattle', 'an advice'.

(vii) Relative pronouns ('whom', 'whose') are avoided to give 'adult education which its main purpose is to help adults . . .'.

(viii) The use of plural is overgeneralised ('luggages', 'advices').

(ix)   Articles and determiners are often omitted ('I am going to post office').

(x)   Pronouns are not always distinguished by gender.

(xi)   Adjectives may be used as adverbs to give 'I can obtain the food easy'.

(xii) Pronoun copying is common ('many of the fish, they have different colours').

(xiii) Negative yes/no questions are confirmed by responding to the form of the question so that the answer to 'he isn't good?' becomes 'yes (he isn't)'.

(xiv) There are invariant question tags, for example 'isn't it?' and 'you wanted to leave for Nairobi, not so?'

(xv)   The interrogative word order is retained in indirect speech to give 'I cannot tell you what is the matter'.

(xvi) There is freer word order so that 'in my family, we are many' becomes common.

It is remarkable how many of these features are also common in other varieties of English. With regard to the similarities in pronunciation, Schmied (1989) points out that, with 20 vowel sounds and 24 consonant sounds, RP is complex compared with many other languages and he predicted that learners would have particular trouble with the differentiation and variation of vowel lengths. New varieties of English appear to solve these problems by doing away with them, along with problems associated with inflectional endings and consonant clusters. It should always be remembered that a tendency towards simplification is evident in the development of 'traditional' English, as illustrated in Chapter 4.

In the final two parts of this chapter I shall consider these two questions:

1. Can English adequately represent African cultures?
2. What linguistic choices do governments have?

8.6 Can English adequately represent African cultures?

This is an extremely complex issue. Mazrui (1973) has argued that English played an important role in the Pan-African movement. He is careful to distinguish between 'Pan-Negroism', whose loyalties were 'ethnocentric', and 'Pan-Africanism', whose loyalties were 'intracontinental' (1973: 62). He notes that 'the towering figures of the 1945 Fifth Pan-African conference were overwhelmingly English speakers' (1973: 63) and this allowed the future President of Ghana, Nkrumah, to argue that it was the first Pan-African conference that promoted African, rather than black, nationalism. The link between nationalism, tribalism and English is also complex. 'Learning English was a detribalising process. If one found an African who had mastered the English language, that African had, almost by definition, ceased to be a full tribesman' (Mazrui, 1973: 66). In Mazrui's mind, however, this was not necessarily negative, as he concludes that English 'helped to detribalise the African's mind and to give it a national dimension' (1973: 70).

In the previous chapter, many Indian scholars and writers argued forcefully that English had become an Indian language in which they could write about Indian cultures. A useful way of exploring this question in the context of Africa, therefore, would be to consider the views of African writers and novelists to see whether they feel that English can be used to express Africanness. As might be expected, writers are not unanimous about this, although it is fair to say that the majority support writing in English about African culture and identity. In this brief summary of their views I shall start with the case for the prosecution – those that feel that Africans should write only in African languages.

In 1959, the Congress of Negro Writers and Artists resolved, among other things, that African countries should not adopt European languages as national languages and that a Pan-African language be chosen for promotion. English was felt to be elitist and the cause of cultural alienation, of 'psychological amputation' (Schmied, 1991: 119). The African language chosen by the congress was the East African *lingua franca*, Swahili. Perhaps one reason why its promotion has not, in fact, extended much beyond the countries of its original usage – the countries of East Africa such as Tanzania and Kenya – is precisely because it is not a Pan-African language. Perhaps the best-known proponent of writing in local languages and opponent of writing in English is the Kenyan writer Ngugi wa Thiong'o (1986/2005). Ngugi originally wrote in his native Gikuyu and reports that, when he was at school, children who used Gikuyu near the school were given the cane and forced to wear a placard round their necks with a sign that read 'I am a donkey' or 'I am stupid'. At the same time, success in English was essential for children who wanted to proceed up the education ladder. A pass in English was a prerequisite to academic advancement. Policies of this type, that forbade the use of the children's vernacular in the school playground or the school itself, may seem outdated and unjust now, but they were common. It is worth remembering that children who spoke the Doric in their schools in Scotland were 'skelpit' for so doing. It may not be surprising that Ngugi's experience in a colonial school system has created a writer who insists that African writers should write in an African language. He feels so strongly about this that he is dismissive of those writers who have chosen to write in English. Of one such, the Nigerian Chinua Achebe, he writes 'it is the final triumph of a system of domination when the dominated start singing its virtues' (2005: 176).

One feels that Achebe would argue strongly against the accusation that writing in English represented singing the virtues of the colonising power. His defence would be that English is an African language and that writing in adapted African forms of English can be both a powerful means of literary expression and a powerful medium for expressing rebellion (Schmied, 1991). Achebe (1975/2005) accepts English as an historical fact and he makes the point that, if sub-Saharan Africa has a 'national' language, then that language is English, as English is spoken in more countries than any other language. He also says that 'while he would love to learn and appreciate many African languages, it is simply impossible to do so' (2005: 170). The African writer should therefore 'aim at fashioning out an English which is at once universal and able to carry his personal experience' (2005: 171). In an oft-quoted passage (cf. Bokamba, 1982: 94), Achebe presents two versions of the same story, one written in an African variety of English and the other in 'Standard' English to show that the African version conveys something essentially African. The opening lines of the two versions, with the African version first, are:

'I want one of my sons to join these people and be my eyes there.'
'I am sending you as a representative among those people.'

Two other lines are:

'The world is like a Mask, dancing. If you want to see it, you will not stand in one place.'
'One has to move with the times or else one is left behind.'

While Achebe promotes the use of an African variety of English and deliberately deviates from standard English and adopts African idioms, he by and large avoids literal word-for-word translations of African vernaculars. Baikolo has concluded after a study of his work that Achebe's 'syntax and phrases spring spontaneously from the Igbo heart without deviating much from current English usage', and he praises Achebe's 'felicitous transliteration of Igbo ideas' (1995: 393).

Other African writers have gone further in their adaptation of English to reflect the vernacular style of a local language. The Nigerian writer Amos Tutuola derives his writing style from the Yoruba oral tradition and, as a result, has been accused by some critics as being semi-literate in English, as his English is 'Yorubised' (Desai, 1993: 6). But the example below seems to capture an innate Africanness, without being 'semi-literate' in any way:

'Now as the father of the lady first asked me for my name and I told him my name was "Father of gods who could do anything in this world".'

(Desai, 1993: 6)

Gabriel Okara is another writer who attempts to translate a vernacular syntax into English, trying to keep as close as possible to vernacular expressions, and who feels that 'African ideas, philosophy, folk-lore and imagery should be translated almost literally' (Desai, 1993: 7). The excerpt below (Bokamba, 1982: 93) illustrates Okara's attempt to capture his native Ijaw syntax, in particular its word order and its fondness for reduplication, in an African English:

> 'When Okolo came to know himself, he was lying on a floor, on a cold cold floor lying. He opened his eyes to see but nothing he say, nothing he saw, for the darkness was evil darkness and the outside night was black black night.'

This raises the question of just how far a writer should go in order to adapt English to local vernaculars. The answer to this, I think, depends on the expected readership. The more local the intended readership, the more 'African' the English can be. And, of course, if the intended readership comprises only speakers of the same language and this is one controlled by the writer, then the writer will write in the local language. This recalls the now familiar identity–communication continuum. But this is not to say that African writers must abandon African English if they wish to reach a global audience. Achebe's fellow Nigerian Wole Soyinka, who was awarded the Nobel Prize for Literature in 1986, has argued that 'when we borrow an alien language . . . we must stretch it, impact and compact it, fragment and reassemble it . . .' (Schmied, 1991: 126). And, in the view of the present author, Okara's attempt to represent the essence of his vernacular in an African English is extremely successful. It is full of menace and mystery. The use of the vernacular also captures the essence of a culture even at a more mundane level. Kachru (1983: 222) quotes Okara's use of the Ijaw expression 'may we live to see ourselves again tomorrow' as an example of a nativised English. This carries a real feeling of the local culture which would be completely lost were Okara to write what would appear in comparison to be a very tame 'goodnight'.

One of the most famous experiments in writing in a uniquely African style is the novel by Ken Saro-Wiwa, *Sozaboy: A Novel in Rotten English*. Saro-Wiwa was a Nigerian activist and member of the Ogoni people who was executed by the Nigerian government in 1995. In the author's note to the novel, Saro-Wiwa explains that *Sozaboy* (soldier boy) was 'the result of my fascination with the adaptability of the English language and my closely observing the speech and writings of a certain segment of Nigerian society' (1985). The book opens:

> Although, everybody in Dukana was happy at first. All the nine villages were dancing and we were eating plenty maize with pear and *knacking tory* under the moon. Because the work on the farms have finished and the yams were growing well well. And because the old bad government have dead, and the new government of *soza* and police have come.

[*knacking tory* means swapping stories; *soza* means soldiers]

Soon, however, things start to deteriorate:

> Radio begin dey *hala* as 'e never hala before. Big big *grammar*. Long long words. Every time.

Before before, the grammar was not plenty and everybody was happy. But now grammar began to be plenty and people were not happy. As grammar plenty, na so trouble plenty. And as trouble plenty, na so plenty people were dying.'

(1985: 3)

[*hala*: literally 'holler' and thus broadcast. Significantly, *grammar* comes to mean government regulations.]

To what extent can English represent African concepts and ways of knowing, the functions that were discussed in the previous chapter on Indian and Sri Lankan ways of knowing? Oladipo believes that they can, and that African world views can be interpreted in languages other than the indigenous ones which constitute the original media of their expression, but that great care must be taken to ensure that alien idioms reflect 'the institutionalised intentions, objectives and practices which inform their supposed African equivalents' (1995: 405).

So, can English be adapted so that it can adequately reflect Africanness? While some African writers argue strongly that it cannot and that English remains a tool of postcolonial domination, the majority feel comfortable writing in an African form of English and feel that it represents an appropriate medium for African literature and ideas. The general feeling is that English can be Africanised and adapted. Desai is in no doubt: 'English today is as much of an African language as it is a British or American one' (1993: 10).

8.7   What linguistic choices do governments have?

Governments are constantly attempting to find the right balance between English and other languages, whether they be regional or local – and not only in Africa. In the context of Anglophone Africa, questions that need to be asked include:

(i)   What role(s) should African languages play in society and education?
(ii)   What role(s) should English play in society and education?
(iii)   How should one balance the mix of languages – should one use one or more of the local languages, a local language and English, or just English?
(iv)   If English is to be taught in schools, which variety of English should be taught?

Schmied (1989) usefully summarises the possible contradictions and tensions inherent in making these choices. If a mother tongue is chosen, this will be seen as restrictive by many stakeholders. First, many parents may want their children educated through English as they feel that this will give their children the best chance of a good education and self-advancement. Second, parents whose mother tongue is not the one chosen as the medium of education will naturally be upset. In Africa this is a major issue. What local language(s) should be used as the media of education in Nigeria where hundreds of languages are spoken? And would not insisting on one or two local languages as media of instruction lead to national disunity in multilingual nations? In South Africa everyone has the right to be educated through their language of choice, although this is significantly tempered by the addition of the words 'where practicable'. Titlestad (1998) reports that, in practice, this means that there have to be at least 45 children at any level who wish for a certain language of instruction.

If English is chosen as the medium of education, on the other hand, then the government can be charged with setting an elitist agenda and of damaging, undermining and devaluing indigenous languages. Then there is the question of which variety of English to choose. If an exonormative model is chosen, the government can be charged with extending the cultural domination of previous colonial powers. If a local variety is chosen, the government can be charged with promoting education in an internationally unviable or unintelligible variety of English. Titlestad (1998) takes this to the extreme by saying that choosing an indigenous variety of English for South African schools would help complete the agenda of the 1953 apartheid government's Bantu Education Act 'by unfitting South Africa from benefiting from the knowledge that English can confer' (1998: 36).

In terms of balance between languages, governments can introduce English as a medium of instruction early on in primary school or just make it a subject for study at primary school and introduce it as a medium of instruction at secondary, or even tertiary level. Or they can require that certain 'science' subjects be taught in English and that 'humanities' subjects be taught in the local language(s).

These are crucial decisions, as there is a definite danger in the over-promotion of English at the expense of local languages, as the experience of Zambia shows. In Zambia, English was introduced as the sole medium of instruction in all primary schools in 1964 and local languages were taught only as subjects. This policy has since been severely criticised for damaging local languages and making them seem inferior to English, the 'source of all knowledge' (Schmied, 1989: 107).

As well as these political questions, there are a range of pedagogical issues to be considered. Which is better for a child's cognitive development: to be taught in one or two languages? Which is better for a child's feeling of self worth and self esteem: to be taught in the language of home or in a language representative of a different culture?

There are also practical considerations. Are there enough proficient and trained teachers to teach in English if this is the decision that is made? It can occur that governments have ruled that an exonormative variety of English be the classroom model and then expect poorly trained second-language speakers of English whose own variety of English is the local variety, or whose level of proficiency is low, to teach it. The result can be an English classroom where the English lesson is characterised by a teacher laboriously translating an English text into a local language and by frequent code-mixing. This is particularly common in rural and poorer schools, of which there are many, and where resources are extremely limited.

Education can stir high emotions. If the wrong choices, or choices that the majority disagree with, are made, opposition, even violent opposition, as in the Soweto uprising of 1976, can be expected. In Sudan, when Arabic, the mother tongue of more than 50 per cent of the population, replaced English as the official language, civil wars ensued (Awoniyi, 1995).

What, then, is the answer? In 1953 a British government document suggested that English was important for Africans for three main reasons, namely: to act as a *lingua franca*; to provide a medium for technical knowledge; and to be a means of contact with world thought (Schmied, 1991: 18). At the time many Africans petitioned for English to be used as early as possible in schools and a dispute arose, similar to the one that began in India in the nineteenth century between the 'Anglicists' and the 'Orientalists' that we reviewed in Chapter 7. Now some so-called 'Anglicists' have moved, in one sense at least, to the Orientalist way of thinking by arguing for a local indigenous variety of English.

There is no easy answer and no answer that will be generally suitable. Each country has to take decisions based on its own specific situation. I consider the issue of the choice of 'which English' in the final part of this book, but, in the context of Africa, my view is that the adoption of an African variety of English is the choice that is both most viable and most appropriate in both Nigeria and South Africa. African Englishes can represent African cultures and thought, while at the same time maintaining international intelligibility. The choice of an African variety of English also undermines the arguments of those who see the choice of English as tantamount to continuing to submit to the cultural domination of 'English'. However, I shall end this chapter with a quote that cautions against officially imposing English in inappropriate contexts. The quote describes the problems that have derived from making English the official language in Botswana's parliament. This is especially significant because, if any institution should allow the use of the common language of its people, it is a democratic parliament:

> In Parliament the official means for conducting the official business and debates is English. The practice is a strain on the verbal competence of most members of parliament, who have not had a high standard of education. To some the use of English is a real impediment to meaningful communication and hinders their contribution to parliamentary debates. The result is that most parliamentarians make up for their lack of proficiency by supporting the evening parliamentary review programme, entitled 'Dikgang tsa Palamente', which is conducted in Setswana. In this programme parliamentarians fight to be allotted time to say to the nation what was communicated inadequately in English during the debates.
>
> (Schmied, 1991: 25)

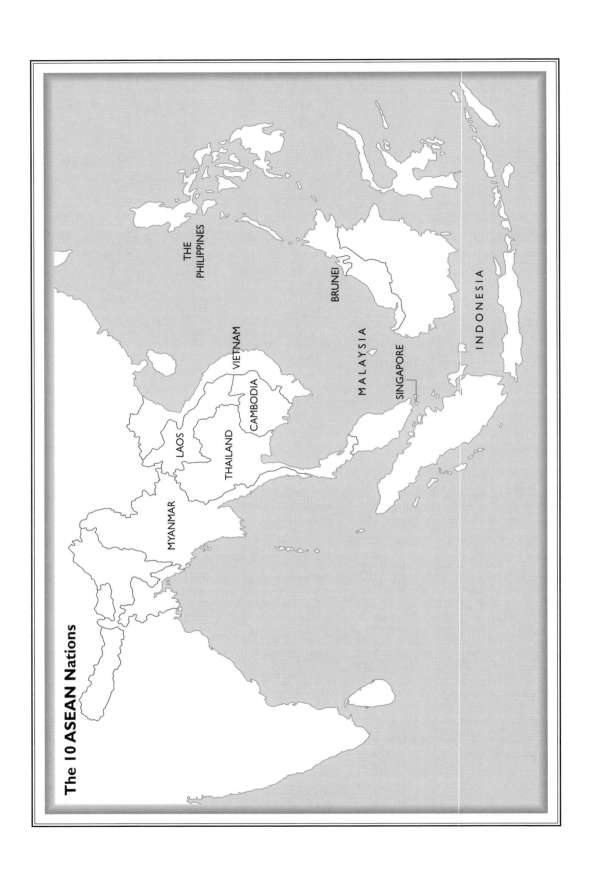

The 10 ASEAN Nations

THE PHILIPPINES

BRUNEI

VIETNAM

CAMBODIA

LAOS

THAILAND

MYANMAR

MALAYSIA

SINGAPORE

INDONESIA

9 Englishes of South-East Asia – colonial descendants?

South-East Asia covers a wide geographical area in which several culturally and linguistically distinct countries are found. These include the countries of the Association of South-East Asian Nations (ASEAN), an organisation which was founded in 1967. ASEAN now comprises the following ten countries, listed here in alphabetical order:

Brunei	Cambodia	Indonesia	Laos	Malaysia
Myanmar	The Philippines	Singapore	Thailand	Vietnam

In this chapter, the situation with regard to the Englishes of Malaysia, Singapore, Brunei and the Philippines will be described. In Chapter 11, the role of English as an international *lingua franca* will be considered with a specific focus on its role in ASEAN. In other words, these two chapters are closely connected, with the first considering the established outer circle Englishes of Brunei, Malaysia, the Philippines and Singapore, and the second considering the expanding circle Englishes of the remaining six ASEAN countries and the use of English as a *lingua franca* in ASEAN as a whole.

9.1 Malaysia, Singapore and Brunei

In 1826 the British established the colony of the 'Straits Settlements' which comprised the major trading posts of Singapore; Malacca, a town on the west coast of peninsular Malaysia; and the island of Penang, off the northwest coast of Malaysia. Predictably, this is where the British established the first English medium schools. The school in Penang was founded in 1816, the one in Singapore in 1823 and the one in Malacca in 1826.

The colonial government both encouraged and imported migrant labour to harvest the country's two great natural resources, tin and rubber. In the second half of the nineteenth century, a 'massive influx of Chinese' arrived to work in the tin mines and workers from southern India were recruited to work on the rubber plantations (Hashim, 2002: 77).

Malaysia and Singapore have shared much of their colonial history and, after independence, were for a short time both part of the Federation of Malaysia, until Singapore's decision to withdraw in 1965. Despite sharing so much colonial history, what is of particular interest is the difference in the roles English has played and continues to play in each country.

At the time of independence in 1957, English and Malay were the official languages of the new Malaysia, but the new government was keen to improve the standing of the Malay population and started to give precedence to the Malay language, Bahasa Malaysia. This was one reason that led to Singapore separating from the Federation of Malaysia in 1965. This difference in attitude to the respective roles of English and Malay can partly be explained by considering the population make-up of the countries. Both Singapore and Malaysia are multicultural and multilingual societies and, in the main, share the same mix of languages and cultures. However, there is a significant difference in the proportional make-up of the populations in each country. The current population of Malaysia is about 20 million. Malays and other indigenous peoples constitute about 60 per cent of this number, with the Chinese (30 per cent), South Asian (8 per cent) making up most of the remainder (Hashim, 2002). In Singapore, on the other hand, the Chinese make up the great majority of the population, while the Malay and South Indian populations form small minorities.

Although the ethnic Malays constitute the largest group in Malaysia, the Malaysian Chinese traditionally held the economic power in the country. On independence, the Malaysian government desired to improve the lot of the ethnic Malays and chose to do so by adopting policies of what might be called 'positive discrimination'. One such policy was the National Language Act, introduced in 1967. It decreed that education, from primary through to tertiary, would, in the main, move to a Malay medium, although certain primary schools could teach in either Tamil or Chinese. All English-medium schools were to be phased out, a process that was completed by the middle of the 1980s. English was no longer a requirement for tertiary education.

The politician most associated with this Malaysianisation policy was Dr Mahathir Mohamed, the Prime Minister from 1981 to 2003. One consequence of the policy to phase out English-medium education was that many tens of thousands of Malaysians, especially the ethnic Chinese, went overseas to English-speaking countries to pursue their education there. Universities in the English-speaking world have done particularly well out of this, as these students all pay international fees and have thus provided the universities with extremely welcome additional funding.

Towards the end of his period of power, Dr Mahathir and others in the government began to show concern at the apparently declining levels of English proficiency and the importance of English is again being stressed. For example, all students wanting to enter Malaysian universities must now pass the so-called Malaysian University English Test (MUET).

Recently it has been estimated (McArthur, 2002) that some 20 per cent of the population of Malaysia understand English and some 25 per cent of those who live in urban areas use it 'for some purposes in everyday life' (2002: 335). It remains a language of prestige and is important in the domains of government, business and the professions (David, 2000).

The history of English in Singapore and its roles today are quite different. By 1947, some 32 per cent of Singaporean school students were studying in English-medium schools. The others were studying in Chinese-, Malay- or Tamil-medium schools. While it might be expected that a country with a large ethnically Chinese majority would promote Chinese-medium schools, the success of the Chinese Communist Party with the establishment of the People's Republic of China in 1949 caused the Singaporean government to view

Chinese-medium education as a possible breeding ground for young communists. Thus the Chinese-medium university was closed. In this context it should be remembered that there was a virtual civil war taking place in Malaysia and Singapore – the coyly termed 'Emergency' – and the main antagonists were ethnic Chinese under the leadership of Chen Ping, who was branded a communist first by the colonial and then by the national government. The upheavals that took place in China in the 1950s and 1960s, culminating in the Cultural Revolution, simply added to this suspicion of Chinese-medium education, especially as the communists seemed to be taking hold in neighbouring Indonesia.

Since 1987, English has virtually been the sole medium of education in Singapore at all levels – 'virtually' because there are a small number of special schools for gifted students that teach through Chinese and English media. So, although English, Mandarin Chinese, Malay and Tamil remain the four national languages of Singapore, the language policy requires all its people to speak English and their own mother tongue. It is a bilingual language policy of 'English + 1'.

While the government has been suspicious of Chinese-medium education, it has encouraged the learning of Mandarin Chinese by Singaporean Chinese, the majority of whom are mother tongue speakers of the dialect of Fujien Province, Hokkien. The 'Speak Mandarin' campaign of the early 1980s has proved remarkably successful, especially in so far as most young ethnically Chinese Singaporeans now fluently converse in Mandarin. But, as I discovered when I was teaching in Singapore in the early 1980s, the success of this campaign has led to unexpected results, not all of them welcome. Before the Speak Mandarin campaign, the school-ground *lingua franca* was a colloquial form of English and/or a form of pidgin Malay. The students all spoke these languages, whatever their ethnic background. After the start of the Speak Mandarin campaign, however, Mandarin quickly became the *lingua franca* of the ethnically Chinese students, but it was an exclusive *lingua franca*, as the ethnically Malay and South Asian students did not understand it. This has led to an unforeseen linguistic division between the majority ethnic Chinese and the rest of the population. The importance of English as the language of Singaporean identity has therefore been heightened further.

A second consequence of the 'English + 1' policy has been the emergence of many students who are not perfectly literate in either English or their '+ 1' language. In terms of reading and writing many students far prefer to use English for two major reasons. First, its script takes less time to learn than the Chinese script. Second, there is a far wider range of writing in English and across different media, including computer-mediated scripts, than in Chinese and certainly more than texts available in Malay and Tamil. This has meant that many students are proficient in the spoken forms of their '+ 1' language but are not adequately literate in it. The problem will be familiar to many teachers working in countries that wish to implement a bilingual educational policy of 'English + 1'. The issue will be revisited in the next chapter in the context of Hong Kong, where the policy is for students not only to be able to write in both Chinese and English but to be able to speak three languages: English and the mutually unintelligible Chinese 'dialects' of Cantonese and Mandarin, or *putonghua*.

The situation in Brunei is different again. A British Protectorate from 1888 until 1984, when it gained full independence, except for the period of Japanese occupation during World War Two, Brunei had earlier been given the chance to join the Federation of Malaysia but elected not to do so (McLellan, 2005). The country has a very small population of only about 300,000 people, the majority of whom are Brunei Malays. Its national ideology promotes the philosophy of a Malay Islamic Monarchy (*Melayu Islam Beraja*) (McLellan, 2005: 15). Brunei Malay is a distinct variety of Malay and students are also expected to learn standard Malay. With regard to English, the government introduced a bilingual education policy in 1985 which promotes the use of both standard Malay and English, but in different domains. Malay is the medium of instruction in the first years of primary school; in later primary and throughout secondary school Malay and English both act as media of instruction, with Malay being used to teach 'humanities' type subjects and English used to teach 'science' type subjects (Jones, 1996). There is only one university, the University of Brunei, where the medium of instruction is primarily English.

Despite these differences in the history and roles of English in the respective countries, the Englishes of Brunei, Malaysia and Singapore share many linguistic features. A selection of these is exemplified below.

9.2   Linguistic features

The English of Singapore and Malaysia has commonly been described in terms of a lectal continuum (Platt and Weber, 1980) which ranges from basilect, through mesolect to acrolect. This can be contrasted with the continuum described for Australian English, operating from broad through general to cultivated (Delbridge, 1999, and see Chapter 6). As I have explained in earlier chapters, I prefer to use terms such as 'cultivated', 'general' and 'broad', as these do not suggest a creole continuum, as this, in turn, suggests that the acrolect is somehow closer to a standard and thus 'better' than the basilect. The avoidance of judgmental terms is particularly important in countries where it can be argued that there are many speakers of the respective varieties of English who are native speakers of it, learning it either as a mother tongue or from a very early age and using it across a range of public and private domains and with one another.

Le Page (1984) has similarly argued that the use of a linear continuum from basilect to acrolect is not appropriate for Singapore and he proposes instead a 'multidimensional one' (1984: 121). It is perhaps helpful to see these continua as being measures of relative formality (Gupta, 1988), with the broad or basilectal stage representing the most informal end. The use of the broad, or basilectal, variety can thus be the most appropriate variety to use in certain contexts. Colloquial varieties are appropriate in colloquial contexts.

Unless otherwise stated, the linguistic features described below represent the variety spoken by well-educated people in relatively formal contexts.

9.2.1   Phonology

The information here draws heavily on Brown and Deterding (2005: 7–14). Singaporean English does not distinguish between pairs of vowels that are distinct phonemes in RP. Thus in the pairs of vowel sounds /ɪ/ and /iː/, /ɑː/ and /ʌ/, /ɔː/ and /ɒ/, /uː/ and /ʊ/, both vowels are short and pronounced more or less the same, so that, for example, the vowel sounds in 'scenic' are pronounced the same as in /sɪnɪk/. The two vowels /e/ and /æ/ are pronounced as /e/, and the diphthong /eɪ/ can be pronounced as a monophthong /e/.

With regard to consonant sounds, the pairs /p/ and /b/, /t/ and /d/, /k/ and /g/, /tʃ/ and /dʒ/, /f/ and /v/, /θ/ and /ð/, /s/ and /z/ and /s/ and /ʒ/ may be pronounced the same, especially when in final position. The notorious dental fricatives are pronounced /t/ and /d/ in initial position and often /f/ and /v/ in final position.

Singaporean English also displays a tendency towards syllable-timing. At the level of the word, Singaporean English may either give each syllable equal stress, or when one syllable is stressed, the stress may be on a different syllable from that stressed in RP. In the following examples, the syllables of 'polytechnic' receive equal stress, while the primary stress of 'Europe' is on the second syllable (Brown and Deterding, 2005: 10):

No, I was from the polytechnic.
Eu*rope*

A difference between Malaysian and Singaporean English is that Singaporean English is non-rhotic, but Malaysian speakers sound post-vocalic /r/ in certain contexts.

In terms of its international intelligibility, relatively formal Singaporean English has proved to be extremely intelligible to speakers of other varieties of English and to people for whom English is not a first language. In a recent study (Kirkpatrick and Saunders, 2005), samples of educated male and female Singaporean speech were played to groups of students studying at a large university in Australia. The groups included first-language speakers of Australian, American and British Englishes and first-language speakers of several other languages including Norwegian, Hebrew, Chinese, Arabic and Afrikaans. The groups listened only once to each sample and were asked to answer comprehension questions on it. They were also asked to say whether they thought the speakers were intelligent and whether they would like to meet them. The great majority had very little difficulty understanding the speakers and, interestingly, based their answers to whether they thought the speakers were intelligent or interesting/likeable on the basis of what they had said rather than on the 'accent' of the speakers. The only people who found it difficult to understand what was being said were listeners whose own proficiency in English was weak, despite being currently enrolled in an Australian university.

9.2.2 **Lexis**

As one would expect, borrowings from local languages are common. This example of a Malay phrase comes from Lowenberg (1991: 367):

'The residents will repair the roofs on a *gotong-royong* basis.' (*gotong-royong* means some form of communal co-operation)

A second example comes from Hashim (2002: 83):

'The corruption case as highlighted under the Road Transport Department's *lesen terbang* is one . . . .' (*lesen terbang* literarally means 'flying licence' and refers to illegal licences)

Other borrowings from Malay include *makan* (food), *kecil makan* (little food, thus a snack, and note that the Malay word order is *makan kecil*), *adat* (traditional law), *kampong* (traditional Malay village), *bomoh* (a traditional Malay medicine man), *amok* (crazy) and *barang* (luggage, bits and pieces). Hybrids are frequent, so '*amok*' combines with 'run' to give 'to run *amok*', which means to become uncontrollable with panic or anger. A '*dadah* addict' is a drug addict.

Some Malay words have seen a shift in their semantic range on transfer into English. Lowenberg (1991) provides these two examples. The first concerns the word *bumiputra*, a key word in Malay politics. It literally means 'son of the soil', but has now come to refer to ethnic Malays, so the semantic range has been narrowed. The second shows the opposite tendency, as the semantic range of the word *rakyat* has been broadened from its original meaning of ethnic rural Malays to the Malaysian people in general.

Semantic shift is also evident when English words become part of Bruneian English and or Brunei Malay. For example the word 'confident' (*konfiden*) has only negative connotations and means over-confident or arrogant. In the same way, 'proud' has only negative connotations and is a translation equivalent of the Malay word *sombong*, which means haughty (McLellan, 2005: 39).

Semantic shift is also evident in English words. If you offer to send someone to the airport, you are offering to accompany them there. In informal contexts, people 'on and off the light' or 'open and close it'. A 'crocodile' refers to a womaniser and derives from a Malay use of the Malay word for crocodile (*buaya*). And Singaporeans constantly enquire of foreigners, 'Can you take spicy food'?

Semantic shift also occurs in certain ordinate and superordinate nouns. For example 'Christian' is a superordinate term in British English and refers to all followers of the Christian religion, no matter to which branch or sect of it they belong. In Singaporean English, 'Christian' specifically refers to Protestants (Deterding, 2000). Similarly, 'alphabet' in English refers to the whole system of letters while in Singaporean English it refers to any one of them. Thus, in Singaporean English, the word 'alphabet' is made up of 8 alphabets.

The different cultural and ethnic mix of the population can be seen from the way different religions refer to special prayer days in English, as the two examples below show:

'9th Moon 24th Day' (female Chinese Buddhist)

'The 6th day prayers will be held at Wada Gurdwara Sahib on 2nd September 2000 between 3pm and 5pm' (male Punjabi Sikh)

(David and Yong, 2002: 172)

9.2.3 Grammar

In common with many other varieties of English, articles are used in fewer environments. While this is a frequent feature in colloquial Singaporean English, as in 'you have pen or not?' (McArthur, 2002), it is also apparent in written texts. Gupta (1988) provides these examples:

'Mortality rate is high', and 'General Secretary is William Wan'

(1988: 42)

Gupta also reports a tendency to use infinitive verb phrases in contexts where a gerund might be used. For example:

'I have great pleasure to report on . . .', and 'I take pride to announce . . .'

(1988: 41)

Other common features found in both formal and informal varieties include differences in preposition usage and the shift of uncountable nouns to countables. Examples of the latter include 'chalks, luggages, sceneries, and slangs' (1988: 42). It is perhaps worthwhile remembering, however, that 'information' is listed as a countable noun in Samuel Johnson's dictionary (see Chapter 4). The invariant tag questions 'is it?' and 'isn't it?' are common, especially in more informal contexts and 'already' can act as an aspect marker as in 'my father already pass away', and 'you finish *makan* already' (Platt, Weber and Ho, 1984: 71).

A further common grammatical feature of these Englishes concerns the marking of past tense forms. In a fascinating study, Platt (1991) showed that there were considerable differences in the frequency of past tense marking and that these depended on three separate variables. The first was the comparative level of education the speaker had received – the more educated the speakers, the more frequently they marked for past tense. The second variable was the phonetic environment in which the past tense marker occurred. Verbs that formed their past tense with a consonant cluster had the lowest degree of past tense marking. Thus a verb like 'walk' whose past tense in standard British English is marked with the consonant cluster /kt/ would not include the final /t/ sound.

The third variable depended on whether the action being described was a single action or one that was iterative or habitual. Platt found that when the speaker was describing a single action (for example, 'I left for Hong Kong last night'), the past tense was marked over 90 per cent of the time. But when the speaker was describing a habitual action (for example, 'Whenever he leaves the lights on I got angry') the past tense was never marked. This supported the findings Bickerton (1981) reported in his study on Guyanese Creole (GC) and Hawaiian Creole English (HCE). He showed that the past tense is marked more frequently for single or 'punctual' events, and far less frequently for habitual or 'non-punctual' events. Examples (translated into English) of non-punctual events include the past continuous ('while we were paddling') and the past habitual ('he kept telling me') (1981: 29).

Variety	Punctual past tense marking	Non-punctual past tense marking
GC	38%	12%
HCE	53%	7%

(1981: 165)

I have argued that the major cause of change is due to contact with other languages, but, if this is the case, how can the many shared features be explained? Crane (1994) pointed out that the simplification of inflections for tense occurred not just in the varieties of English where the mother tongues of speakers had no tense inflection, but also in varieties of English where the mother tongues of the speakers did inflect for tense. He therefore proposed that the similarities across varieties are due to a 'pan-linguistic grammatical simplification process' (1994: 358). It may be that both theories – language contact and 'pan-simplification' – can be accommodated by suggesting that many of the local languages that have influenced English themselves share many grammatical features. Theories of universal grammar may help shed light on this. For example, a feature of Singaporean English that appears to be caused by influence from local languages is 'subject dropping'. This not only occurs in informal settings but also in formal written texts (Deterding, 2000). This looks likely to be caused by direct influence from Chinese languages as these are, unlike English, 'pro-drop' languages that allow for no noun to be in subject position. For example, the Modern Standard Chinese for 'it's raining' is *xia yu* (literally 'down rain'). British English is a non-pro-drop language and thus requires a noun in subject position in order for it to be grammatically acceptable. So a dummy subject has to be brought in to give the grammatically acceptable 'it's raining'.

The headline below from the *Singapore Straits Times* newspaper provides an interesting example of this 'pro-drop' feature of Singaporean English (Deterding, 2000):

'Hurt girlfriend with lighted butt'

As Singaporean English is a pro-drop language, this is grammatically acceptable and the Singaporean reader automatically provides a subject, probably something like 'Boyfriend' here so that the headline means 'her boyfriend hurt his girlfriend with a lighted (cigarette) butt'. In British English, however, subject dropping is not possible. The headline will be interpreted as a subject noun phrase and the reader will need to provide a predicate for the sentence. This necessarily completely alters the meaning of the sentence. 'Hurt girlfriend with lighted butt (subject) jumped into bath to put herself out (predicate)' becomes a grammatically acceptable sentence of British English.

Second, the preference in Singaporean English for paratactic over hypotactic constructions may stem from differences in the parameter setting of universal grammar, as this occurs in many varieties of English, including African. Thus the Chinese stylistic preference for parallel conjunctions (Kirkpatrick, 1995) can be seen in the written English of many Singaporeans so that sentences like the following are common:

'Though it may not be a direct translation, but it is more acceptable in English.'

(Deterding, 2000: 206)

The use of certain particles in Singaporean English (such as 'lah' in the examples below), however, looks to be a direct transfer from local languages, rather than from a different parameter in the universal grammar of the local languages. This particle use is therefore specific to the Englishes of Singapore, Malaysia and Brunei:

'I didn't buy the dress lah'

'For Chinese New Year, we make jam tarts, jelly, love-letters, all lah'

(Platt, Weber and Ho, 1984: 57/63)

'But still, try lah'

(Hashim, 2002: 88)

In sum, features that are shared by many new varieties of English can be explained by the transfer of parameter settings in universal grammar. Features that are specific to one variety can be explained by the transfer of a language-specific feature into the new variety.

9.2.4 Code-mixing

In multilingual countries code-mixing (the use of more than one language or variety intra-sententially, i.e. in the same utterance or sentence) and code-switching (the use of different languages or varieties inter-sententially) is common and natural.

Despite its frequency, or perhaps because of it, some scholars and self-appointed guardians of linguistic morality view both code-mixing and code-switching as a sign of linguistic poverty or deficiency and rail against it. Code-mixed English Malay has been given the negative term *bahasa rojak*. *Rojak* is a type of Indonesian mixed salad dish, so *bahasa rojak* means mixed language. Its use is frequently condemned in the local media (McLellan, 2005: 45).

One reason for assuming that a code-mixed variety is in some way inferior to a 'pure' one is that is has been commonly assumed that code-mixed texts are formed with one language providing the grammatical framework and the second providing lexical items. This has been challenged in a recent study of language use in a Brunei internet discussion forum (McLellan, 2005). McLellan has shown that code-mixing is systematic and that code-mixed and code-switched texts, far from being deficient, are linguistically extremely sophisticated. He has also convincingly argued that many of the code-mixed texts show a more or less equal amount of grammar and lexis from both languages. In order to be able to produce texts such as the examples below the user must be fluent in both English and Malay and also know how to combine them to create a third code. The first example contains more English, the second more Malay. The Malay components are italicised. The 2 after *barang* signifies a plural marker *barang barang*, many items of luggage or 'stuff':

'Frankly speaking, *baiktah jangan dibali barang 2 yg kena* auction *atu, bukannya apa,* if we buy them, in a way, we are helping those who have used *buit ketani* for their personal interest to pay for their debts. *Mana tia yang dulu* the famous 7 *org atu. Inda kedengaran.* Has the trial started? It's so sad, isn't it, how our beloved country *jadi cemani.*'

'As for me, Bruclass *ani* my mind opener *walaupun ada masanya* idea *atu inda sehati dengan* contributors. I have also been proud *meliat idea-idea yang diusulkan menunjukkan anak2 Berunai ani pintar dan befikiran. Mungkin cara penyampaian seseorang atu berbeda* and *ada mesanya tunggang tebalik, panjang* (like me) and *payah kan dicompre-hend*, but at the end of the day it's one opportunity *untuk diorang meluahkan isihati demi kepentingan Negara. Samada diterima atau inda atu terserahlah.*'

(McLellan, 2005: 270)

In his study, McLellan found that texts of this type co-existed with monolingual Malay and monolingual English texts. He has proposed that these code-mixed texts constitute a systematic third code or variety and suggests that the relation between Malay, English and code-mixed texts of the type exemplified above is 'complimentary, perhaps even as interdependent' (2005: 177).

Hashim (2002: 86) illustrates a different type of code-switching with this excerpt from a short story, 'Everything's arranged', by the Malaysian writer Siew Yue Killingsley. In the excerpt below, the author code-switches between English of different levels of formality. This type of code-switching is common in all varieties of English. The more colloquial variety is in italics:

'Sitting in the lounge, watching the distracting and excited girls rushing by with packed cases, longing to go home to some decent food, Rukumani asked Devanayagam, '*This time you think you can write or not? Can send to Amy's house what.* My mother likes her mother. I can easily go there to get your letters. *But I think better you don't put my name outside. Can just put "Miss Amy Wong".* She knows your writing and won't open.'

The above excerpts and examples show that, while the roles of English in the three countries differ, English is used in a wide variety of domains and by different types of people in all three. The importance of identity is common, however. In the context of Malaysia, Hashim argues that the features of Malaysian English are important in 'establishing . . . national identity' (2002: 92). In the context of Brunei, Ramly, Othman and McLellan conclude that Bruneians 'would like to echo the claim that they have some control over English but that English has no control whatsoever over them' (2002: 105).

But it is, of course, not quite as simple as that. As earlier chapters have illustrated, in any multilingual and multicultural society, there will always be intense argument over the role of specific languages. In a recent study on the relationship between language and identity, Lee (2004) investigated how the acquisition of English had influenced the identities of three well-educated Malaysian women of different ethnic backgrounds. She found that there was wide difference of opinion between the three. The Malaysian Tamil subject asserted that it was essential for her to know Tamil in order to appreciate her cultural heritage. The Straits Chinese subject felt that languages were 'just assets in one's repertoire of skills and the more one knows the better' (2004: 117). The third subject, an ethnic Chinese who speaks Hainanese and Cantonese, but not Mandarin, deliberately chose to speak English at all times when in the presence of Mandarin-speaking Chinese. This was because she had been criticised at times in the past for not being fully Chinese, because she could not speak Mandarin. She herself felt that one did not necessarily have to speak Chinese to be Chinese. Lee concludes that there are no right and wrong answers and as educators 'we must teach tolerance and the right to agree or disagree . . . at the same time we must be aware of the dangers of ethnocentrism and we must teach an appreciation of our cultural diversity and empathy for others . . . no matter what tongue we speak, alien or mother' (2004: 124).

This complexity can also be seen in the development of Malaysian literature in English. Quayum (2003) points out that, with the 1967 National Language Act and subsequent amendments to it, English and writing in English fell out of favour. The Act raised the status of Bahasa Malaysia, and *Sastera Melayu* or Malay literature, because of its symbiotic relationship with the language, became the national literature, while literatures in other languages, including English, 'were but *Kesusasteraan sukuan* or sectional literatures' (2003: xvii). Writers who wrote in English moved to write only in Malay. One such, Mohammed Haji Salleh, recalling the view of the Sri Lankan poet Wikkramasinha, mentioned in Chapter 7, is quoted by Quayum as asking, 'should I lick the hand that strangles my language and culture?' (2003: xv).

With the importance of English for national development again recognised, attitudes to English are changing and 'the earlier hostilities towards the language, fresh from the memories of colonial oppression and exploitation, have slowly eased and subsided' (Quayum, 2003: xviii).

Two examples of Malaysian poetry in English, one by Mohammed Haji Salleh himself, are included on the accompanying CD. In the next section, the situation in the Philippines is considered.

9.3   The Philippines

The linguistic background and colonial history of the Philippines provides an illuminating example of the development of a new variety of English. The Philippines is made up of a population of some 72 million people who together speak some 85 Malayo-Polynesian languages and live on some 7,000 islands. The country was named after Philip II of Spain, and it was a colony of Spain from 1521 until it came under American rule in 1895. Like the Cameroon, therefore, which was colonised by both the French and the English, the Philippines has experienced two colonial masters. This particular combination of colonial influence has been described as combining 'monarchical Catholic Spain' with a republican 'quasi-imperial United States' (McArthur, 2002: 344).

Within three years of coming under American control, seven schools were opened in Manila by the American military and 'public education . . . was an essential component of military strategy . . . and throughout the American colonial period, English was systematically promoted as the language that would "civilise" the Filipinos' (Martin, 2002: 201–2).

In 1901, six years after the beginning of American rule, English-medium education was introduced, with English being the medium of instruction for all schools (Gonzalez, 1997). In 1935 the Philippines became a self-governing commonwealth and received independence in 1946. At the time of independence its colonial history was evident in the establishment of both English and Spanish as national languages, along with the local language Tagalog (Filipino).

Foreshadowing the bilingual policy introduced into Brunei in 1985, the government of the Philippines introduced a similar policy of bilingual education in 1974. English became a school subject at primary level and a medium of instruction for science and maths at secondary level. Bautista summarises this by saying Filipino was for 'culture-loaded' subjects and English for 'culture-free' ones (2004: 4).

The increase in the numbers of Filipinos claiming to speak English shows that the education policies have been successful. In 1901, English was spoken only by a very few, but by the 1980 census, 64.5 per cent of the population claimed to be able to speak English (Gonzalez, 1997: 29). Despite this, Thompson has argued that the future of English is bleak as, on the one hand, it is no longer regarded as useful for socio-economic advancement and, on the other, 'once an intellectual version of Filipino is accepted for a wide variety of scientific, technical and professional purposes, English will die out except among a select few' (2003: 265). However, this view is not shared by Filipino scholars. Garcia (1997) feels that translations of scholarship into Filipino would be far too costly and time-consuming. This is an important point and is relevant to other languages, as it would simply be impossible to translate all the articles currently published in English in academic journals. Decisions about which journals and which articles to translate would have to be made. She also disagrees with Thompson's claims that English is not important for socio-economic advancement. Her view is that English remains the preferred language, not only in science and technology, but also in government, business, commerce and industry, and that it is still the language of socio-economic mobility and advancement. Gonzalez (1997) argues along similar lines and predicts that demand for English will not only continue but actually increase for two reasons. First, Filipino academics will have to continue to rely on American sources for their scholarship. Second, as English is so useful for the export of human resources and as so many Filipinos work overseas as contract workers, there is a great demand for English 'especially at the lower socio-economic levels' (1997: 36). A third possible reason for the increased use of English in the Philippines is the role that English plays as a *lingua franca* in ASEAN and this will be described and explored in Chapter 11.

Gonzalez (1997: 39) concludes that the 'revivification' of English will be represented by Filipino English which will be marked by an attenuated phonological system, 'Filipinisms' and local collocational rules, and a fully restructured system of tense, aspect and articles (1997: 36). The next section of the chapter describes a selection of these features.

9.4   Linguistic features of Philippine English

9.4.1   Phonology

Gonzalez has claimed that the first language of speakers of Philippine English (PE) is 'almost always recognisable, even among the elite' (1991: 324). He is referring to being able to identify the first language of PE speakers from their accent. He also points out that 'almost from the beginning, Filipinos learned English from Filipinos and the seeds of what we now call Philippine English began' (1997: 26–7). As will be seen in the next chapter, phonological variation is even more evident in the case of Chinese speakers of English.

Nevertheless, certain phonological features have been identified for Philippine English, many of which occur in other varieties.

As McArthur (2002: 344ff.) notes, PE is rhotic and has a tendency towards syllable-timing. He describes its intonation as 'singsong'-like. There is no phonemic distinction between the /ɪ/ and /iː/ or between /ʊ/ and /uː/ and the diphthong /oʊ/ is sounded as /ɔː/.

The following tables of the vowel and consonant sounds of cultivated Philippine English are taken from Gonzalez (1997: 32–3).

The vowel and consonant sounds of cultivated Philippine English

i̦			u	
(I)			(∪)	
		(ə)		
ey				(o)
e				o
	(æ)	a		

p		t	c	k
b		d	j	g
	(Ø)	s	š	h
	(ð)	(z)	(ž)	m
		n		
		l		
	m	n	ng	
		l		
		r		
	w	y		

9.4.2 Lexis

As would be expected, the vocabulary of Philippine English derives from a range of phenomena including semantic and part-of-speech shift, loan translations, coinages and creative innovations, compounds and hybrids. Unless otherwise indicated, the examples below come from Bautista (1997b: 49–72).

The adoption of certain brand names to refer to the articles in general is one example of semantic shift. For example 'pampers' refers to disposable nappies in general and 'colgate' to toothpaste. A similar process can be seen in other varieties of English where 'hoover' has come to refer to all vacuum cleaners and 'xerox' to all photocopying machines.

Part-of-speech shifts can be seen in the following examples:

'Sorry I'm late, it was so *traffic*'
'Why are you so *high-blood* again? What's upsetting you?'

Examples of new coinages are 'carnapper' (car thief), 'holdupper' (thief) and 'cockfighter' (someone who raises cocks for cockfighting). Compounds include 'captain ball' (team captain), 'green joke' (for blue joke – possibly a yellow joke in Chinese English), and 'phonepal'. Hybrids – where a compound is formed of words from different languages – are common: '*buco* juice' (the juice of a young coconut), '*pulot* boy' (a tennis ball boy) and 'common *tao*' (an ordinary Filipino). Words for local items of flora and fauna, food and culture naturally occur in Philippine English. This example comes from Butler (1997: 119) and represents an excerpt from the novel *View From the Middle* by Asuncion David Maramba:

> 'What have operated in our lives – negative values like a never-ending *utang na loob* (debt of gratitude) etc., or positive values like *kasipagan, katapatan* (industry, honesty) etc., or are they two sides of the same coin, now up, now down, like *cara y cruz* (heads or tails).'

9.4.3 Grammar

Gonzalez (1997: 39) was quoted above as saying that Philippine English is restructuring the tense and aspect systems. Certain tenses are thus used in distinctive contexts (McArthur, 2002). For example, PE speakers use the present perfect where other varieties would use the past simple, so that a PE speaker might say 'I have seen her yesterday'. For example:

> 'In a recent Senate hearing probing questionable conduct, former President Estrada *has claimed* it was . . .'

> (Pankratz, 2004: 80)

The past perfect is often used where others might use a present perfect or past simple:

> 'Have some pupils tell they class what *they had observed*'

> (Pena, 1997: 92)

> '. . . Sen. Francis Pangilinan *had already started* sponsoring the proposed . . . Act'
> (Pankratz, 2004: 80)

A second example is the PE use of the present continuous to refer to habitual actions as in the sentence 'he is going to school regularly'.

Word order can also be distinctive as Philippine English favours a 'verb – adverb – object' sequence as in the examples 'let the pupils read part by part the selection . . .' and 'interpret orally the selection'. The interrogative order is retained in imperatives as in 'ask what are boys fond of playing' (Pena, 1997: 91).

In her investigation into distinctive features of PE, Bautista (2005) identified three potential candidates. She then analysed corpora collected by the International Corpus of English (ICE) to see if these features occurred in other varieties of English.

The first feature she looked at was the PE speaker use of 'one of the +N (singular)' phrase as in the sentence 'That's *one of the related problem* we will also be discussing'. However, she discovered that this usage is also common in other varieties of English and that it is actually more frequent in Hong Kong, Indian and Singaporean Englishes than in PE.

The second 'typical' feature of PE she investigated was the use of the word 'majority' without a preceding article, as in 'But a survey done by Pulse Asia shows *majority of their respondents* want President Estrada to keep his post'. Again, however, she found that this usage occurs more frequently in Indian English and, importantly, that it only occurs 30 per cent of the time in PE. In other words PE speakers use an article with 'majority' 70 per cent of the time.

The final feature she investigated was the distinctive PE use of 'wherein' as in the following two examples:

> 'This practice is still being done in several universities in the US okay *wherein* they have a quota for different racial groups'

> 'Yes one potential danger if you have fall-outs from the volcanic eruption is you get a very irritating skin disease *wherein* you have li.. a freckle-like uh spots.'

This usage of 'wherein' did prove to be distinctive and was far more frequently used in PE than in any other variety, especially in spoken PE. Only Indian English was found to use 'wherein' more than very occasionally, but its use was nowhere near as frequent as in PE. Bautista suggests that this distinctive use of 'wherein' in PE might be parallel to the use of the Filipino particle *na*. This is commonly transferred to PE:

> 'And I don't like her reasoning *na* she doesn't wanna pay me because it's not her priority because I have money.'

Bautista's study illustrates the value in using large corpora, like those collected by ICE, in identifying distinctive and/or shared features of varieties, as it allows researchers to analyse the use of specific features across a wide range of varieties of English and allows researchers to identify which features are shared across several varieties and which may be specific to just one. Such studies can therefore help determine which features are shared across varieties – and thus possibly caused by their transfer from parameter settings in universal grammar – and which features are specific and thus possibly caused by their transfer from just one language.

9.5 Literature in PE

The Philippines already had a flourishing literature by the time the Americans arrived. Despite the existence of literature in the native languages, however, it was not taught in the colonial classroom as colonial policy was not to teach local languages in the schools. English remained the sole language of public schools until 1940 and the literary canon taught in the schools was exclusively colonial or 'Anglo' and included Longfellow, Lincoln, Emerson, Defoe and Shakespeare (Martin, 2002: 203).

This led to an appreciation of 'Western' writing and a rejection of traditional Filipino fine writing. Martin cites the Filipino Head of the Department of English of a major Philippine university writing in 1936:

'. . . in writing there are certain qualities of the English language which are difficult of assimilation in an Oriental country like ours; for whereas the best English writing demands the crispness, sharpness, severity and economy of expression, the Oriental manner of speaking and writing calls always for wordiness, ornate language, a "fine writing" – all these being very suggestive of pleonasm and surplusage.'

(Martin, 2002: 210)

Some Filipino writers currently writing in English appear to feel that the English they write in must be correct in this sense of being crisp, sharp and economical. In a writers' forum held in 1993 (Bautista, 1997a: 163–76), several of the participants pointed out that they chose not to write 'Filipinisms'. One of the participants, Cristina Pantoja-Hidalgo, suggested that a possible reason for this was that many Filipino writers were teachers and they were thus conscious of correct classroom English (Bautista, 1997a: 170). Other writers took a different stance. Gemino Abad argued that the English he used was distinctively Filipino, saying, 'English is ours. We have colonised it too' (Bautista, 1997a: 170). In similar vein, F. Sionil Jose recalled a discussion with an American editor in which the editor asked if there was anything Jose would like him to do. 'And I said, you can correct my grammar and correct anything, but don't make me less a Filipino' (Bautista, 1997a: 168). But it is hard to understand how 'correcting' the 'grammar' and 'everything' would result in anything other than making the author 'less a Filipino'.

These conflicting views are instructive, as they illustrate that, even in a country that has an established variety of English, there is still hesitation about seeing it as a worthy medium for literature. This serves as a reminder that, along with the complexity over the possible causes of the linguistic features of varieties of English, the extent to which these varieties are considered acceptable and appropriate by their own speakers is as varied as the socio-cultural and linguistic contexts in which they have developed.

China

10 Emerging Englishes: Hong Kong and China

Introduction

While China and Hong Kong are today part of the same country under China's 'One Country, Two Systems' policy, the history and roles of English in both places have been quite distinct, especially during the period between 1842 and 1997 when Hong Kong was a British colony. In this chapter, I shall briefly outline the history of English in Hong Kong and then China, and compare the roles that English has played and is playing there. Linguistic features of Hong Kong English (HKE) and Chinese English (CE) will be described and the extent to which they can be considered varieties of English in their own right will be discussed. Finally, predictions about the future of HKE and CE will be made.

10.1 English in Hong Kong

Hong Kong became a British colony in 1842 at the conclusion of the first Opium War, fought between Britain and China. The 1842 Treaty of Nanjing was signed at the end of the war and also opened up the Chinese cities of Amoy (Xiamen), Canton (Guangdong), Fuzhou, Ningbo and Shanghai, as these cities became the so-called treaty ports in which the British and other Western nations could conduct trade.

British traders had, in fact, been trading in Canton from the beginning of the nineteenth century. Bolton (2003) explains that there were three different groups of English-speaking traders involved. The first group were employees of the East India Company, at the time the most powerful trading company in the world. The second group were traders who had their main offices in England and Scotland and later established very successful trading companies, such as Jardine Mathieson. The third group comprised American traders.

These traders communicated with the Chinese in a form of Chinese pidgin English. One reason for the development of this pidgin was that, in the early days, the Chinese forbad the teaching of Chinese to foreigners and only allowed a certain group of Chinese – the middlemen or compradores – to interact with the foreigners. This pidgin English was considered something less than a proper language. Bolton (2003: 159) cites a European trader as calling it an 'uncouth and ridiculous jargon'. Nevertheless, it remained the primary means of communication between the two sides for several decades. The following examples of this 'Canton jargon' come from Morrison's 1834 glossary and are taken from Bolton (2003: 154ff.). Some of these terms, *fan kwei*, for example, are still common:

Canton jargon	Meaning
can do?	will it do?
chop-chop	very quickly
chow-chow	food, to eat
cow-cow	to be noisy and angry; an uproar
fan kwei	foreign devil
nex' day or tomorrow nex' day	the day after tomorrow
pidgeon (pidgin)	from 'business'
that no makee good pidgeon	the thing is ill done

The first schools established in Hong Kong were missionary schools. St Paul's College (1851) was the first and, in 1862, the government-run Central School was established. This later became Queen's College. Although these schools were run by a combination of missionaries and the government, their curricula appear to have been enlightened. Many of the missionaries were 'orientalists' and students of Chinese philosophy and culture. As Bolton argues, the reason why Chinese language and culture were taught in most mission schools was because many of the largely Protestant educators who set up the first missionary schools had 'a profoundly orientalist interest not only in the Mandarin language but also the dialects of South China' (2003: 84). Missionaries were responsible for many early translations of the Chinese Classics and also compiled the first dictionaries. The mission schools thus taught Chinese language and literature and, in most, the students were taught through Chinese (Boyle, 1997). The first principal of Central School, Frederic Stewart, emphasised that 'schools should be secular and should give strong support first to Chinese education' (Pennycook, 1998: 109). Pennycook goes on to say that Stewart held remarkably liberal views on education, but argues that his policies, 'although apparently based on liberal educational ideals, suited the colonial administration better than the more extreme Anglicist or Orientalist policies advocated by others' (1998: 112). To view Stewart's educational policies solely as promoting colonial ideals seems a little harsh. Indeed, Pennycook contradicts his own argument, as he has earlier pointed out that the Governor of Hong Kong, Hennessy, had been shocked to discover how few of the boys in Hong Kong schools spoke English well and asked for Stewart's policies to be altered so that English would be promoted. In the event, little change took place so that a later Governor, William Robinson (1891–8), was equally shocked to find 'that after fifty-five years of British rule, the vast majority of Chinese in Hong Kong should remain so little anglicised' (Boyle, 1997: 173). It was only in 1894 that Central School moved to English as a medium of instruction along with a name change to Queen's College (Boyle, 1997).

Key events and dates in the role of English in Hong Kong before its return to Chinese rule in 1997 include the establishment of the English-medium University of Hong Kong in 1912. This remained the sole university until the establishment of the Chinese-medium Chinese University of Hong Kong in 1963. By offering a Chinese-medium university, the government hoped to increase the number of students electing to enter Chinese-medium secondary schools. However, as there was an English entrance exam, it transpired that students from English-medium schools were more successful in gaining entry even to the Chinese University. As a result, the number of Chinese-medium schools actually declined in the years immediately after 1963 (Boyle, 1997).

It was not until the Official Languages Ordinance of 1974 that Chinese was made a co-official language with English in all domains, except for law. The Ordinance did not define Chinese, but it was taken to mean spoken Cantonese (Johnson, 1994). However, English secondary schools remained the overwhelming choice for parents. The 1982 Llewellyn report into education, authored by education experts from Britain, the USA, Australia and Germany, recommended a shift to mother-tongue education in the early years of schooling 'accompanied by formal teaching of English as a first foreign language' (Bolton, 2003: 91). This resulted in a series of further reports published by the Education Commission in which the use of Cantonese as a medium of instruction was strongly recommended. As, however, the government eventually left the medium-of-instruction decision to school principals, the great majority of secondary schools remained English-medium. Many classes were characterised by lessons taught in mixed Cantonese–English code.

Despite the 1990 Education Commission's view that the ideal proportion of Chinese-medium to English-medium schools was 70:30, the actual figures showed that while over 90 per cent of students were indeed in Chinese-medium primary schools, over 90 per cent were in English-medium secondary schools (Johnson, 1994). A great number of these English-medium schools, however, remained so only in name. Although the textbooks and exams were in English, much of the actual teaching was done in Cantonese and a great deal of class time was spent in translating English textbooks into Chinese. Instruction was actually in mixed code or Cantonese and followed a 'textual explanation approach' (Luke and Richards, 1982: 50). I myself observed a number of such classes when I was teaching in Hong Kong in the late 1970s.

Just months before Hong Kong's return to Chinese rule, the colonial government moved from its position of allowing principals to decide which medium of instruction would be used in their schools and decreed that only 100 secondary schools, out of a total of some 460, would be allowed to continue to use English as medium of instruction. The remainder would teach in Cantonese. This, predictably enough, was met with public opposition and, as a result, the government slightly increased the number of English-medium secondary schools to 114. Bolton (2000) has suggested that this sudden decision to decree mother-tongue education after so many years of a *laissez-faire* attitude was primarily aimed at preserving Cantonese against its bigger Chinese official 'brother', *Putonghua*. This shift was also designed to help implement the new language policy of 1995, which was 'to develop a civil service which is biliterate in English and Chinese and trilingual in English, Cantonese and *Putonghua*' (Bolton, 2000: 270).

This policy has been continued by the new Hong Kong government. Beijing wants Hong Kong to be an international city rather than a Southern Chinese one. 'It is our policy to promote biliteracy and trilingualism. Hong Kong . . . needs to promote the wider usage of basic English. As part of China, Hong Kong people should also learn to speak fluent *Putonghua*' (see Bolton, 2003: 200). The government has also recognised that this switch to Cantonese-medium schools means that students will need extra help with their English. To this end, each Cantonese-medium school received extra funding to hire a native speaker of English as an English teacher. (I shall discuss these 'native-speaker teacher' policies in Part C of the book.) The current government's recognition of the importance of English can also be seen through the subsidies which are available for members of the workforce to improve their English through attending courses (Li, 2000). Written English is still the language of civil service documents, the legal system and the police force and it remains the main language of textbooks and lectures in most of the eight universities (Bolton, 2003).

Throughout Hong Kong's colonial history and beyond, its people have maintained a consistent mercantile and pragmatic attitude to English (Sweeting and Vickers, 2005). Boyle sums this up by saying 'Hong Kong Chinese have always wanted English' (1997: 176).

10.2 Hong Kong English – variety or interlanguage?

Many scholars have argued that Hong Kong Chinese do not use English for intra-ethnic communication and that this means that Hong Kong English does not have the linguistic environment in which to develop as a new variety. For example, Luke and Richards recall the treaty port days in arguing that Hong Kong is a place where two largely monolingual communities exist 'with a small group of bilingual Cantonese functioning as middlemen' (1982: 51). They thus conclude that English in Hong Kong derives its norms from British and American English rather than possessing local norms. 'There is no such thing as Hong Kong English' (1982: 55). This view is largely shared by Johnson, as he suggests that Hong Kong Chinese do not use English among themselves and thus that the idea of a Hong Kong variety of English 'has received little support' (1994: 182). The best-known local scholar who espouses this view is Li. He argues that English is not used by the Chinese in Hong Kong for intra-ethnic communication so 'indigenous forms have not developed' (2000: 50). So, while the great majority of Hong Kong Chinese see the need for English, they learn it as a school subject and feel an inhibition to use it among themselves. Thus 'the language learning environment in Hong Kong is not at all conducive to the development of communicative and linguistic competence in English' (2000: 56). English in Hong Kong is exonormative. Its typical 'features', in Li's view, should be seen as errors not systematic features of a new variety.

This position has been challenged, most notably by Bolton (2000, 2003). He argues that the knowledge of English in the general population expanded greatly in the 1980s and 1990s, with the 1996 census showing that 38 per cent of the population (currently some 7 million) claimed to know English. He also argues that the notion of a Chinese community that converses only in Cantonese is a myth. Instead he argues that Hong Kong is a multilingual society with much greater linguistic and ethnic diversity among non-Chinese in Hong Kong than previously understood along with greater linguistic diversity among the Chinese community. To suggest, therefore, that Hong Kong comprises only two speech communities, Cantonese-speaking Chinese and English-speaking expatriate, 'would be a gross simplification' (2003: 90).

There is no doubt that Hong Kong is multilingual in the sense that many languages are spoken there. However, the role of English as a *lingua franca* is not as pronounced or obvious as in places such as Singapore, primarily because the overwhelming majority of the people are Chinese, most of whom speak Cantonese. This is not to say, however, that English is never used among the Chinese-speaking majority. In a comparative study of the use of English in the workplace of companies in Kuala Lumpur and Hong Kong, Briguglio (2005) identified several interesting differences. She found that the personnel in the Kuala Lumpur company used English more than the Hong Kong personnel in all speaking and personal interaction tasks, but that the Hong Kong personnel used English more than the Kuala Lumpur personnel in all writing and reading tasks, with the exception of writing and reading formal reports and writing recruitment literature. The results showed that over 95 per cent of the Hong Kong personnel used English to write and read emails and faxes, and that over 65 per cent used English to write letters, memos and informal reports. And while the Hong Kong personnel used English less frequently in oral communication with their fellow workers when compared with their Malaysian counterparts, some 33 per cent used English regularly on the phone and 20 per cent in face-to-face conversation with fellow workers. This would suggest that English plays important roles in the Hong Kong workplace.

A sense of political uncertainty in the period leading up to the 1997 handover of Hong Kong to China has also increased the use of English among Hong Kong Chinese. Some 10 per cent of Hong Kong Chinese emigrated overseas, primarily to English-speaking countries (Li, 2002b), but many have returned to Hong Kong where they are referred to as 'astronauts' in HKE. Their time overseas has given them and their children an international perspective and much more confidence in English. Thus Bolton is able to argue that Hong Kong students 'negotiate their internationalism through English and mixed code, and increasingly through electronic media such as the internet' (2003: 202). It should also be pointed out that many Hong Kong families employ Filipina maids, and the *lingua franca* between the family and the maid is English. Indeed, Filipina maids often take on the role of English tutor to the family's children.

A further reason why English may play a greater role among Hong Kong Chinese than commonly allowed has to do with their sense of identity as Hong Kong people. When Hong Kong was a colony it was perhaps unique in providing a place of refuge for many Chinese who wished to escape the conditions, both political and economic, of their own country. There was mass migration from China to Hong Kong, not only at the time of the establishment of the People's Republic of China in 1949, but on several occasions since then. As Li has pointed out, the immigrants to Hong Kong 'volunteered to live under a foreign flag in preference to their own' (2002b: 40). The subsequent introduction of Hong Kong identity cards helped give these people a sense of separate identity from mainland Chinese. The extent to which English helped create this separate sense of identity among educated Hong Kong Chinese is, as illustrated above, a hotly contested topic, but there can be little doubt that the Hong Kong Chinese viewed the colonial administration of Britain as providing a 'benevolent, non-intrusive government and a politically stable shelter' (Li, 2002b: 40). English was thus not associated with colonial oppression but with economic and social mobility, primarily through education, and possibly, for some, Hong Kong identity.

In summary, English has come to play an increasing role not only in Hong Kong itself but also among Hong Kong Chinese and so, therefore, it is possible that a Hong Kong variety of English does exist. Certainly, HKE appears to meet at least three of Butler's criteria for an emerging variety of English. The five criteria are (Butler, 1997: 10):

(i)   a standard and recognisable pronunciation handed down from one generation to another;

(ii) particular words and phrases which spring up usually to express key features of the physical and social environment and which are regarded as peculiar to the variety;

(iii) a history – a sense that this variety of English is the way it is because of the history of the language community;

(iv) a literature written without apology in that variety of English; and

(v)   reference works – dictionaries and style guides – which show that people in that language community look to themselves, not some outside authority, to decide what is right and wrong in terms of how they speak and write their English.

That criteria (i) and (ii) are met by HKE will be illustrated below and the discussion above shows that English in Hong Kong has historical roots. The fourth criterion – a literature – will be considered below. As for the fifth, this criterion is only likely to be met some time *after* the variety has been established. Australian English is a prime example of this, as the dictionary of Australian English, *The Macquarie* (of which, incidentally, Butler is the Executive Publisher), was first published only in 1981, some 200 years after Captain Cook first arrived in Australia. No one would argue, however, that Australian English was not a recognised variety before 1981. As demonstrated in Chapter 6, Australian English was a recognisable variety at least by the beginning of the twentieth century.

10.3 **Features of HKE**

10.3.1 **Phonology**

With regard to Butler's first criterion, Hung does not think that 'there is any dispute about the existence of an identifiable HKE accent, which is just as easily recognisable as Indian, Singaporean or Australian English' (Hung, 2000: 337). He has described the vowel and consonant sounds of HKE (2000: 337–56) and shown that HKE speakers operate with seven vowel contrasts compared with the 11 of British speakers of RP. The four vowel sounds that are distinguished in RP but not in HKE are:

a) the vowel sounds in RP 'heat' and 'hit' are both sounded as /ɪ/ in HKE

b) the vowel sounds in RP 'head' and 'had' are both sounded as /ɛ / in HKE

c) the vowel sounds in RP 'hoot' and 'hood' are both sounded as /u/ in HKE

d) the vowel sounds in RP 'caught' and 'cot' are both sounded as /ɔ/ in HKE.

While HKE speakers use only seven simple vowel contrasts, they have eight diphthong contrasts (2000: 347). These are the diphthongs in 'hate' /eɪ/, 'height' /aɪ/, 'house' /aʊ/, 'coat' /oʊ/, 'toyed' /ɔɪ/, 'here' /ɪə/, 'hair' /ɛə/ and 'poor' /ʊə/.

Hung concludes (2000: 354) by saying that HKE phonology exists with systematic features of its own, that the phonemic inventory of HKE is considerably simpler than older varieties of English, both in its vowel and consonant systems, and that, although HKE phonology shows influence from both Cantonese and English, it needs to be investigated on its own terms.

10.3.2 Lexis

Many of the lexical items identified below also occur in Chinese English and, as with other varieties, HKE vocabulary stems from several sources. One rich source is the coinage or innovation of new terms (Bolton, 2003: 212ff.). Examples include 'Canto-pop' (Cantonese pop music), 'Chinglish' (Chinese English) and '*tan tan* noodles'.

Words of specific cultural importance often appear in compounds. In Chapter 6, the many compounds made with 'bush' in Australian English were noted. In Hong Kong and Chinese Englishes, two such key words are 'dragon' and 'temple', both occurring in a wide range of compounds that describe culturally specific phenomena, such as 'dragon boat', 'dragon dance', 'dragon pot', 'dragon cup' and 'dragon gate', and 'temple bell', 'temple altar,' 'temple compound', temple festival' and 'temple priest' (Butler, 2002: 153–4).

Borrowing also affords a rich source of HKE words and include *cha siu* (a type of barbecued pork), *cheongsam* (a type of dress) and *gwai lo* (foreign devil).

Expressions in HKE that derive directly from Cantonese include the phrase 'return back' (*waan4 faaan*) and the italicised parts of '*no matter* you pursue. . .' (*mou4 leon6*) and 'laziness is *my largest enemy*' (*zeoi3 daai6 ge3 dik6 jan4*) (Li, 2000: 52–3). The numbers in the Cantonese versions refer to specific tones.

Uncountable nouns in older varieties of English become count nouns in HKE, for example 'aircrafts', 'equipments', 'staffs', 'alphabets', 'audiences' and 'researches'.

Other examples of part-of-speech shifts include the shift from intransitive to transitive verbs as in 'they always laugh me' and 'he didn't reply me' (Li, 2000: 53).

10.3.3 Grammar

Li analysed the written work of his university students and identified the following common features of their written English (2000: 53ff.). Note that Li's view is that these are actually errors and representative of an interlanguage rather than systematic features of HKE. This explains the way in which he describes these features.

a) Non-tense-marking in certain contexts. Li's example is: 'Luckily I am now a university student. I *decide* not to join the activities I am interested in.'

b) Failure to use the passive or pseudo passives: 'In the 'Reading Section', *it divided* into three parts . . .'

c) Intransitive passives: 'That accident *was happened* at 6pm.'

d) Failure to use the 'Adj for NP to V' structure: '*You are impossible to stay* here overnight.'

e) Inappropriate post-modifying clause structure after 'There Be NP': 'There are *a lot of people died.*'

f) Independent clause as subject: '*He was willing to stay* surprised us all.'

g) Periphrastic topic construction: '*In the above examples, it shows* that learners. . . .'

He also identifies the common response to negatively phrased questions in spoken HKE, which has also been identified in many other varieties of English. For example:

Invigilator: James, you're not cheating are you?
Student: Yes. (meaning: You're right. I'm not cheating.)

What is interesting here is that some of these features occur in many other varieties of English, although Li treats them as errors. The criteria to use in distinguishing between features of learner English or an interlanguage and features of a new variety of English remain elusive. I shall suggest some in the next chapter.

10.4 Literature in HKE

Does Butler's fourth criterion, a literature 'written without apology', exist in HKE? *Renditions* is a Chinese–English translation journal published in Hong Kong. Its main content comprises the translations of Chinese writing of various types into English to make them available for an English readership. It is instructive, in the context of the debate about whether a Hong Kong literature exists, to ask whether a Hong Kong literature is thought to exist in *Chinese*. It is interesting, therefore, that in 1988 *Renditions* published a special double issue on literature written in Hong Kong. In raising the question 'Is he or she a Hong Kong writer?', the editor, Eva Hung, felt that no consensus had yet been reached, but that, in the past few years, Hong Kong literature had become a 'hot topic' (Hung, 1988: 7). And as she points out, the special edition showed that Hong Kong literature possessed a richness and diversity, 'qualities which reflect the heterogenous culture of the territory' (1988: 8).

Almost a decade later, a second edition of *Renditions* (1997) was devoted to Hong Kong. By this time the editors, Eva Hung and David Pollard, appeared more convinced that a distinctive Hong Kong literature did indeed exist, as they wrote, 'In producing an anthology of Hong Kong literature of the nineties . . .' (1997: 5). In other words, a Hong Kong literature written in Chinese is now accepted. The question remains as to whether a Hong Kong literature written in HKE exists. Vittachi certainly uses colloquial HKE and mixed code to effect in his writing (see Vittachi, 2000, for example). Xu Xi, one of several Hong Kong writers who write in English, says that, although she is a Hong Kong person who writes about Hong Kong in English, what that English is, is for someone else to decide (Xu Xi, 2000). There are a number of Hong Kong authors writing in English, including the poets Louise Ho and Agnes Lam, but whether they write in an English that can be classified as distinctively HKE is open to question. (Readers can refer to poems by both authors in the Appendix, but please note that these have not been recorded.) In my own view, it is not as distinctive as the English employed by the Chinese writer Ha Jin, examples of whose writing are illustrated later in this chapter, and it is to China that I now turn.

10.5 English in China

The first recorded contact between British traders and the Chinese took place in 1637 and was recounted by one of the traders in *The Travels of Peter Mundy* (Bolton, 2003). But it was not until the late eighteenth and the beginning of the nineteenth century that contact became more systematic. Needless to say, the early schools and colleges were established by missionaries, but, as was the case in Hong Kong, many of these taught Chinese language, literature and philosophy. Adamson (2004) has provided a useful account of the development of English teaching in China and of Chinese attitudes towards English. This chronological summary is taken from an earlier work (Adamson, 2002: 232).

1911–23	intellectual revolution; English for ideas/philosophy
1923–49	English for diplomacy and interaction
1949–60	English for science and technology only
1961–66	first renaissance – English for modernisation and international understanding
1966–76	Cultural Revolution; English speakers are suspect
1976–82	slow recovery; English for modernisation
1982–present	English highly desirable and strongly promoted in school curricula

As the chronological table above illustrates, English has variously been seen as a conduit for Western science and technology, a conduit for Western ideas that will assist in the modernisation of China and international understanding, or as a language whose speakers represent the 'enemy' if they are foreigners and someone suspicious if they are Chinese. Currently English is seen as extremely important for the modernisation of China and for international understanding and influence. The current attitude towards English is the most positive in Chinese history. With regard to the period of intellectual revolution (1911–23), it should be noted that other European languages, in particular Russian and German, have been influential in introducing new ideas into China. The intellectual debate was between the 'Anglo' philosophies of men such as Russell and Dewey and the 'European' philosophies of men such as Hegel and Marx. The European philosophies eventually triumphed, with a Chinese interpretation of Communism becoming the national ideology in 1949.

Not surprisingly, therefore, Russian was the first foreign language from 1949 until the relationship with Russia deteriorated from the late 1950s. Since then, the first foreign language has been English, but with attitudes towards it shifting in the ways indicated above.

Even during those periods when English was officially classified as being the language of suspect forces, many educated and urban Chinese maintained a wish to learn it. While I was a postgraduate student at Fudan University in Shanghai during the final stages of the Cultural Revolution in the mid-1970s, I was frequently approached by Chinese who wanted to practise their English discreetly. On one memorable occasion I was approached by a man who whisperingly wanted to know whether I knew much about the Royal Navy of Elizabeth I.

Today the desire to learn English among the educated and urban Chinese is astounding. The number of English teachers has increased from an estimated 850 in 1957 to well over half a million today (Bolton, 2003) and the number of Chinese learning English probably outnumbers the total population of the United States and Britain combined. It seems inevitable that this number of people learning and speaking English will lead to a distinctive Chinese variety of English. Indeed the existence of Chinese English has been the subject of debate among Chinese scholars since the beginning of the 1980s (Du and Jiang, 2001). Wang (1994: 7) has defined Chinese English as 'the English used by the Chinese people in China, being based on standard English and having Chinese characteristics'. In the next part of this chapter, features of Chinese English (CE) will be described. Unless otherwise noted, these are taken from Xu (2005).

10. 6 Features of Chinese English (CE)

10.6.1 Phonology

Gonzalez (1997) argued that the first languages of speakers of Philippine English could be identified. While it may not be possible to identify accurately in every case the mother-tongue dialects of speakers of CE, speakers of CE currently have a range of accents that are determined to a large extent by their mother-tongue dialects. It has already been noted that speakers of Hong Kong English speak with an easily identifiable accent and that the influence of Cantonese phonology can be detected. By definition, speakers of CE come from all over China and, as the Chinese language has seven major dialect groups and many more sub-varieties, it follows that speakers of CE may have different accents dependent upon their mother-tongue dialect. Little research has yet been conducted into this and here I shall not attempt to claim any distinctive phonological features that are common to all speakers of CE, except to say that CE speakers have a tendency towards syllable-timing.

10.6.2 Lexis

Transliteration of Chinese words provides a rich source of words for CE. These include *pinyin* (the romanised script for Chinese characters), *Putonghua* (Modern Standard Chinese), *yamen* (feudal administrative office), *dazibao* (big character poster), *tai chi* (physical exercise like shadow-boxing), *feng shui* (architectural tenets, literally wind–water) and many others including *ganbei* (literally 'dry glass'), which is what you are supposed to do when you have a glass of *maotai* (white spirit) in front of you. A recent transliteration that forms a hybrid compound is '*xiaokang* society', a society that ensures that all can become slightly better off in the future.

Direct translations from Chinese into English of 'things Chinese' or Chinese cultural concepts are also a rich source of words. These include the 'four modernisations', 'one country, two systems', 'running dogs', 'paper tiger', 'to get rich quick is glorious', 'iron rice bowl', 'open-door policy', 'barefoot doctor', 'the three represents theory' and 'Project 211' (the policy to establish 100 key universities in China in the 21st century), to name just a few.

Direct translations of metaphors also add a special flavour to CE. These examples come from Ha Jin's writing (Xu, 2005: 85):

'a flowered pillowcase' (someone who is good-looking but otherwise useless)
'you can't squeeze fat out of a skeleton' (you can't get blood out of a stone)

and this memorable sentence:

'The three of them wear the same pair of trousers and breathe through one nostril.'

(Zhang, 2002: 310)

Nativised English words are also common, and these often show signs of semantic shift. For example, the English word for a particular card game, 'poker', has become *pu-ke*, but this refers to card games in general.

Other 'English' words take on specific culturally Chinese meanings. Examples of compounds with 'dragon' and 'temple' have already been provided. Another example is 'face', in its distinctively Chinese meaning, referring to the crucial importance of maintaining someone's sense of self-esteem and position. A Chinese cultural value that is referred to in CE by the original Chinese word is *guānxi* (relationships/contacts) and an example of the way this is represented in CE is provided later in the context of an excerpt from a Ha Jin short story.

'Lover' in CE has a wider semantic range than in other varieties of English and includes the notion of 'spouse', as in the following example:

'People are supposed to know exactly the physical conditions of their *lovers*,' Yao said.

This rather startling remark was made in the context of a regulation to abolish the requirement for engaged couples to undergo premarital medical tests in favour of privacy protection. The word 'lover' in this context is closest to *àirén* (spouse) in Modern Standard Chinese (Xu, 2005: 58).

Two words that are of particular interest are 'comrade' and 'individual'. In CE 'comrade' was originally the standard form of address and is a direct translation of the Chinese word *tongzhi*, itself a translation from the Russian. It represented an attempt to see everyone as equal, as required in Communist thinking. Its meaning in CE has shifted significantly in recent years, however, as it now refers almost exclusively to homosexuals, although, curiously, it is still used in its original sense to refer to the highest leaders in the Party hierarchy. The meaning of 'individual' has also shifted in CE. Originally it carried the negative connotation of selfishness but has recently taken on a more positive meaning, aligned to the Anglo interpretation of the word to mean someone with a 'sense of independence and competition' (Xu, 2005: 60). This shift in meaning is reflected within Chinese society. For example, the Communist Youth League has decided to drop its exemplar of selfless Communist Party spirit, the boy-scout-like Lei Feng, and replace him with that Western symbol of individual pluckiness Mickey Mouse (Hing, 2005: 56). It will be interesting to see which meaning of individualism will finally become the default meaning in CE and how long Mickey Mouse will hold a place in the Chinese Communist Party pantheon. The success of the recently opened Disneyland in Hong Kong suggests Lei Feng's days are truly numbered.

10.6.3 Grammar

In an analysis of a variety of data that included Chinese newspapers in English, fiction written in CE and spoken conversational data, Xu (2005: 315ff.) has identified the following grammatical features of CE, many of which parallel features apparent in other varieties of English. Each feature (in bold) is followed by an example:

Adjacent default tense (ADT)
Last year, I *write* a letter . . . I *write* two letters every week

Null-subject/object utterances (NS/O)
Sometimes _____ just play basketball, and sometimes _____ go to the Beijing library, and sometimes _____ just play some games on computer.

We can see movies, and other activities about English.
Yes, I like _____ very much.

Co-occurrence of connective pairs
Yes, *although* it's not as big as Beijing, *but* I like it, because I was born in it.
Because in the canteen of our school, it is crowded at the first of this semester, *so* we wouldn't like to go . . . go there to have our lunch or supper, *so* we choose some small res . . . restaurant to have our food.

Subject pronoun copying
Some of my college classmates they like to dress up very much, and they don't like to study very much.

Yes-No response
Researcher: You mean your hometown is not so crowded?
Informant: *Yeah*. Not so crowded.

Topic–comment sentence structure
You know, I think *this society* (topic), the people get more and more practical (comment).

Unmarked object subject verb (OSV) word order
So, um . . . I think the love is important, and *the money I don't care*.

Inversion in subordinate finite wh-clauses
I really don't know *what is International English*.

Nominalisation
a) **Head nominalised noun phrases**
   investment in the sectors of education, health and culture in rural areas

b) **Premodification nominalised noun phrases**
long-term land-use rights

c) **Postmodification nominalised noun phrases**
the top priority given to deepening reform in rural areas

d) **Paratactic compound nominalised noun phrases (NPs of equal weight)**
rural prosperity and the well-being of farmers

e) **Hypotactic compound nominalised noun phrases (one NP subordinate to the other)**
the guiding principle for the development of agriculture

10.6.4 Pragmatics and cultural conventions

Kirkpatrick (1996) has shown that a modifying–modified sequence is a preferred sequencing norm in Modern Standard Chinese and Xu shows that this is transferred across into CE as in the following example:

'Because many farmers lack adequate knowledge and experience to distinguish counterfeit goods they are generally more vulnerable.'

(Xu, 2005: 318)

This is not to say that the alternative sequence cannot be used, simply that it is marked in CE when it is so, as in the following example:

'In Shangdong province, Pingyuan county, Zhanghua town, most seed-raising farming families would never be bothered by the matter of selling seeds, *because the Seed Association of the town has taken up 90% of the corn seeds sales*.'

(Xu, 2005: 145)

This has implications for communication between speakers of CE and other varieties of English, as the marked form in British English becomes the unmarked form in CE. Conversely, the marked form in CE is the unmarked form in British English.

Further findings identified by Xu that are of relevance to cross-cultural communication include the frequency with which Chinese interlocutors use what Xu has termed 'ancestral hometown discourse'. It is clearly considered polite to talk about one's hometown when meeting someone for the first time. Xu (2005: 189) summarises the possible things one can say about one's hometown and ask about someone else's. Topics in square brackets were less commonly discussed:

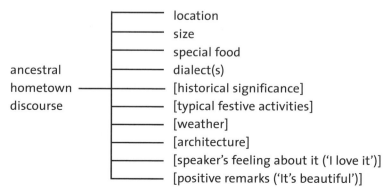

The writings of the Chinese writer Ha Jin provide an excellent source for identifying both the linguistic features of CE and how key Chinese cultural values are reflected in CE. Although Ha Jin currently lives in the United States, he writes about life in China from the point of view of a Chinese person and uses a distinctive type of English in which to do this. He can thus be considered a Chinese writer who writes in a Chinese English vernacular rather than as a new breed of American writer, in much the same way that the Pakistani novelist Sidhwa described herself as a South Asian writer writing in a Pakistani English vernacular and distinguished herself from the new breed of British writers of South Asian origin (see Chapter 7 and Sidhwa 1996: 239). As Zhang has argued, the Chineseness of Ha Jin's fiction is achieved through 'the creative adoption of the English language, and the innovative recreation of the sensations of his native experiences' (2002: 306). The example below shows how Ha Jin uses English and how the key Chinese cultural value of *guānxi* (influence gained from interpersonal relationships) is realised through his writing:

> 'Every morning from then on, Jiang Bing got up early and went to the riverside to buy fish. Sometimes he bought a silver carp, sometimes a pike, sometimes a catfish; once he got a two pound crucian, which he smoked. Each day he cooked the fish in a different way, and his dishes pleased the director greatly. Soon Jiang Bing ran out of money. When he told Nimei he had spent all their wages, she suggested he withdraw two hundred yuan from their savings account. He did, and day after day he continued to make the fancy dishes . . .
>
> A few times Director Liao wanted to pay Nimei for the fish, but she refused to accept any money from him, saying, "It's my job to take care of my patients."
>
> Gradually the director and Jiang Bing got to know each other. Every day after Liao finished dinner, Jiang would stay an hour or two, chatting with the leader, who unfailingly turned talkative after a good meal.'

The story continues:

> 'Director Liao was going to leave the hospital in two days. He was grateful to the couple and even said they had treated him better than his family.
> On Tuesday afternoon he had the head nurse called in. He said, "Nimei, I can't thank you enough!"
> "It's my job. Please don't mention it."
> "I've told the hospital's leaders that they should elect you a model nurse this year. Is there anything I can do for you?"
> "No, I don't need anything,' she said. 'Jiang Bing and I are very happy that you've recovered so soon."
> "Ah yes, how about Young Jiang? Can I do something for him?"
> She pretended to think for a minute. "Well, maybe. He's worked in the same office for almost ten years. He may want a change. But don't tell him I said this or he'll be mad at me."
> "I won't say a word. Do you think he wants to leave the hospital?"
> "No, he likes it here. Just moving him to another office would be enough."

"Is there a position open?"

"Yes, there are two—the Personnel and the Security sections haven't had directors for months."

"Good. I'm going to write a note to the hospital leaders. They'll take my suggestion seriously. Tell Young Jiang I'll miss his fish."

They both laughed.'

Xu (2005: 177ff.) explains how this excerpt shows how Nimei, in collaboration with her husband Jiang Bing, manipulates the *guānxi* network with Director Liao:

> Nimei is the head nurse, while Director Liao is her patient. This bureaucratically defined 'nurse–patient' relationship is not of any apparent *guānxi* or significance. However, Director Liao is not just a patient, he is also a director 'whose department decided their [the hospital leaders'] promotions and demotions'. To Nimei, there is some sort of hidden pragmatic *guānxi* to explore. . .Director Liao is 'tired of the liquid stuff'—'rice porridge and egg-drop soup' served by the hospital canteen, so he asks the head nurse Nimei for 'something else for a change', preferably 'fish', thus rendering Nimei an opportunity to set up *guānxi* with Director Liao. Since what is in her mind is her husband's promotion, she naturally wants her husband Jiang Bing to get involved in the *guānxi*. So she asks him to cook fish for Director Liao.
>
> In this way, Jiang Bing is able to become involved in the *guānxi* with Director Liao. And although developing and nurturing the *guānxi* is expensive and demanding on the part of Nimei and Jiang Bing, it is well worth the 'investment'.
>
> (Xu, 2005: 177)

10.7 Conclusion

By referring back to Butler's five criteria for a new variety of English, it can be argued that HKE meets criteria 1, 2 and 3, with criterion 4 debatable. Chinese English meets criteria 2, 3 and 4, but the first criterion may not be applicable to Chinese English, given the different dialect mother tongues of its speakers. That Chinese English already meets these criteria is quite remarkable given the relatively short time in which the Chinese have embraced the learning of English on a wide scale. At the same time, recent studies into Chinese attitudes to CE (see Kirkpatrick and Xu Xi, 2002; Hu, 2005; Lin, 2005; Xu, 2005) have also shown that Chinese speakers of English are shifting towards an acceptance of CE as a variety. These points, together with the sheer numbers of speakers of CE, strongly suggest that Chinese English is soon likely to become the most commonly spoken variety of English in Asia.

But at what price? First, English is now being taught in Chinese primary schools throughout the country and it is not clear how effective that teaching can be, especially as there is a chronic shortage of trained teachers. Second, the demand for English has seen parents, especially those in urban areas, having to sacrifice and make savings in order to be able to afford to send their children to increasingly expensive private English classes. There is, I believe, a need for research into the sacrifices that 'normal' Chinese families face in order to ensure their child receives adequate tuition in English. Research is needed into the impact of changing levels of English-language proficiency on local, regional and global labour markets, social mobility and status, political activism, traditional culture and family life. Research is also needed into the consequences both of the growing use of English and of the huge industry which has grown up to teach people English. While China would be an excellent site for such research, comparable research is needed throughout the world.

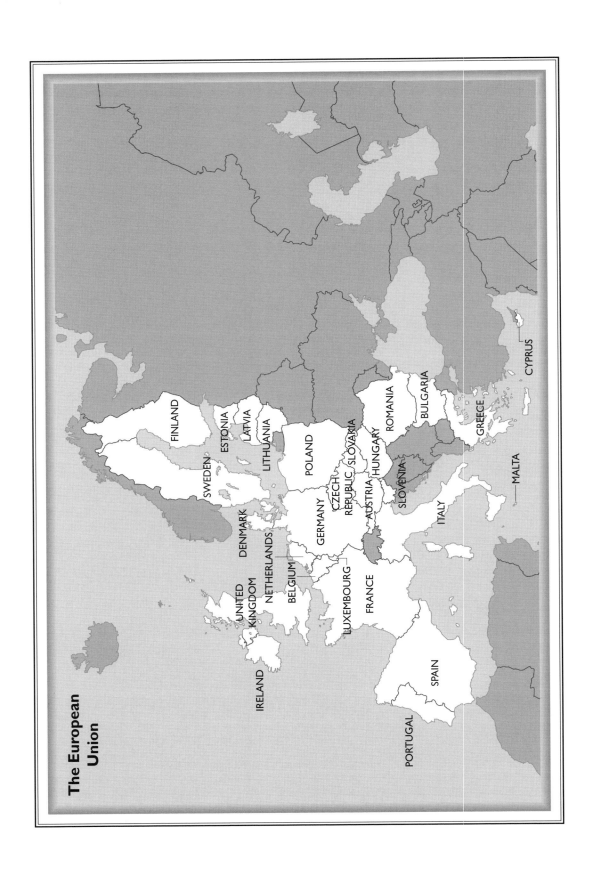

The European Union

11 English as a *lingua franca*

English is used throughout the word as a *lingua franca*. That is to say, it is used as a medium of communication by people who do not speak the same first language. Despite this extremely widespread and common function of English, analysis and descriptions of *lingua franca* Englishes are rare, although there is increasing interest in English as a *lingua franca* (ELF). In this chapter I shall consider the role of ELF in a specific setting, the Association of South-East Asian Nations (ASEAN), and describe the linguistic features and communicative strategies of English when used as a *lingua franca* by speakers from countries in ASEAN. This description will include the extent to which people who use ELF in ASEAN are mutually intelligible. The findings for ASEAN ELF will form a basis for a comparison with the features and role of ELF in other settings, in particular the European Union.

11.1 ASEAN and English

The Association of South-East Asian Nations (ASEAN) was established in Bangkok in 1967. It currently has ten member states: Brunei, Cambodia, Indonesia, Laos, Malaysia, Myanmar, the Philippines, Singapore, Thailand and Vietnam (for a map of this region see p118). A useful recent overview of English language teaching trends in each of these countries is provided by Ho and Wong (2003).

The role of English in ASEAN is as a *de facto lingua franca* (Krasnick, 1995). Although this obviously privileges those member states who can be considered outer circle countries, largely due to their earlier status as colonies of Britain (Brunei, Malaysia and Singapore) or the United States (the Philippines), the decision to adopt English as a *lingua franca* was considered so natural that the delegates in Bangkok did not even debate it (Okudaira, 1999). Since then, two attempts have been made to make other languages official languages of ASEAN: on one occasion, Indonesia suggested that Bahasa Indonesia be adopted; on the other, Vietnam suggested 'their' 'colonial' language, French, should be adopted. Neither suggestion was taken up.

ASEAN provides English language using contexts that are of great potential interest. First, the four outer circle countries have developed local Englishes, namely Brunei English, Malaysian English, Philippine English and Singaporean English. These were described in Chapter 9. Five of the remaining six nations, Cambodia, Indonesia, Laos, Thailand and Vietnam, can be classified as being in the 'expanding circle'. This leaves

Myanmar, which would have been classified as an outer circle country in the years before General U Ne Win's coup in 1962. Since then, it has remained a military dictatorship and has been a virtually closed country. English was removed from the curriculum until a change in policy took place that led to a moderate revival of English in the mid-1980s. At that time a total of five British-government-financed 'Key English Language Teachers' (KELTs) were assigned to tertiary institutions in Yangon and Mandalay, of which I was one. In any event, the universities have been closed for a great deal of the time since the riots of 1988, in which some 8,000 people died, and this has slowed down the revival of interest in English.

The use of English as an inter-regional *lingua franca* raises the question of mutual intelligibility. If ASEAN is characterised by different varieties of English that include both a number of new varieties and a range of 'expanding circle' Englishes, to what extent do people who use it as a *lingua franca* within ASEAN understand each other? It also raises the question of whether an ASEAN variety of English is developing. In other words, do the Englishes of ASEAN speakers share any distinctive linguistic features and, if so, what are they? Or, will ELF be characterised by variation, given the different varieties of English currently spoken in specific ASEAN countries together with the different linguistic backgrounds of the speakers?

11.2   ASEAN ELF

The findings that form the basis of the following discussion come from recordings of ASEAN nationals who were attending a two-week ELT teacher training course at the Regional Language Centre in Singapore (RELC) in 2004 and 2005. Each group was recorded for about 20 minutes. They were asked to begin their conversation by discussing their impressions of Singapore and then to consider the ELT situation in their home countries. In fact, the groups covered more topics than this and no group found themselves silently wondering what to say or who should speak next.

Four of the five groups comprised three speakers and one had four. The groups were made up as follows:

Gp 1:   an ethnically Chinese Bruneian female (Brunei), a Philippina female (P1), a Thai male (T) and a Vietnamese female (V)

Gp 2:   a Singaporean female (with Punjabi as an L1) (SP), a female from Myanmar (M1), and a Laotian female (L1)

Gp 3:   a Cambodian male (C1), an Indonesian male (I1) and a Singaporean female (with Malay as an L1) (SM)

Gp 4:   an Indonesian female (I2), a female from Myanmar (M2) and a Cambodian female (C2)

Gp 5:   an ethnically Chinese Malaysian male (MC), a Laotian male (L2) and a Philippina female (P2)

There were two people each from Cambodia, Indonesia, Laos, Myanmar, the Philippines and Singapore and one person each from Brunei, Malaysia, Thailand and Vietnam. The speakers thus comprised people from both outer and expanding circle countries.

Detailed results of this research have been reported elsewhere (see Kirkpatrick, 2006b; Deterding and Kirkpatrick, 2006), so here I shall simply report the overall findings.

11.3   Linguistic features of ASEAN ELF

11.3.1   ASEAN ELF syntactic (tense and inflection) uses

The present simple was by far the most commonly used tense with ASEAN speakers and accounted for 61 per cent of all the tenses used. The past simple was the next most common, accounting for 18 per cent of the total, with modals accounting for 12 per cent. Some verb forms, including, for example, the present perfect passive, the past continuous and the past perfect, were used extremely rarely. This raises the question whether students in certain contexts should spend much classroom time on these 'rare' tenses.

The majority of participants use a minimal number of non-standard forms (NSF). The only participants whose NSFs in tense use constitutes more than 6 per cent of their output are the Indonesian and both Cambodians and Laotians. If these uses are non-systematic, it would suggest that these five be classified as learners of English rather than highly expert users. By considering the actual language they use, however, it might be possible to identify uses that are qualitatively different from the NSFs made by the other participants. If this proves to be the case, it could be argued that the language used represents 'learner errors', while the NSFs made by the others are actually systematic variations that occur in their varieties of English. After all, if standard British English were to be taken as the overall norm, then, as illustrated in Chapters 4 and 5, American and Australian speakers produce a wide range of non-standard forms. The specific uses uttered by the Indonesian (I2) and the Cambodian (C2) are listed below. A discussion of the nature of the specific language uttered by these two speakers follows. I shall suggest that the NSFs used by the Indonesian speaker **are** systematic, but that those used by the Cambodian **are not**, and that the Cambodian's uses may therefore provide a criterion for distinguishing between a fluent speaker and a learner. This is a key question for all varieties of English and recalls Crystal's conundrum about the problems involved in describing Old English, quoted in Chapter 4, 'Which bits of the variation are random error and which reflect some aspect of the sociolinguistic situation of the time?' (2004: 50).

The Indonesian speaker used NSFs when forming 7 present simple, 14 past simple and 1 present perfect form. The Cambodian speaker used NSFs when forming 7 present simple, 2 past simple and 1 modal form. A summary of the uses of both speakers is provided below. This is followed by an excerpt in which both participate, in order to illustrate the points being made:

The Indonesian's (I2) NSFs are:

Present simple tense

7 NSFs out of a total of 119 uses:

'Singapore and Indonesia *is* very close' (concord)
'if the class trip *finish* before eleven' (no '-s' marking)
'I'm looking for on Sunday that's why I *try* to' (adjacent default tense)
'most of stuffs in Singapore have'(?)
'what company belongs to' (incorrect collocation – lexical?)
'what Silk Air belongs to' (incorrect collocation – lexical?)
'because we *get* new knowledge' (are getting)

Past simple tense

14 NSFs out of 43 uses. They are:

'Mrs X already *give* to us'
'yesterday I *check*'
'I already *spend*'
'I left my house that's because I *have* to travel'
'and then I *spend* one night and my niece drove me to'
'I waited for the official who *pick* me up'
'and then did nothing just *sit* and I *check*. . .that's why I just *sit* and *take a rest*'
'you taste you taste grammar already'
'the temperature dropped dramatically so we have to and we have to'

Present perfect

1 NSF out of 8 uses. It is:

'you have never *see* before'

It should be noted that the Indonesian (I2) also uses the present continuous 5 times, the present passive 3 times and the past perfect once without using NSFs.

The great majority of the NSFs identified in I2's speech can be explained by non-marking of the verb form for tense in situations where the time has already been established by the context. The verbal inflections simply aren't necessary for making meaning in these contexts. Phonological causes for the non-marking of tenses are also present. For example, the non-marking of 'picked' in 'pick me up' is likely to be caused by the phonological environment. Deterding has shown that native speakers routinely drop final /t/ and /d/ in their speech in this way in certain contexts (Deterding, 2006).

Importantly, I2 shows expertise in the use of the tense system, while at the same time breaking rules she clearly knows. 'Sit', 'check', 'sit' and 'take a rest' are all unmarked for past tense, but this cannot possibly be explained by saying the speaker does not know the rule. In the excerpt provided later, for example, she uses the past tense 17 times, but chooses not to mark it only on 4, possibly 5 occasions:

The Cambodian's (C2) NSFs are:

Present simple tense
7 NSFs in 42 uses. They are:

'I *get* used to it' (I am getting / I have got)
'if we *has* no time then we just go there' (concord)
'comparing to other countries —— still expensive' (no subject, no copula)
'in the time maybe they brought there *is* not the other food' (adjacent tense)
'Silk Air *is belong* to' (use of copula 'is' and no '-s' inflection)
'I will go next years I *am glad* to be there' (adjacent tense)

Simple past tense
2 NSFs out of 18 uses. They are:

'how long *have you waits* for them?' ('-s' inflection for past)
'as the one *that's pick* me up said' ('-s' inflection on pronoun, no inflection on verb)

Modals
1 NSF out of 14 uses. It is:

'so we should *makes* any plan' ('-s' inflection on verb stem)

Other NSFs
This speaker also uses what I have called 'epenthetic' '-s' inflections. For example:

'there are a lot of*s* kinds of fruits'
'one day*s* you will have one day'
'an hour*s*'
'I also arrived earlier*s* than'
'I will go next year*s*'

There is evidence here of language use of a qualitatively different kind from I2's language. This may signal a learner of English. In particular, rather than *simplifying* the inflectional system by the routine non-marking of tense forms in contexts where it is not required for meaning, C2 *complicates* it by *adding* inflections in an apparently idiosyncratic or random way. For example, her utterances 'how long have you wait**s** for them?', 'the one that'**s** pick me up', and 'so we should make**s** any plan' all *add* inflections in places where they are not required. These 'complicating' additions may be signals of learner English.

C2's English also suggests other 'learner' features where she *adds* features that are not required. For example the added 'epenthetic' /s/ sounds under 'Other NSFs' above are not used by any of the other speakers in these conversations.

The excerpt below comes from the conversation in which an Indonesian (I2), a Cambodian (C2) and a Malaysian (M) were involved. Relevant parts are in bold. The complicating additional inflections, which I am suggesting as possible markers of learner

English, are also underlined. The extract, along with others, can be heard on the accompanying CD.

I2: **I waited]** for the official **who picked** (/pik/) me up ok er and **then I tried** to look for the official but because er er **the plane you know landed** so early so (ehm uh oh) the **official hadn't come yet** (C2: ehm) yeah

M: what a pity (laugh)

I2: er er I I I **had to stay** in the airport and **then did nothing** (C2: ehm) **just sit and I check the placard** of (ehm) RELC (M: ehm) ok and er and **I couldn't see that's why I just sit and take a rest** . . . what about you what time

C2: how long **have you waits** for them

I2: just an hour

C2: an **hours** (I: an hour) oh oh

I2: ok **I enjoyed** the arcades you [know

M: and] then **how did you get here**

I2: er no the official

M: **came late**

I2: er **that I met** ok the er **came late** (laugh) yeah because **the flight was earlier** than the (eh) schedule (oh) so ok **I just er waited** for him an hour in the airport yeah er finally I **met him** (ehm) at one o' clock (laughter) **that's it**

M: luckily **you arrived** [safely

C2: I] **also arrived** *earliers* than the exact time (I2: oh ok) as the **one that's pick** me up (ehm) **said but luckily I met him** (laugh)

11.3.2 ASEAN ELF phonological features

The following features of pronunciation appear to be part of an emerging ASEAN ELF. For a fuller discussion see Deterding and Kirkpatrick (2006). It should be emphasised, however, that these features do not always occur.

The dental fricatives /θ/ and /ð/ have been identified by Jenkins (2000: 137) as prime candidates for exclusion from her Lingua Franca Core, as alternative pronunciations of these sounds seldom cause confusion. Indeed they are commonly pronounced /t/ and /d/ by some native speakers and this is the case with the speakers from the Philippines, Myanmar, Singapore, Laos, Cambodia and Vietnam.

The consonant sounds /f/ and /p/ tend not to be distinguished in Malay and Tagalog (Deterding and Poedjosoedarmo, 1998: 174, 224) and this also occurs occasionally with speakers from Vietnam (e.g. 'fractical' for 'practical'), Laos (e.g. 'grouf' for 'group'), and the Philippines (e.g. 'fersonal' for 'personal').

The simplification of final consonant clusters is common, for example 'firs' (T), 'Eas' (SP), 'wol'(world) (C1) and 'expec' (I1).

The data also provides many instances of a tendency towards a lack of reduced vowels, for example 'method' /meθɒd/, (T), 'officially' /ɒf. . ./ (I1), 'compare' /kɒmp. . ./ (Brunei) and 'graduates' /græÄjuːeɪts/ (P1).

There was also a tendency not to reduce prominence where this (de-accenting) might be expected. In these examples, the italicised words are given equal stress and prominence by the speakers:

> 'we have the government *schools* and the private *schools*' (Brunei)
> 'I love *teaching* and I enjoy *teaching*' (M1)
> 'It was meant for only a h- a *holiday* a three day *holiday*' (T)
> 'Erm *English* is very new and very few people speak *English*' (C1)

Examples of syllable-timing, where each syllable in the utterances takes more or less the same time to produce, include:

> 'all the theories are different when you go to classroom teaching actually' (P1)
> 'I still speak dialect to my father right now but I speak Mandarin to my mother' (Brunei)
> 'I guess get shipped to other countries' (SM)
> 'Er in Cambodia we do not classify them as er . . . ability in English' (C1)
> 'I bought in the Muslim restaurant' (I1)

The use of these features did not disrupt communication in the conversations. Indeed, there were relatively few breakdowns in communication throughout the data. Miscommunication was caused, however, by misinterpreting pronunciation. In the following example M2 hears 'rooms' as 'food':

I2: what about your rooms
M2: er
I2: you feel OK any [problems
M2: I] find the taste er quite ok (ehm) but er like yours is I think er . . . er . . . the rice a little bit sticky (C2: ehm) in our country we don't er eat er rice as sticky as that rice here er ehm and then ehm how shall I say er . . . and then vegetables er maybe er the same vegetables we eat (C2: ehm) in our country (I2: ehm) but er the price for them is also expensive (laughter) I think because I prefer eating vegetables (I2: ok) I prefer vegetables er than (I2: OK) to meat er
I2: ok what I'm asking is about room . . .

One occasion when communication broke down completely was when fellow participants couldn't make out what L2 was saying:

L2: you know at the time that ehm tsunami occurs they there were some problem in my country (P2: ehm)
MC: what problem
L2: yeah we've some problem we have big holes /horns/ in in some areas
MC: horns? Sorry
L2: horn you hornt
P2: hornt
L2: yeah big horn
MC: (laugh) sorry

P2:   what's a horn?

L2:   H-O-L-E something like this

MC: holes oh **you mean** hole in the ground.

In the following example, initial misunderstanding was not caused by pronunciation, but by the lexical choice of 'sit' on the part of I1. This example also shows a participant providing the correct lexical item. SM's primary motive is to engender communication rather than to correct the speaker. The Indonesian speaker accepts the correct word immediately:

I1:   so how long do do they have to **sit** in the junior high school and senior high school?

C1:   ehm I've been teaching there for two years after my graduation er from (..) er

I1:   no I mean er er how many years do students have to **sit {SM: stay} to stay** in the junior high school {C1: ehm} and the senior high school?

C1:   er in in in Cambodia er /s/ junior high school starts from grade seven

In summary, the varieties of English spoken by the participants did not cause many breakdowns in communication. Indeed the conversations are characterised by mutual understanding. The group below, however, did experience breakdown in communication, but the major cause of this was the relative lack of proficiency of one of the participants (L1). I now turn to the communicative strategies which the participants in this interaction adopted to overcome this.

11.3.3 ASEAN ELF communicative strategies

The excerpt below illustrates the most serious breakdown in understanding in the entire data. The SP and M1 participants are prepared to try a range of repair strategies, in particular the patient rephrasing of the original question. No underlying tone of irritation or impatience is evident, despite SP rephrasing the question in five different ways and M1 suggesting a possible answer on behalf of L1.

SP: eh huh ehm do the do the children you know in er in your country those who come from a very poor families {L1: yes} are they given financial assistance?

L1:   ehm

SP: are they in in terms of money?

L1:   ehm

SP: I mean does the government support them?

SP: ok is there is there like you know those children who are very poor and their parents cannot afford to send them to school? {M1: eh hm} does the government actually given them assistance?

M1:   yeah the government will ass/ɪt/ I think so {SP: eh hm} your government will as /sɪt/
        (two second silence)

SP: example you know like buying uniform for them or textbooks and paying for their school fees

L1:   I th I think they don't do like that yes {SP: oh is it?} only the family or parents

SP: can afford

L1:   yes afford them er for example {ehm} in the (..) er countryside some studen cannot learn because er it's hardly for them to er go to school /n/ {SP: eh hm}

While this is an extreme example, it exemplifies the patience of the participants in rephrasing and applying a range of repair strategies. This underlines the cooperative nature of the interaction and this cooperation is seen across the data. Participants in these ELF interactions strive to understand each other and help out where they can. These findings mirror those for ELF in Europe (see Firth, 1996), which will be considered later.

11.4 ASEAN ELF conclusion

With regard to the use of tense and inflection, this limited data set shows that the present simple tense is by far the most common tense constituting 61 per cent of all tense uses. The past simple accounts for 18 per cent of all uses and modals 12 per cent. No other tense accounts for more than 3 per cent of usage and many for far less even than that. Generally speaking, there is relatively little syntactic variation and far less than was identified in Chapter 4 among native speaker varieties. Only 5 per cent of the present simple and 1 per cent of the past simple uses, for example, might be marked as incorrect by someone using a native speaker model as the standard. Most of these uses actually represent the way these speakers use tense in spoken interaction. Marking past is not necessary when the past is made clear by the context, for example. Similarly, concord (and plurals) may remain unmarked. Some speakers make different types of mistakes, however, and these may signal that they are learners. In particular the *addition* of inflections in contexts where they are not needed is a potential marker of learner English. The simplification of syntax by not adding inflections where the time or meaning has already been established by the context are features of new varieties of English and mirror the way inflections have become simpler within traditional English itself.

There is remarkably little syntactic variation and a reason for this is considered later in the chapter. Despite the relative lack of variation, it would be impossible to describe ASEAN *lingua franca* English as a single systematic system that could be codified and then used as a model for the ASEAN English language classroom. Rather than being a systematic code, ASEAN *lingua franca* English comprises a number of separate systems. There are, nevertheless, very few instances where speakers fail to understand each other. These examples of ASEAN *lingua franca* English are characterised by mutual understanding, cooperation and tolerance of variation. It is this mutual intelligibility and the ways in which the participants strive for it that have important classroom implications and I discuss these in detail in Part C of the book. I now turn to a brief discussion of the role and description of ELF in Europe.

11.5 The European Union (EU) and English

The European Economic Community, as it was then known, was established by the Treaty of Rome on 25 March 1957. At the time, only six European countries were members:

Belgium, France, Germany, Italy, Luxembourg and the Netherlands (for a map of this region see p154). Over the years there have been changes of name and more and more countries have joined so that today it is known as the European Union and comprises 27 countries[1], with two more currently applying to join.

The main objective of the original EEC was to rebuild the European economy after the devastation of World War Two (Ammon, 1996). Germany's defeat in the war was also reflected in the decrease in the number of countries which studied German. Several northern European countries downgraded German and upgraded English as a school subject (Ammon, 1996: 250). Before the war, German had been the major *lingua franca* in Eastern Europe. When this became the 'Eastern Bloc', controlled by the then Soviet Union after the war, German was replaced there by Russian. In turn, the collapse of the Soviet Union in 1990 saw a revival of interest in German, but also an upsurge of interest in English. For example, in the Czech Republic English is now seen as the 'language of higher education, science and world-wide communication' (Ammon, 1996: 253).

English is the most widely used language of wider communication in Europe. It is taught more than all the other European languages put together (Görlach, 2002). It is the major foreign language for business in all EU countries, preferred for negotiations and dominant in academic publishing almost to the exclusion of all other languages (Ammon, 1996: 253), and is 'by far the most important language of scientific and scholarly conferences' (Ammon, 1996: 260). The domination of English in academic publications is startling. For example, in 1950 all contributions to the 'oldest specialist journal in the field of behavioural science', *Zeitschrift für Tierpsychologie*, were in German. By 1984, 95 per cent were written in English (Viereck, 1996: 20). The European Science Foundation's working language is English and its journal *Communication* is exclusively in English (Ammon, 1996). The dramatic shift to English in the academic domain means that European languages are not developing appropriate scientific terms (Hoffmann, 2000: 10). And the move from German into English has raised concerns that a once powerful European *lingua franca* is being reduced to a sub-variety, used only in restricted local domains (Görlach, 2002: 16).

It is not just in the domains of business, education and science, however, that English is increasing its respective roles. Dollerup has argued that the 'present hegemony of English in Europe is primarily due to the entertainment industry, and only secondarily to war, technological lead, science and political domination' (1996: 26). For example, some 80 per cent of the films shown in Western Europe are imported from either Britain or the USA.

English is also, along with French, one of the working languages of the EU. While each country's national language is an official language of the EU and there are thus 23

---

[1]   These are: Austria, Belgium, Bulgaria, Cyprus, the Czech Republic, Denmark, Estonia, Finland, France, Germany, Greece, Hungary, Italy, Ireland, Latvia, Lithuania, Luxembourg, Malta, the Netherlands, Poland, Portugal, Romania, Slovakia, Slovenia, Spain, Sweden and the United Kingdom. The two applicant countries are Croatia and Turkey. For a general introduction to the EU, see the website www.europa.eu.int.

languages[2], in effect English plays the major role, for, apart from being one of the working languages, it is also the most commonly used 'link' language for interpreters and translators in the EU. This is not hard to explain, as there are likely to be many more people who are bilingual in, for example, Greek and English than in Greek and Danish. Thus the majority of interpreters will use the English interpreter's English version of a Greek delegate's speech as the basis from which to interpret the speech into Danish (or any other language). For informative accounts of the complexity of the translation process in the EU, see Dollerup (1996) and Tosi (2003).

Yet, while English is now the most important *lingua franca* of Europe, the position of English within the countries of Europe differs considerably (Hoffmann, 2000). In Scandinavia, Belgium and the Netherlands, English has an extremely high profile and is almost like a second language. In contrast, in the countries of southern Europe – Spain, Portugal and Italy, for example – it has less of a presence, although that presence is growing. English is growing in importance even in Turkey, where it is considered important both for work and education (Hoffmann, 2000: 8). The overall picture appears to be of a bilingualism or multilingualism with English as one of the languages. The majority of Europeans, excluding native speakers, learn English in schools, while the reduction in the numbers of students learning other European languages is worrying. So 89 per cent of students study English with French next at 32 per cent and then German with 18 per cent. There is no increase in the number of European students learning Italian and Spanish and 'Danish, Dutch, Modern Greek and Portuguese are badly neglected' (van Essen, 1997: 97). At the same time, Spanish and Italian students who traditionally have learned French are taking up English at the expense of French in increasing numbers (van Essen, 1997). In summary, English is spreading because of its value in so many different domains. Increasingly, young Europeans are able to communicate with each other in English. 'Students need little encouragement to study English as its utility is so clearly evident' (Labrie and Quell, 1997: 22).

Does this mean that a variety or varieties of 'Euro-English' will develop, or will English be a *lingua franca* marked by variation of the type described above for ASEAN ELF?

11.6 **Euro-English and/or ELF**

Most scholars agree that the increased use of English in Europe will lead to a variety or varieties of Euro-English, although their emphases and predictions differ. Modiano believes that a Euro-English will be 'legitimised, codified, standardised' (Jenkins, Modiano

---

[2] The 23 official languages are: Bulgarian, Czech, Danish, Dutch, English, Estonian, Finnish, French, German, Greek, Hungarian, Italian, Irish, Latvian, Lithuanian, Maltese, Polish, Portuguese, Romanian, Slovak, Slovene, Spanish and Swedish. Irish is to become an official language in the near future. The discrepancy between the number of official languages and countries is explained by French and German being national languages of more than one country. Britain's *Independent* newspaper reported on 10 November 2005 that three non-official EU languages – Catalan, Basque and Galician – could be used at official EU meetings and in official EU correspondence.

and Seidlhofer, 2001: 13). Seidlhofer agrees, saying it should be possible to describe European ELF 'and eventually also to provide a codification which would allow it to be captured in dictionaries and grammars and to be taught' (Jenkins, Modiano and Seidlhofer, 2001: 14). Jenkins, however, is more cautious, preferring to argue for a core of Euro-English features, but allowing the development of different varieties of Euro-English, each with its distinctive features. For example, French English 'will probably have an unrounded vowel sound in the word "hot" so that it sounds more like "hut"' (Jenkins, Modiano and Seidlhofer, 2001: 18). One would certainly expect that the pronunciation of Euro-English would be influenced by the first language of their speakers, in much the same way that Indian English or Chinese English is so influenced. But will a range of nativised Englishes develop in Europe? Dollerup is certain that Euro-English will develop, but unsure whether it will be represented by one or several varieties (1996: 35). Cenoz and Jessner (2000b) feel a non-native variety of Euro-English is emerging. Goethals, on the other hand, seems certain that different varieties will develop. 'Flemish English is as recognisably different from the Dutch English in the Netherlands as from the German or French Englishes' (1997b: 110). Berns takes a similar view. In predicting that English will become the 'primary language' of the European Union, British English will be a mere 'sub-variety' along with French, Dutch or Danish Englishes (1995: 9–10).

11.7 Research into ELF

The communicative strategies of speakers of ELF are aimed at ensuring cooperation and preserving face. For example, Firth (1996) analysed a corpus of telephone calls from two Danish international trading companies that exclusively involved non-native speakers. The level of English competency among the interactants varied and participants occasionally openly acknowledged their lack of English competence. In his analysis, Firth noted that 'participants demonstrate a remarkable ability to *systematically* and *contingently* – and on the basis of quintessentially *local* considerations – attend and disattend to a range of anomalies and infelicities in their unfolding interaction' (1996: 243). A principle associated with this is what he calls the 'let it pass' (1996: 243) concept by which participants, if they are unsure of what the other speaker means, will, instead of seeking immediate clarification, let it pass in the expectation that the meaning will become clear as the conversation unfolds. This may even require using the unknown phrase or word in one's own speech. Firth terms this the 'make it normal' concept (1996: 245). As an example he shows that, although the listener does not understand the term 'blowing' in the context in which it is used, he nevertheless incorporates it into his turn:

A: their bricks get u:::h(.) *blow*ing uh [like the balloons],
B: [yah that's it] yeah the bricks g- get blowing and uh they had. . .

(1996: 247)

Similarly, any 'mistakes' are allowed to pass as long as the meaning is understandable from the context. However, if the information is necessary for the interaction to be completed successfully, then 'perceived problems must be dealt with immediately, rather than being allowed to pass' (1996: 250). In general, Firth noted people's extraordinary ability to make sense of what was being said. Firth concludes that further research is needed to investigate the 'universality of such notions as the (dis)preferred construction of turns, and the function of "accounts", laughter, silence and hesitation phenomena, reformulations and repair' (1996: 255). Meierkord (2000) also found that participants in ELF interactions worked to preserve the face of all participants and to ensure each other of a benevolent attitude. The strategies reported by Firth and Meierkord are also found in the ASEAN ELF interactions described earlier.

Perhaps the best-known grammatical study into ELF is Jenkins' work into the phonology of international English (2000). This is of particular pedagogic value, as she has identified a '*lingua franca* core' which shows, among other things, which sounds and aspects of pronunciation hinder mutual intelligibility and which do not. I consider this further in Part C. James (2000) is investigating the use of ELF in the Alpine-Adriatic region of Europe. The syntactic features which he has identified appear remarkably similar to the features that have been described above and in earlier chapters on specific varieties of English. These syntactic features display a tendency towards simplification including the conflation of certain tenses and the absence of certain morphological markings. These features appear to be non-essential for mutual intelligibility.

Seidlhofer is collecting the Vienna–Oxford International Corpus of English as a Lingua Franca (VOICE). She has listed (2004: 220) the following typical 'errors' of ELF that do not appear to hinder communication. Again, all these have appeared earlier and in descriptions of nativised varieties of English:

(i)   dropping third person present tense '-s'
(ii)   confusing the relative pronouns 'who' and 'which'
(iii) non-L1 use of the definite and indefinite pronouns
(iv)   not using correct tag questions
(v)   inserting redundant prepositions
(vi)   overuse of certain verbs of 'high semantic generality' ('do', 'have', 'make' etc.)
(vii) replacing infinitive constructions with *that*-clauses
(viii) overdoing explicitness (as in 'black colour')

The major cause of misunderstanding is 'unilateral idiomicity', where idiomatic speech of one speaker may not be understood by others (2004: 220).

In an investigation into the use of English as an international *lingua franca*, Meierkord (2004) obtained data comprising 22 hours of informal spoken data, primarily of students from both outer and expanding circle countries who were studying at British universities. She analysed the data for syntactic variation and classified the syntax of the speakers as 'regular' (i.e., following native speaker norms), 'marked' (i.e. following nativised norms) or 'doubtful' (deviating from both native and nativised norms) (2004: 118). She found that 94 per cent of the utterances of the outer circle speakers were regular and was surprised by this, as 'it contradicts the assumption that speakers would carry the characteristics of their nativised varieties into the English lingua franca interactions' (2004: 119). She also found that 95 per cent of the expanding circle speakers' utterances were regular, but was not surprised by this, as they had been taught either British or American English. These findings did not take into account the utterances of less competent speakers, 22 per cent of which 'diverged grammatically from British English or American English' (and presumably nativised norms also) (2004: 119). She also found that speakers adopted processes of simplification and regularisation. This is not the syntactic simplification referred to in my study of ASEAN ELF above, but here refers instead to the tendency of speakers to split up their sentences into small simple units and to avoid compound sentences and hypotaxis. Regularisation refers to the tendency of speakers to 'front' the topics under discussion, as in these two examples:

'Three years you have had to do'
'My unit, it's not that special you see'

(2004: 214)

Meierkord expressed surprise at the lack of variation displayed by her outer circle speakers in these international ELF interactions. But perhaps this is not surprising at all. English operates as a *lingua franca* at a number of different levels, including local, national, regional and international. Apparently paradoxically, the more localised the use of English as a *lingua franca*, the more variation it is likely to display. Conversely, the more international its use, the less variation it is likely to display. This can be explained by reference back to the 'identity–communication continuum'. When used in a local setting, ELF will display identity markers. Thus code-switching and the explicit used of nativised norms can be expected. When used for international communication, on the other hand, speakers will consciously avoid the use of local and nativised norms and expressions. Thus, in the ASEAN ELF data, the only use of code-mixing occurred in the conversation that included a Singaporean and Indonesian, when they referred to Singaporean English as *rojak* English. *Rojak* is an Indonesian-Malay word that usually refers to a kind of Indonesian mixed salad and the term was familiar to both of them, but not to the third member of the conversation, a Cambodian.

SM: in school in the class I will try? to speak good English in fact we are supposed to speak good English {I₁: ehm} so I will switch you know ehm {I₁: ehm} in the class I'm I am a teacher I see myself as a teacher we have to {C: yes} show good example {I₁ : eh hm} so ehm there's no way that I will speak Singlish to my kids {I₁ : eh hm} not in class yeah er not in class not in school {I₁ : eh hm eh hm} but ehm like what you said just now NAME when we go back to our friends {I₁ : (laugh) ok} and all that {I₁: laugh} all the English {I₁ : laugh} and Singlish are all {I₁ : laugh} mixed together {I₁ : all right} like *rojak*

I₁: oh like *rojak* right like that

SM: yes you know *rojak* right

I₁: yes it's fruits mi[xed

SM: all] mixed up together

I₁: all right all right {SM: yeah} ok oh all right

With this single exception, avoiding the use of terms that might not be familiar to other participants was a strategy adopted by all the participants in their use of English for wider regional communication. A conversation between Malays, Singaporeans and Bruneians, on the other hand, would be peppered with code-switching and nativised features, as all participants would have at least some familiarity with the local cultures and languages. Meierkord's (2004) finding that the syntax of her outer circle subjects displayed such little variation may be because they were using English for international communication with people who would not have been familiar with the cultures of Africa or India. Thus they would consciously excise nativised norms and cultural references from their speech.

11.8 **Conclusion**

I have suggested that the 'identity–communication continuum' can explain why ELF, when used for international communication, is likely to display relatively little variation. In contrast, the more localised its use, the more variation it is likely to display, in the form of nativised and local norms. I have also suggested a possible morphological criterion for distinguishing between features of learner English and new varieties of English, namely that learners may add inflections where they are not needed, while a tendency for all varieties of English is towards the simplification of the inflectional system.

In the case of ASEAN ELF, the results of early research suggest that speakers have little difficulty in communicating with one another, despite the inherent differences in the Englishes that each speaker brings to the interaction. However, a great deal more research into the linguistic features and roles of ASEAN ELF is needed. A second point of note is that there has been comparatively little ill-feeling over the adoption of English as the *de facto lingua franca* of ASEAN. It seems unlikely that this will change, especially if the prediction made in the earlier chapter about China's use of English for regional and international communication is fulfilled. This does not mean, however, that research into the roles of English and attitudes to it is not needed. Localised empirical research into these matters is vital, so that a picture of the ways English impacts on the lives of people, both positive and negative, can be documented. For example, case studies in specific ASEAN countries are required to test the current belief that the use of English as a *lingua franca* continues to be accepted so pragmatically.

In the case of English in Europe, there seems little doubt that it will continue to increase its position as the dominant *lingua franca*. Whether this will result in varieties of European Englishes, or in a single variety of Euro-English being used as a *lingua franca* can only be determined by further research. The extent to which it is 'stifling' (Görlach, 2002: 1) other European languages by steadily encroaching on more and more domains also needs to be researched, as do European attitudes towards English, especially the attitudes of the young.

In more general terms, research in ELF is needed to investigate if and how its speakers use ELF in what Halliday has called the 'mathetic' way (1978: 54 –6). In contrast to the pragmatic uses of language that demand responses and represent a way of participating in a situation, the mathetic uses of language do not demand a response, but represent a way of learning and arise out of the personal and heuristic functions of language. In other words, the ways speakers of a new variety use the language to make meaning and create their own versions of reality must be a key question for the researcher. This issue was discussed in Chapter 7, in the context of Indian and Sri Lankan scholars transmitting local and traditional knowledge.

What then is the likelihood or possibility of English providing a mathetic as well as a pragmatic function when it is used as a *lingua franca*? It may be argued that its very role as a *lingua franca* means that English can only serve the pragmatic functions when so used. It may also be argued that this is true of all languages that serve as a *lingua franca*. However, *lingua francas* that are used for communication between peoples of related languages and cultures – such as Bahasa Indonesia in Indonesia and Modern Standard Chinese in China, for example – can surely provide the mathetic functions perfectly adequately, as their speakers share, in some fundamental sense, a view of the world. And when English is used as a *lingua franca* among people who share the same cultural values and where their variety of English has become their primary language, as is the case with Australian Aboriginal English, for example, then there is no doubt that the variety can perform mathetic functions. But if it is argued that new varieties of English must develop mathetic functions as well as pragmatic ones in order to become accepted and established as new varieties, then speakers who come to *lingua franca* communication using their own varieties of English will be using varieties of English that see the world in different ways. So can ASEAN ELF provide both pragmatic and mathetic functions? With regard to the use of English as a *lingua franca* in Europe, the answer to this question would appear to be yes, as it has taken over the academic domain from other European languages. However, much more research is needed in this particular area before definitive answers can be given.

In the next part of the book, Part C, I summarise the key points raised in Part B, and then consider their implications for English language teaching.

Part C: Implications

12 **Summary of key themes**

In this chapter, the major linguistic and sociolinguistic themes identified and discussed in Parts A and B will be summarised. This will focus on the causes of linguistic variation and the development of Englishes on the one hand, and the sociolinguistic causes and explanations for the spread of English on the other. For example, can Phillipson's (1992) theory of Linguistic Imperialism (see Chapter 3) adequately account for the current widespread use of English, or is local demand for English the underlying reasons for its current role as the world's international language?

12.1 **Linguistic variation and the development of Englishes**

There are countless varieties of English and these varieties perform countless roles in an extraordinary range of contexts and domains. Yet, despite the number of varieties and the variation within and between them, the linguistic causes of this variation are comparable for all of them. That is to say, a major cause of variation is contact with other languages. As illustrated throughout Part B, this is as true of the way English and varieties of English developed in Britain, as it is of the way the so-called new varieties of English have developed or are continuing to develop. Thus traditional English owes many of its current linguistic features to its contact over several centuries with Latin, Scandinavian languages and French. This change is constant, so that many other languages continue to influence the way 'traditional' English is developing. In the context of inflections, for example, a major change has been a tendency for the inflectional system of English to become simpler over time, so that the English of today contains far fewer inflections than Old English did.

Similar influences and tendencies can be seen in the development of new varieties of English. All have developed in contact with other languages and all have displayed a tendency towards syntactic simplification or regularisation of one sort or another. Any differences are merely differences of degree, rather than differences of type. As Mufwene (2001, and see Chapter 5) has argued, the differences in linguistic features between Black and White varieties of American English can be explained by the different linguistic features of the languages that have influenced them – African-American English has been influenced more by African languages, white varieties by European languages. But both Black and White varieties have been influenced to some extent by both African and European languages.

The varieties of English that have developed in outer circle countries have also been influenced by contact with other languages. The influence of local languages upon these indigenised varieties of English, such as Indian, for example, may be greater than their influence upon inner circle varieties, such as Australian, for example; but both Indian and Australian English can be said to be nativised varieties, in that both have developed linguistic features that reflect local cultures and ways of speaking. The Englishes of Britain are clearly also nativised varieties in that they reflect the cultural norms of their speakers.

Some scholars (see Chapters 3 and 11, for example) have argued that new varieties of English will become so influenced by contact with local languages that they will develop into different languages and will become mutually unintelligible. While this has happened in certain contexts with the development of languages such as Nigerian Pidgin English, for example, the need for people to be able to communicate beyond their own speech communities has ensured the maintenance of varieties of English that are internationally intelligible. This can be explained by the identity–communication continuum (see Chapter 1), presented again below.

The identity–communication continuum illustrates two major functions of language: for communication; and to establish identity. It shows that when speakers wish to highlight their identity and membership of a speech community, they will choose to use a highly localised, informal variety of English. Or, if they wish to identify themselves as members of a specialist profession, they may use a highly specialised variety or register for this purpose. These varieties are likely to be unintelligible to people outside the particular speech community. As Smith has pointed out, 'Our speech and writing in English needs to be intelligible only to those with whom we wish to communicate in English' (1992: 75). When used locally and to signal identity within a speech community, the variety of English will display a wide range of distinctive phonological, lexical, syntactic and cultural features. When used in order to communicate across speech communities, however, the variety will display far fewer distinctive features. This helps explain the comparatively wide range of variation in the local dialect of Scottish English, the Doric (Chapter 4), as against the comparatively narrow range of syntactic variation found when English is used as an international *lingua franca* (Meierkord, 2004, and see Chapter 11).

Figure 1: The identity–communication continuum

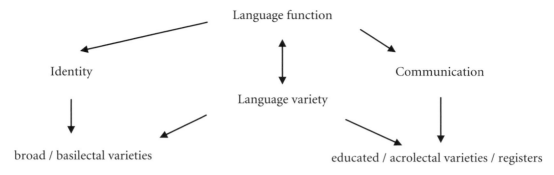

A remarkable fact connected to the development of so many varieties of English in so many different linguistic and cultural contexts is that so many of these varieties *share* a large number of linguistic features. Below is Schmied's list of shared phonological and syntactic features of African Englishes (1991: 58ff., and see Chapter 8). As so many of these features have also been described in other varieties of English, such as Indian (Chapter 7), Singaporean and Filipino (Chapter 9), I include the list again here:

Common linguistic features of African Englishes

Pronunciation

(i)   Fricatives tend to be avoided.
(ii) Length differences in vowels are levelled and not used to distinguish meaning.
(iii) The central vowels /ʌ/, /ɜː/ and /ə/ as in 'but', 'bird' and 'about' become more open as in /ɔ/, /ə/, and /a/.
(iv) Diphthongs tend to become monophthongs, so that /eɪ/ and /əʊ/ become /e/ and /o/ respectively.
(v)   Consonant clusters either drop consonants or insert vowels to split them.

Grammar

(i)   Inflectional endings are not always added to the verb but general, regular and unmarked forms are used instead.
(ii) Complex tenses such as the past perfect and certain conditionals tend to be avoided.
(iii) The use of verb+*ing* constructions is extended to all verbs resulting in examples such as 'I am having your book' and 'I was not liking the food in the hotel'.
(iv) Phrasal and prepositional verbs are used differently, for example 'I will pick you at 8 o'clock tonight.' (= 'I will pick you up at 8 o'clock tonight')
(v)   Verb complementation varies freely to give phrases such as 'allow him go' and 'they made him to clean the whole yard'.

(vi)   Noun phrases are not always marked for number and case or are treated differently, to give 'informations', 'a cattle', 'an advice'.

(vii)   Relative pronouns ('whom', 'whose') are avoided to give 'adult education which its main purpose is to help adults. . .'.

(viii)   The use of plural is overgeneralised ('luggages', 'advices').

(ix)   Articles and determiners are often omitted ('I am going to post office').

(x)   Pronouns are not always distinguished by gender.

(xi)   Adjectives may be used as adverbs to give 'I can obtain the food easy'.

(xii)   Pronoun copying is common ('many of the fish, they have different colours').

(xiii)   Negative yes/no questions are confirmed by responding to the form of the question so that the answer to 'he isn't good?' becomes 'yes (he isn't)'.

(xiv)   There are invariant question tags, for example 'isn't it?' and 'you wanted to leave for Nairobi, not so?'

(xv)   The interrogative word order is retained in indirect speech to give 'I cannot tell you what is the matter'.

(xvi)   There is freer word order so that 'in my family, we are many' becomes common.

In Part B, further distinctive phonological features were identified. For example, many varieties of English have a tendency towards syllable- rather than stress-timing, and this is also true of many African varieties. Specific varieties will also display distinctive phonological features. It explains why speakers' accents can often tell listeners where they come from. This happens at an individual level as well, which is why it is possible to identify a close friend from the sound of their voice alone.

Many of the grammatical features listed above appear in other varieties of English. There are two possible explanations for this. The first is that the similarities across varieties are due to a 'pan-linguistic grammatical simplification process' (Crane, 1994: 358, and see Chapter 9). This accords with the process of inflectional simplification through which traditional English has passed and would account for the frequency of the non-marking of tenses, which is listed first in Schmied's catalogue above.

A second possible explanation for the 'regularity' of these features is that they are derived from parameter settings in Universal Grammar (UG). UG proposes that all languages share a basic grammatical system which is mapped onto language through certain parameter settings, but that these differ across languages. 'While the principles of UG lay down absolute requirements that a human language has to meet, the parameters of UG account for the syntactic variation between languages' (Cook and Newson, 1996: 55). However, many languages can share the same parameter settings. One example of a parameter setting is whether a language insists on some form of noun in subject position (non-pro-drop languages) or whether it does not (pro-drop languages). British English is a non-pro-drop language, but many other languages such as Arabic, Chinese and Italian, are pro-drop. Cook and Newson (1996: 55) give this example from British English and

Italian respectively, where the English version requires the subject 'I', but the Italian version does not:

I am the walrus

'Sono il tricheco' (am the walrus)

In Chapter 9, I suggested that one reason why Singaporean English does not require a subject – as in the headline 'Hurt girlfriend with lighted butt' – is because it has been influenced by Chinese, which is a pro-drop language. Thus, varieties of English that have been influenced by pro-drop languages may themselves become pro-drop languages.

A second parameter of UG concerns the 'presence or absence of syntactic movement' (Cook and Newson, 1996: 27). British English requires movement but other languages do not. For example, it is possible to change a Chinese or Malay sentence into a question simply by adding some form of interrogative particle, but in English the word order needs to change. For example, the Malay sentence:

Dia nak pergi ke Kuala Lumpur. (He is going to Kuala Lumpur.)

can be turned into a question by the addition of 'kah':

Dia nak pergi ke Kuala Lumpur-kah? (Is he going to Kuala Lumpur?)

(Cook and Newson, 1996: 27)

The English question form, on the other hand, requires a change of word order from 'He is' to 'Is he'.

It has been shown in the previous chapters that many varieties of English do not require a change of word order in order to form questions and this may be explained by their speakers' first languages not requiring word order change in the same way that British English does. Linked to this is the concept of a language's Principle Branching Direction (PBD). The PBD of a language 'refers to structures such as relative clauses, adverbial subordinate clauses and sentence complementation and the way they are generated in relation to a head' (Flynn, 1984: 106). Chinese is principally left-branching so prefers the clause sequence in complex sentences of subordinate to main. British English is principally right-branching so prefers the clause sequence in complex sentences of main to subordinate (Kirkpatrick, 1996). Thus Chinese *prefers* a compound cause–effect clause sequence of 'because clause, therefore clause', while English *prefers* a 'therefore clause, because clause' sequence. In a neutral or unmarked context, Chinese speakers are therefore more likely to say 'because it was raining, the match was cancelled', while English speakers are more likely to say 'the match was cancelled because it was raining'. In Chapters 9 and 10, this 'because–therefore' sequence was shown to be preferred in both Singaporean and Chinese English respectively, a preference that can be explained by the transfer of PBD from the first language to the local variety of English.

As a final example, languages differ in the way grammatical relations operate at sentence level. For example, Chinese is a topic-prominent language in which the grammatical relation 'topic–comment' (e.g. 'apples [topic], I like [comment]') plays a major role, while in British English the grammatical relation 'subject–predicate' (e.g. 'I [subject] like apples [predicate]) plays a major role (Li and Thompson, 1976). Thus the subject–predicate sentence 'the leaves on that tree are big' may be rendered in Chinese as a topic–comment sentence, 'that tree, leaves big' (Kirkpatrick, 1996). The transfer of a preference for 'topic–comment' structures may explain why so many varieties of English allow sentences which Schmied has called 'pronoun copying' and 'freer word order', as in his examples (xii) and (xvi) above.

The twin phenomena of 'pan-simplification' and the transfer of parameter settings from local languages to the relevant variety of English may therefore explain why so many varieties of English share so many linguistic features. In addition, however, varieties of English possess features that do distinguish them from others. Their very distinctiveness sees them regarded as stereotypical features of the variety in question. For example, the use of the '*lah*' particle in Malaysian and Singaporean English, and the use of 'wherein' in Philippine English (Chapter 9) are seen as stereotypical features of these two varieties.

Language contact therefore affects the relevant variety of English in different ways. A natural tendency towards simplification coupled with the transfer of parameter settings of UG mean many features of a developing variety of English will be shared by others. However, the transfer of linguistically specific features from a local language to the variety of English will result in genuinely distinctive features in that variety. As the description of the varieties throughout Part B has demonstrated, certain phonological features transferred from local languages will also make speakers of that variety distinctive – and in many cases this distinctiveness will be reflected in local varieties as much as the national variety. Lexical and cultural features also contribute in major ways to the distinctiveness of any variety.

A major conundrum in the description of new varieties of English concerns the lack of criteria for determining whether a linguistic feature that differs from an established norm is indeed a feature of a new variety of English or whether it is a feature of learner English. Bamgbose (1998: 13) has suggested five factors that can be used to determine whether an innovation is a norm:

(i)   how many people use it?
(ii) how widely is it used?
(iii) who are the people who use it?
(iv) where is the use sanctioned?
(v)   is the use accepted?

It is worth recalling that this is a conundrum that faces scholars who are trying to describe Old English (see Chapter 4), as well as those scholars who are engaged in the description of new Englishes. And, indeed, Bamgbose's criteria present problems. First, it is not clear how many people have to use the feature and in which contexts etc. before it can be classified as a norm. Second, as I argued in Chapters 6 and 10, codification of a feature may mean that it is an established norm, but the converse does not hold: the fact that a feature has not been codified does not mean that it is not an established norm. Arguing otherwise would be like demanding to see someone's birth certificate before admitting that they existed. Third, if the codification is prescriptive in intent, a feature that is codified may not be commonly used at all. It may simply be that the codifier feels that it should be. In Chapter 11, I tentatively suggested one linguistic criterion for distinguishing between learner and 'new' English. If a speaker simplifies the inflectional system of English in ways identified above (lack of tense marking in certain contexts, for example), this is likely to be a feature of a 'new' variety of English. If, on the other hand, the speaker makes the inflectional system more complex, either by adding inflections to the wrong word or by adding them where they are not necessary, this is likely to be a feature of learner English. One obvious way of avoiding this conundrum is to ensure that the informants or subjects providing the data are themselves expert users of the variety in question. All too often research into new varieties of English and into *lingua franca* English includes speakers who are not proficient speakers. For example, involving first year university students in places like Hong Kong is unlikely to provide data from which a reliable description of Hong Kong English can be obtained, as many of these learners will not be expert users of the language. Indeed, if I were to base a description of Australian English on the written work of first year Anglo-Australian university students, I would find many features that differed from established norms. It is essential then that descriptions and analysis of varieties of English and *lingua franca* be based on the language of expert users.

12.2   Sociolinguistic features and the spread of Englishes

In Chapter 3 I briefly reviewed Phillipson's theory of Linguistic Imperialism (LI) (1992). Here I return to this and discuss it in the light of the findings presented in Part B of this book. It is important to reiterate the key tenets of LI, and in order to ensure that these are expressed in his own words, I quote from Phillipson's response (1997) to Davies' critique (1996) of LI:

> Linguistic imperialism is a theoretical construct, devised to account for linguistic hierarchisation, to address issues of why some languages come to be used more and others less, what structures and ideologies facilitate such processes, and the role of language professionals.
>
> Linguistic imperialism is a subtype of linguicism, a term which Tove Skutnabb-Kangas coined (1988), and is used to draw parallels between hierarchisation on the basis of race (racism), gender (sexism), and language (linguicism).
>
> Linguicism can be intralingual and interlingual. It exists among and between speakers of a language when one dialect is privileged as standard. Linguicism exists between speakers of different languages in processes of resource allocation, vindication or vilification in discourse of one language rather than another – English as the language of modernity and progress, Cantonese as a mere dialect unsuited for a range of literate and societal functions – (. . .)

> Linguistic imperialism takes place within an overarching structure of asymetrical North/South relations, where language interlocks with other dimensions, cultural (particularly in education, science and the media), economic and political.
>
> (Phillipson, 1997: 239)

Fishman, Conrad and Rubal-Lopez (1996) set out to discover, in a systematic way, the changes in the status and functions of English in the period 1940–90 in 20 countries. The authors responsible for reporting on these countries were also asked to react to Phillipson's theory and ask whether any increase in the use of English could be seen as the result of Linguistic Imperialism. Some of their findings have been reported in Part B. In his summary, Fishman himself made the following points:

> With regard to which languages were used as media of education, only four of the twenty countries conducted primary education primarily in English (or another exoglossic European language). The four countries were Cameroon, India, Nigeria and Papua New Guinea. In contrast, twelve places (Cuba, the European Union, Israel, Malaysia, Mexico, Puerto Rico, the Canadian Province of Quebec, Saudi Arabia, Sudan, Sri Lanka, Tanzania and Uganda) used local languages for primary education. Three countries – Kenya, the Philippines and South Africa – used a mixed model, whereby both English and local languages were used in primary education. In contrast, however, English is commonly used in higher levels of education, especially at tertiary level. It was also found that English is used as either an official or co-official language in eleven of the twenty places surveyed. English is more common in higher reaches of society in the domains of science, commerce and industry and is least common in the local dimensions of society. There is thus a functional division of labour between English and local vernaculars, and there is no evidence of linguacide.
>
> (Fishman, 1996: 637)

As Conrad argues in the same collection, 'if the agenda was really for English to replace local languages, the policy has failed miserably' (1996: 26). Fishman concludes that the main drivers behind the current spread of English are socioeconomic factors and that it is more linked to countries' engagement in the modern world economy 'than to any efforts derived from their former colonial masters' (1996: 640).

In Chapter 3, I also briefly described the work of Brutt-Griffler and her view that English 'owes its existence as a world language in large part to the struggle against imperialism, and not to imperialism alone' (2002: ix). Far from forcing its colonial subjects to learn English, British colonial policy was, in large part, to provide an English education only for the elite rather than to offer it to the great majority of the population, who were to be educated in the local languages. This policy did not mean that pupils should learn only English. On the contrary, elite education was bilingual and included the learning of local languages. As reported in Chapter 10, this was even the case in the majority of missionary schools in Hong Kong, where the curriculum was divided between Chinese language, Chinese literature and English (Bolton, 2003). To argue, then, that the colonial government imposed their language at the expense of local languages is to ignore the facts.

As Brutt-Griffler has argued, the role played by colonial subjects is crucial to understanding how World Englishes have developed. 'Asians and Africans transformed English from a means of exploitation into a means of resistance' (2002: 65). In other words, the colonised adapted the English language and used it for their own ends. Many instances of this have been provided in Part B, where several writers were quoted attesting to their ability to 'colonise' English and make it theirs. I review a selection of these quotes below. The Indian author Raja Rao wrote in the foreword to his seminal and iconic piece *Kanthapura*, published in 1963, 'We shall have English with us and amongst us, and not as our guest or friend, but as one of our own, of our castes, our creed, our sect and of our tradition' (quoted in Srivastava and Sharma, 1991: 190, and see Chapter 7).

D'Souza argued that English has been Indianised by being 'borrowed, transcreated, recreated, stretched, extended, contorted perhaps' (2001: 150, and see Chapter 7).

The well-known Indian novelist Anita Desai agrees. She emphasises that Indian life is an amalgam of many languages, cultures and civilisations that form 'one very compactly woven whole' (1996: 221). She has found English 'flexible, elastic, resilient, capable of taking on whatever tones, rhythms and colours I chose' (1996: 222, and see Chapter 7).

I also quoted a number of writers who expressed the opposite view, the Sri Lankan poet Wikkrammasinha, the Malaysian poet Mohammed Haji Salleh and the Kenyan writer Ngugi wa Thiong'o, to name just three.

The Nigerian writers Achebe and Soyinka, however, have argued that English is an African language and that writing in adapted African forms of English can be a powerful means of literary expression. 'When we borrow an alien language . . . we must stretch it, impact and compact it, fragment and reassemble it . . . (Soyinka, cited in Schmied, 1991: 126, and see Chapter 8).

Despite Pennycook's claim that 'cultural constructs of colonialism' continue (1998: 27), the evidence presented above suggests that the colonial experience is foreign to an increasing number of people, especially younger people who no longer see English through a postcolonial lens. As Görlach (2002: 10–11) argues:

> The use of English has apparently become totally detached from the concept of colonial oppressor's language in Africa and Asia (. . .) English is regarded as having been a vital asset in the fight for independence and it has eminent advantages as a nation building language in multilingual nations.

All this would suggest that Phillipson's theory of Linguistic Imperialism has been overtaken by recent international developments. Linguistic Imperialism was more directly applicable in many countries in the period after the end of World War Two, but the globalisation phenomenon of recent times has complicated the issue of language choice, so that other factors need to be considered. Thus, English is now not used by speakers in outer circle countries today solely because it was imposed upon them by British colonial policy. The quotes above strongly suggest that, for many people in outer circle countries, English is used in a wide number of domains because they consider the nativised form of the language to be their language. English is no longer considered a 'colonial' language. Even during the time of colonialism, in certain places English was seen as a language through which people could mount their own resistance to colonialism. In some African countries, for example, it was seen as a language of liberation and it is still used as a language of resistance against indigenous regimes throughout the world (see Chapter 8).

As has been illustrated in Part B, English is also used for a range of pragmatic and personal reasons. It is used because the people see how useful it is for social and economic advancement. It is used because it is the language of international trade. It is used because it is the major language of technology, education and popular culture. I reiterate Li's views on this in the context of Hong Kong:

> English helps one access more information and people – through higher education, on the job, in cyber space and international encounters. In writing, English has a greater potential to help one reach out to wider audiences compared with other languages. In this light, rather than a tool of hegemony, English may be looked upon as a resource to enhance the learners' linguistic repertoire, which in turn has good potential for enriching their quality of life through higher education and professional development.
>
> (Li, 2002b: 55, and see Chapter 10)

This pragmatism is also evident in expanding circle countries, as we saw in the case of the extraordinary and increasing desire for English in the countries of the European Union, South-East Asia and China (Chapters 10 and 11).

The argument that English has spread because of demand as well as hegemony appears powerful. However, this does not mean that the spread of English is always benevolent. The arrival in any linguistic setting of a language for which there is so much demand is likely to affect the role and status of the other languages. So, we need to ask, for example, whether English has spread at the expense of local languages? The answer to this question depends very much on the contexts in which English has become established. In Britain itself, English has been a 'killer' language. As the importance of English increased throughout Britain, it became the language that people needed to know in order to gain employment. People then began to learn it and started to lose their own languages. A long-term process developed that saw a monolingual community in Language A gradually becoming a bilingual community in Language A and English, and finally becoming monolingual again, but in English (Burchfield, 1994b). In this way, English replaced local languages in many parts of Britain. A comparable process can be seen in settlement colonies. As described in Chapter 6, for example, an original 250 Australian Aboriginal languages have been reduced to fewer than 50 and, at the same time, Australian Aboriginal English has become the language spoken by the majority of Australian Aboriginals.

In outer circle countries and in those where English also plays an important role, such as the European Union, English tends to be learned as an additional language and its speakers are bilingual, or more probably, multilingual. Görlach argues that, while English has never completely replaced a European language outside Britain (2002: 16), it will stifle European languages in that it will take over functions currently served by European languages. He cites Germany as a country where German may be reduced to a kind of dialect

(2002: 16), in particular in the field of education and scholarship, a fear shared by Ammon for German and other European languages (1996). In Chapter 10, a number of other scholars were cited expressing similar concerns. Certainly research is needed into the role academic English is playing in international scholarship. This is not simply a question of having to write in a language that is not one's own in order to disseminate one's scholarship or ideas, unfair and onerous as that this may be. The need to write following an empirical-scientific knowledge paradigm and in 'Anglo' rhetorical styles can greatly disadvantage those unfamiliar with both, as was discussed in Chapter 7 in the context of India and Sri Lanka. This is also a major concern of Ammon (2000), who argues that the second language writer is seriously and unjustly disadvantaged when seeking publication in mainstream Anglo-American journals. We need to develop ways of ensuring that the dissemination of knowledge can flow from outer and expanding circle countries to inner circle ones in order to counteract the current mostly one-way flow of knowledge from the inner circle, in particular the United States, to the outer and expanding circle. As suggested in Chapter 7, research is needed to see whether English is being shaped and adapted to local rhetorical styles so that traditional and indigenous knowledge – whether this be medical or technological or philosophical – can be successfully disseminated to the inner circle and globally through English.

When used as an international *lingua franca*, however, English tends to become an additional language. This does not mean that it has no effect on local languages. Clearly it takes over domains in which local languages previously operated. And while Bisong (1995) has argued that English has not replaced any local languages in Nigeria, a detailed ethnographic study conducted at a local level has provided evidence that English is replacing the Emai language in a region of southern Nigeria (Schaeffer and Egbokhare, 1999). This kind of localised empirical study is the type of research that is crucially needed in order to establish the influence that English is having on local languages in outer and expanding circle settings (see also Martin, 2005). It is likely, for example, that the need to learn English will have an effect on the maintenance of smaller languages, especially if they have no written tradition, as is the case with Emai. This is because children will not only need to learn English but also a major local language which itself will act as some form of *lingua franca*, whether that be Igbo in Nigeria, Swahili in East Africa, Bahasa Indonesia in Indonesia or Putonghua in China. The need to learn two languages may well mean that priority is placed on the learning of these at the expense of local languages, especially as children move away from rural areas, where the local language is used, into the cities. So, while it can be argued that it is national *lingua francas* – whether these be English or Swahili or Putonghua – that are the killer languages, the need to learn English in these settings may serve to push local languages further down the pecking order of importance. What is clear is that many languages that are spoken by relatively small populations are dying or have already died (Skutnabb-Kangas, 2000; Dalby, 2002).

Further issues that need to be addressed in any consideration of the demand for English upon people and nations include the amount of sacrifice or cost that is required for the learning of English. How much are parents willing, or being asked to, pay in order to ensure that their children learn this apparent passport to social and economic improvement? To what extent does the learning of English actually provide such a passport to the rapidly increasing number of school children who are now learning English all over the world? What are the implications of this desire and demand for English for local, national and international labour markets? There has been little research into questions of this nature, but such research is needed.

In addition to reviewing the work of Phillipson (1992) and Brutt-Griffler (2002) on reasons for the spread of English, in Chapter 3 I also reviewed the theories of the ways English has developed in outer circle settings. I pointed out that scholars such as Kachru (1992a, b), Moag (1992) and Schneider (2003a) agreed in general terms that new varieties of English pass through a series of stages, starting with a reliance on exonormative varieties and a prejudice against the local variety through to the stage where the local variety receives local acceptance and becomes the classroom model. And, as was pointed out in Chapter 1, it is important to remember that prejudice against the local variety, even by speakers of it, is also common among speakers of so-called native speaker varieties. Moag also suggested that in some cases – and he gave Malaysia and the Philippines as examples – a decline in the use of English might be seen. As illustrated in Chapter 9, however, in the case of both Malaysia and the Philippines, far from a decline, there has been an increase in the use and roles of English and this increase is likely to continue, although Malaysia did see a decline in the 1960s and 70s. Indeed this increase in use can be seen not only in outer-circle countries but also in those of the expanding circle, where I have suggested that nativised varieties are also developing, as in the case of Chinese English, for example. This is interesting as Schneider expressed the hope that, while his model was based on postcolonial Englishes, 'In principle it should be possible to apply the model to most, ideally all of the Englishes around the globe' (2003a: 256). It will be remembered that Schneider has identified five phases. The first, the foundation phase, occurs when English first arrives; the second, the phase of exonormative stabilisation, is characterised by a dependence on the variety spoken by the settlers; the third, the nativisation phase, occurs when the variety of English takes on local lexical and cultural features leading to phase four when this newly formed indigenous variety becomes accepted as the local standard. The final stage, differentiation, signals not only the emergence and acceptance of the local variety in all domains, but also sees the emergence of different local varieties that may mark ethnic identity, for example.

Are these the phases that expanding circle varieties go through? If we consider China, it would be difficult to justify that there was a 'foundation phase' as such, in the same way that there was in inner and outer circle countries. By the same token, the second phase of 'exonormative stabilisation', during which there is a dependence on the variety 'spoken by the settlers', makes little sense when there were no settlers, although, in expanding circle countries the model of English used for the teaching of English is always, by definition, an exonormative one, at least in the early stages. It does appear, however, that the next three phases may accurately describe the process through which Chinese

English is going. Based on the evidence provided in Chapter 10, I would argue that it is currently somewhere between Schneider's phase two and phase three. This corresponds with Kachru's second phase, which sees the co-existence of exonormative and local varieties.

A second potential difference in the development of expanding circle Englishes is the speed with which they can develop. Given the extraordinarily high current demand for English, certain 'expanding circle' Englishes – European Englishes and Chinese English, for example – are likely to develop at a far greater pace than did their outer or inner circle counterparts, remembering that it took some 200 years to pass before *The Macquarie Dictionary* of Australian English was published. If we argue that China's interest in English really only took hold in the 1980s (Chapter 10), it seems highly unlikely that we shall have to wait until 2180 for the first dictionary of Chinese English, especially given China's emerging status as an economic super-power.

In this chapter I have reviewed the key themes established in Parts A and B of the book. I have briefly summarised the linguistic causes of variation and the development of Englishes, and discussed the reasons for the spread of English across the world. I concluded that local demand for English is at least as powerful a cause for its current spread as any imperial or post-imperial imposition of it upon unwilling speakers. In the next chapter I consider the implications of these issues for English language teaching.

13 Implications for English language teaching

In this chapter I shall consider the implications for language teaching of the variation that exists within and across Englishes and the way that it has developed and spread in the context of the choice of model for the language classroom in outer and expanding circle countries (see also Kirkpatrick, 2007, 2006a). Currently, one of the following two alternatives tend to be chosen: either to adopt an exonormative native speaker model or to adopt an endonormative nativised model. The possible reasons and the advantages and disadvantages for the various stakeholders in choosing these models will be considered. These choices are never absolute, of course: a country, ministry or institution may choose one model for one context and another for another. It is possible for an outer circle or expanding circle country to choose an *exonormative* nativised model. I shall also discuss the possibility of using a *lingua franca* model in certain contexts and conclude the chapter by providing a list of skills required by English language teachers. It follows that TESOL courses should provide these and TESOL employers should insist upon them.

13.1 Choosing an exonormative native speaker model

This is the choice that most outer and probably all expanding circle countries have made. There are several reasons for this. The first is that these native speaker models have prestige and legitimacy. They have a history and, most importantly, they have been codified. This means that grammars and dictionaries are available, useful reference tools for teachers and learners alike. Codification also brings with it the notion of acceptance as a standard – learness can be tested and evaluated against codified norms and standards. Thus Bamgbose has pointed out that, for nativised varieties, 'The importance of codification is too obvious to be laboured' (1998: 4).

A second reason for choosing an exonormative native speaker model is that English language teaching materials based on such models are readily available. English language teaching publishers are constantly commissioning new courses and reprinting successful old ones. However, most publishers seek to publish for a mix of global markets for their English language teaching courses and localised markets, producing market-specific courses for the latter.

Linked to this is the massive English language teaching industry that exists in the US and Britain. American and British organisations compete for contracts to provide English language teaching expertise in countries throughout the world. The English language teaching market is so important that it is common to find senior government ministers promoting it on behalf of their respective ELT industries. It is inevitably sometimes tempting for them to claim a 'market advantage' in that they can provide native speaker teachers, and thus appear to claim some extra value in a native speaker model.

A third reason for the choice of a native speaker model is that Ministries of Education around the world are keen to be seen to be providing the 'best' for their people. By insisting on a native speaker model, ministries can claim to be upholding standards and providing students with an internationally recognised and internationally intelligible variety of English, although, as I have illustrated earlier, native speaker models are not always easily understood in international communication.

But does the choice of an exonormative native speaker model really advantage the people for whom the choice is most significant: the teachers and the learners?

13.1.1 Advantages and disadvantages

As implied above, there is no doubt that the choice of a native speaker model advantages the American and British English language teaching industries. They can sell materials, provide training and courses, place native speaker teachers and develop international examination and testing systems. All this is financially beneficial for the parties concerned.

The choice of a native speaker model obviously also advantages native speaker teachers. They have become in great demand throughout the world. The demand for native speakers is so high in many places that being a native speaker is the only qualification that many teachers require. Thus native speakers who have no specialist training in English language teaching are routinely employed by schools, institutions and universities all over the world. I know from personal experience that many Chinese universities currently employ native speakers to teach English to a wide range of students and that only a small minority of these teachers have teacher training qualifications. That teachers only need to be native speakers is often explicitly stated in advertisements. When the South Korean government decided to employ 1,000 native speaker English teachers in its schools, the Korean *Herald* carried the advertisements reprinted below (emphasis added) (Kirkpatrick, 2002a: 220):

> Type 1 teachers require a Certificate in TESOL **or** three years full-time teaching experience with a graduate degree in TESOL **or** experience and interest in Korean culture and language.
>
> Type 2 teachers only have to be native speakers of English with a bachelor's degree in any field.

In other words, even the higher grade teachers only actually require 'experience and interest in Korean culture and language', however defined.

In a teacher recruitment advertisement placed by an ELT company in Japan, a prospective applicant simply needed to be 'a people-oriented, professional-minded university graduate'. In the same issue of the newspaper, an ELT recruitment company was also recruiting for teachers to teach English in Japanese schools. Such teachers needed to be 'enthusiastic, energetic graduates' and 'must like children'; 'No teaching or TEFL experience is required'.

It would seem pedagogically risky for such companies to recruit and employ untrained native speakers as English language teachers. And it is disturbing that these companies are recruiting untrained teachers (who 'must like children') to teach children, given the child protection measures that operate in other areas of education. This recruitment of untrained native speakers needs to be challenged on both pedagogical and moral grounds.

In some countries around the world, the choice of a native speaker model can also advantage those institutions and schools which can afford to hire native speakers, who, even when untrained, can command a far higher salary than even well-trained and highly proficient local teachers. This can happen when groups of learners of English in an outer or an expanding circle country display a prejudice against the local model and a preference for a native speaker model (see for example, Kubota, 1998).

If the choice of a native speaker model advantages native speaker teachers, it can also disadvantage non-native speaker local teachers for several reasons. Firstly, the choice of an exonormative model automatically undermines the value and apparent legitimacy of a local teacher's own model of English. Secondly, teachers are required to teach a model which they themselves do not speak, which can severely reduce their sense of self-confidence (Medgyes, 1994). Such a lack of self-confidence may be accompanied by a related feeling of resentment, especially when they themselves are highly trained, if an untrained native speaker teacher appears in the school who then becomes the 'source' of knowledge about *the* model purely on the strength of being a native speaker. How would such a situation be received by teachers in inner circle countries? It is diverting to imagine the reaction of Australian English language teachers, for example, if they were told by their government or institution that the model they would be required to teach was American English and that untrained American native speakers would be employed, at higher rates of pay, to demonstrate the model.

The choice of a native speaker model may also disadvantage local teachers if the choice of the model is tied to a choice of methodology associated with native speaker teachers. Two tenets of native speaker English language teaching methodology are that English should be taught monolingually – this despite there being 'no principled reasons for avoiding the L1 in the classroom' (Cook, 2001: 157) – and that the ideal teacher is therefore a monolingual native speaker (Braine, 1999). That is to say that English should be the sole language of the classroom and a teacher who is monolingual is thus an ideal teacher, precisely because s/he cannot resort to the use of other languages in the classroom. The teacher's linguistic paucity ensures the sole use of English in the classroom.

Belief in these two tenets further undermines the value of multilingual local teachers. Their knowledge of the language of their students, far from being seen as a strength, is seen as a weakness. As they know the languages of their students, they will inevitably resort to it in the classroom, runs the argument and this thus violates the first tenet.

In fact, however, being multilingual and knowing the language of their students should be seen as important strengths for any language teacher for a range of reasons (Cook, 2002; Skutnabb-Kangas, 2000). First, such teachers have had the experience, not only of learning a language as a second language, but learning the language they are now teaching. This experience gives them an understanding of the potential difficulties their students might have and an empathy with their students (Medgyes, 1994). Second, it would seem important for a language teacher to have knowledge of more than one language. It is hard to conceive of any other field in which a powerful part of the profession could seriously argue that teachers with limited knowledge of the subject should be employed ahead of those with wider knowledge of it. But when arguing that monolingual native speakers are ideal language teachers, the language teaching profession is in danger of doing just that. The great majority of English language learners are at least bilingual (Brutt-Griffler, 2002). Bilingual students benefit from and respect bilingual teachers.

In some circumstances, however, certain students may be advantaged by the choice of a native speaker model. In particular, students who have the opportunity to visit or study in inner circle countries would clearly benefit from being taught by a well-trained native speaker teacher who has first-hand knowledge of the culture and manners of the relevant inner-circle country. Students who go to study abroad in English-medium universities comprise the major part of this group and it would appear obvious that such students would benefit from using as a model the English variety spoken in the country to which they are going. However, this is more complex than it seems for at least four reasons. First, many of the academic staff of the host university will be 'foreigners'. For example, many universities in English-speaking countries employ a significant number of academics recruited from other inner-circle countries and from many outer-circle ones. In some disciplines, 'Anglo' academics represent a minority on the staff. Second, the local student body will speak a broad, informal variety of English characterised by local and 'student' slang, while the international student body will speak a wide range of varieties of English. Third, the host country, especially if it is Britain or the United States, will be home to a wide range of regional dialects (see Chapters 4 and 5). Finally, the host country is likely to have a mixed multicultural population, many of whom will speak a 'localised' version of their own variety of English. For these reasons, the belief that students going, for example, to Australia, Britain or the United States will be advantaged by learning an idealised version of the respective native speaker model is not necessarily true.

It also needs to be pointed out that students who are learning English in order to study in English-speaking countries only constitute a very small minority of the sum total of English learners. The great majority of learners of English are children studying in state-run schools that range from well-resourced urban schools to poorly resourced rural schools, of which the latter, unfortunately, represent the majority. As I shall argue below, the choice of a native speaker model does not necessarily advantage such students.

The choice of a native speaker model can also disadvantage the great majority of students if the chosen model is seen as unattainable by the students (Honna and Takeshita,

1998) and *the students feel that this is so*. This also leads to an unwillingness to experiment with the language and results in:

> . . . Japanese students' passive attitudes in using this language as a means of international and intercultural communication. They are ashamed if they do not speak English as native speakers do

(Honna and Takeshita, 2000: 63)

As Cook has pointed out:

> If L2 learners feel that the chief measure of L2 success is passing for native, few are going to meet it. Both teachers and students become frustrated by setting themselves what is, in effect, an impossible target.

(2002: 331)

This feeling can be devastatingly de-motivating for students. Adopting a native speaker model and then hiring native speakers to model it simply serves to let the students know that the model can only be attained by people who look and sound very different from themselves. This also carries the clear message that teachers who do look and sound like them are unable to produce the required model. Students will wonder what chance they will have if even their teachers can't manage it. Again, it is hard to conceive of any other field in which the learners are implicitly informed that, not only can they never achieve the goal that the curriculum has set for them, but that this goal is even beyond their own teachers. Students who are continually evaluated against unrealistic, unattainable and inappropriate models will soon become disheartened and disillusioned.

A native speaker model is thus potentially disadvantageous, not only when it is unattainable, but also when it is *inappropriate* for all but a minority of students. Throughout this book, the development of local nativised Englishes and the roles of English as a *lingua franca* have been described. Outside inner-circle countries, English is most commonly used by and between bilingual or multilingual people. These users thus do not need an inner-circle native speaker model as much as they need to be able to communicate effectively across linguistic and cultural boundaries. Teaching a native speaker model that includes inner-circle linguistic and pragmatic norms and inner-circle cultures is thus not appropriate for many learners of English in non-inner circle countries. The role of English in the European Union (EU) and in the Association of South-East Asian Nations (ASEAN) (see Chapter 11) would appear to indicate that learners need an English language teaching curriculum that teaches them about the cultures of the people they are most likely to be using English with, and how to compare, relate and present *their own culture* to others. In the context of ASEAN, students are likely to need ELT materials that provide information about ASEAN cultures and how their own culture relates to and differs from others in ASEAN. In this way, the major focus of the curriculum becomes Asian cultures. 'The English standard becomes an Asian standard' (Kirkpatrick, 2002a: 215), and this includes both linguistic and pragmatic norms. Potential texts for an ELT curriculum could include comparative cultural topics such as a discussion about the comparative roles of Buddhism and Islam in Thailand and Indonesia, comparative linguistic and pragmatic norms, such as a comparison of the different ways of addressing, greeting and farewelling in ASEAN cultures and topics that explore the roles and status of English in ASEAN.

Curricula of this type already exist in the EU. One of the aims of 'Networking English/European language learning in Europe' (NELLE) is to promote materials about European cultures and values and 'to develop awareness of English as a supplementary language of communication in Europe and as a means to the richness of other cultures' (Goethals, 1997a: 61). Of course, Britain is a member state of the EU so there is good reason for European students to learn about British English and British culture, but not as a model, rather 'as an example of a national variety of European culture and civilisation' (van Essen, 1997: 99).

I have argued that adopting a native speaker model of English for outer and expanding circle countries advantages the American and British ELT industry and native speaker teachers. As far as non-native teachers are concerned, however, it is greatly disadvantageous, as it devalues their potential strengths as English language teachers and undermines their self-confidence. For the most important people, the students, the choice of a native speaker model can benefit those who have specific reasons for learning inner-circle models of English. For the great majority of learners, however, the choice of a native speaker model is both unattainable and inappropriate. What then are the advantages and disadvantages of adopting a local endonormative model of English?

13.2 Choosing an endonormative nativised model

Countries most likely to choose an endonormative model are outer-circle countries in which the local variety of English has become socially acceptable. Even in such countries, however, there is often fierce debate over this. For example, while Nigerian English is the classroom model in Nigeria, there are still those who oppose this (see Chapter 8). It is also only relatively recently that a country such as Singapore with its well-established variety of English has moved from insisting on a native speaker model to one which is internationally intelligible. Countries of the European Union, on the other hand, have been far more ready to accept what might be called a *lingua franca* or 'bilingual' model (van Essen, 1997) and I discuss this approach later.

13.2.1 Advantages and disadvantages

Local teachers are obviously advantaged by choosing the local model, as they are, by definition, speakers of that model. This legitimises their model of English and thus increases their self-confidence and self-esteem. The choice of a local model also empowers local teachers in a number of other ways. With the choice of the local model, the multilingual competence of the teacher is both recognised and can be exploited in the classroom. The two tenets concerning the monolingual teacher and the monolingual classroom are discarded in favour of the multilingual teacher and the use of languages other than English in the classroom. In particular, as teachers know the language of their students and have had the experience of learning English as a second language, they can use their shared linguistic resources in the classroom while, at the same time, understanding the language learning problems that their students might face. Instead, therefore, of being made to feel linguistically inadequate because of their inability to speak a native speaker model, they can now feel proud of their multilingual skills and put these to use in the classroom.

In addition to sharing the linguistic repertoire of their students and being able to exploit this in class, local teachers are also familiar with the educational, social and cultural norms of their students and, importantly, the school system as a whole. They understand the roles expected of them as teachers in their particular culture and how these roles interact with the expected roles of students. This clearly benefits both them and their students. In summary, it is hard to see how, in these language learning contexts, a monolingual native speaker could be preferred over a multilingual teacher who speaks the local variety of English and has 'native' familiarity with local cultural and educational norms. The choice of a monolingual native speaker becomes even more perplexing when that person is not trained, but when the multilingual local teacher is.

The education system as a whole is also advantaged both pedagogically and financially by the choice of a local model and local teachers. Resources that would otherwise be spent on employing native speaker teachers can go towards the training of local ones. This is money well spent, as local teachers will remain in the system. Schools and students will benefit from their increasing expertise and experience. Hiring native speakers, on the other hand, brings little long-term benefit to the students or schools. Native speaker teachers tend to take short-term contracts and then return to their own countries. Furthermore, those that are monolingual are likely to be less able to contribute to the life of the school or institution in the ways routinely expected of local teachers.

An advantage for governments of adopting a local model and thus the local teacher is particularly significant in the context of the fear that the learning of English brings with it the learning and adoption of alien values and cultures. I have argued that the spread of English has more to do with local demand than 'Anglo-American' policies, but there is no doubt that American values and culture, for example, have permeated most corners of the world, primarily through the reach of popular American culture. Local teachers are less likely than American teachers, for example, to be purveyors of American cultural values. Why then would governments who fear the encroachment of alien cultural values upon their own insist on recruiting native speakers to be teachers of English in their own countries? As Goethals has pointed out, most European English teachers are multilingual and European. This, in Goethals' words, 'weakens their anglophilism . . . and favours sensitivity to English as an international language' (1997b: 110). In the same way, local teachers of the local variety are far less likely to promote 'Anglo-American' values in the language classroom. A monolingual native speaker, on the other hand, is more likely to do so. By employing local teachers to teach the local model, governments may therefore not only advantage their teachers and students, but also safeguard what they feel is unique and precious in their own society and culture.

In certain contexts, the choice of the local model can also directly advantage the students. The model is now both attainable and appropriate. Students now have role models in the form of their teachers and they can get on with the business of language learning without worrying that, whatever progress they make, they will remain unsuccessful. Instead of being forbidden to speak their own language in the classroom, they can exploit their own multilingualism in the classroom in their learning of English. Multilingualism becomes the language learning asset it should be.

To turn to possible disadvantages inherent in the choice of a local model, a major drawback arises if the local model has not yet been codified and there are no grammars and no textbooks or materials based on the local model. A possible solution suggested by some scholars (see McKay, 2002) is that a native speaker variety could be used as a *norm* rather than as a model. That is to say that a native speaker variety becomes a benchmark against which to measure the production of learners. Learners are not expected to mimic the native speaker model precisely but to produce sounds and utterances that do not stray too far from the norms in the native speaker model. This solution does give rise to some questions, however. First, as we have seen in Chapters 4, 5 and 6, native speaker varieties differ significantly from each other in terms of phonological, lexical and grammatical features. The *norms* of each of these varieties stand some linguistic distance away from each other. How far from a norm can a learner be allowed to travel, therefore? Apart from the issue of intelligibility, which I consider below, there seems to be no definitive answer to this question. In the end, it will not make much difference whether students will be evaluated against a native speaker norm or a native speaker model. Native speakers will remain the source of 'correctness' and this greatly disadvantages both local students and local teachers.

The fear that learners may not be internationally intelligible underpins the argument for adopting a codified model. However, as I have argued throughout this book, this fear is unfounded. First, as long as speakers have a genuine motivation to communicate across cultural and linguistic boundaries, they will be able to communicate. Second, many local varieties of English are syllable-timed, and these have been shown to be more easily intelligible than the stress-timed varieties of native speakers (see Chapters 9, 10 and 11). Third, a native speaker model is unattainable in any case and this makes any argument about the relative international intelligibility of such a model frequently irrelevant.

The advantages of choosing a local model in outer-circle countries where the local variety has been codified and has become socially acceptable in both informal and formal domains appear obvious. On the other hand, in outer-circle countries where the local variety is currently only acceptable in informal domains, or in expanding-circle countries, the disadvantages of choosing a local model may outweigh the advantages.

But is there a case for an expanding-circle country to use, as its model, a codified nativised variety of English? In the case of Indonesia, for example, there would appear to be a strong argument for the adoption of the exonormative but *nativised* model of Malaysian English for several reasons. First Malaysia and Indonesia share many linguistic and cultural features. Both countries have more or less the same national language (Bahasa Melayu/Bahasa Indonesia) and, while both countries are multicultural and multi-ethnic, both are predominately Muslim countries. Indonesian English can be expected to share many linguistic and cultural similarities with Malaysian English therefore. Other advantages for Indonesia in the adoption of Malaysian English as a classroom model would be that Malaysian English language teachers would provide a more economic and culturally knowledgeable source of language teachers than native speakers imported, say, from neighbouring Australia. Added to this, the South-East Asian Ministers of Education Organisation (SEAMEO) has established the Regional Language Centre (RELC) in Singapore. One of RELC's aims is to promote collaborative English language teaching within ASEAN. All these apparent advantages need to be weighed against political and cultural sensitivities, however. The geographical and cultural proximity of Indonesia and Malaysia, coupled with their closely connected histories, might make it difficult for either country to accept scholarly expertise from the other.

Would the choice of an exonormative but nativised model be more advantageous than not in an expanding country such as China? In Chapter 10, I argued that although China was an expanding-circle country following Kachru's classification, a Chinese variety of English was developing there and developing faster than has been the case in outer-circle countries. In such contexts, it seems inevitable that the local endonormative model will become the one used in classrooms. This is already the *de facto* position in many parts of China as local Chinese English language teachers have no option but to teach the model they themselves have learned. It would be sensible for the government to move to make this the official position as well as the *de facto* one. In this way, teachers and learners would enjoy the advantages associated with choosing a nativised model itemised above.

In Japan, the situation is different, as the development of Japanese English is unlikely to proceed as quickly as in China. This is partly because the Japanese ELT profession has been so strongly influenced by American teachers. But there really are two quite different 'Englishes' in Japan. The first is an institutionalised variety based on an American native speaker model. This is the variety that students struggle to learn in schools. Kubota has predicted that the English taught and learned in Japan will continue to gravitate towards inner-circle varieties and to promote Westernisation 'while failing to provide global sociolinguistic perspectives' (1998: 302). The presence of this institutionalised variety on the school curriculum has led Tsuda to argue that English is being imposed upon the Japanese in a process he has called *eigo-shihai* (English domination) (1997: 22). However, Kubota's plea that the ELT curriculum should be extended to include varieties and cultures other than British and American has been heard, at least in certain quarters. Professor Honna of Aoyama Gakuin University, and the editor of the journal *Asian Englishes*, has long argued against the use of a native speaker model for Japanese schools (see above) and has been influential in promoting the idea of English as an Asian language. As part of this, he has encouraged the hiring of speakers of Asian Englishes from outer-circle countries such as the Philippines, Singapore and India to work as English language teachers in Japan. His goal is to show Japanese learners that English is as much an Asian language as an Anglo-American one and that English can be owned by Asians, and varieties of English that reflect Asian rather than Anglo cultures can develop. This idea has been taken up and promoted by Professor Yoshikawa and others in the recently established Department of World Englishes at Chukyo University (Yoshikawa, 2005).

The second variety of English that exists in Japan is quite unlike the institutionalised variety taught in schools. Stanlaw (2004: 291) quotes Ono's definition of Japanese English as 'the English which internalises a Japanese language system and a living system of the Japanese and which grows with Japanese culture'. This Japanese variety of English is a 'creative force in Japanese sociolinguistics and in various forms of artistic expression' (Stanlaw, 2004: 299). This creativity is evident in advertising, pop culture and internet usage. It can also be seen in the creation of words. Stanlaw (2004: 37–43) gives a number of interesting examples, two of which are: *ron pari* (London–Paris), which means being cross-eyed, as it refers to someone with one eye on London and the other on Paris; and *peepaadoraibaa* (paper driver), which refers to someone who has a driving licence, but seldom actually drives. Despite its existence and its inventiveness, it will be a long time before this variety of Japanese English becomes formalised and taught in schools. Yet a move towards adopting, as a learner target, a Japanese variety of English that allows for international communication could greatly enhance the prospects of successful language learning in Japanese schools.

In summary, the advantages of choosing a local model in outer-circle countries in which the local variety has already gained widespread social acceptance outweigh the advantages of choosing a native speaker model. Above all, such a choice advantages local teachers and the great majority of the students. In other situations, the choice over which variety to adopt must depend on the local context, including the reasons why people are learning English and the extent to which a local endonormative model is appropriate.

However, the concern over the lack of codification of many new and developing varieties of English remains. An alternative to both a native speaker and a nativised model is to adopt what might be called a 'bilingual' or 'lingua franca' *approach* to the teaching of English, and I consider this below. In such contexts, the teachers themselves and other expert users of English with which the learners can readily identify can become the 'models' for the learners. This may help overcome the concerns associated with the lack of a codified model.

13.3   Choosing a *lingua franca* approach

In Chapter 11, the features and roles of English as a Lingua Franca (ELF) in ASEAN and the EU were described. I noted that the many varieties of English that *lingua franca* speakers bring to any regional or international *lingua franca* interaction make it difficult to describe or codify a *lingua franca model* as such for the classroom. However, a *lingua franca approach* based on the goal of successful cross-cultural communication could be advantageous to both teachers and students. Such an approach would need a curriculum which would include at least three strands. First, students would need to be alerted to which linguistic features cause particular problems of mutual intelligibility (see James, 2000; Meierkord, 2004; Seidlhofer, 2004; and Chapter 11). In this context, Jenkins' work on the phonology of international English is of particular pedagogic value (2000, 2002). She has described a 'Lingua Franca Core' to 'provide EIL (English as an International Language) with a core intended to guarantee the mutual intelligibility of their accents' (2005: 126).

This provides a list (see Jenkins, 2002, 2005: 126–7) of segmental and non-segmental features that alerts learners to features of pronunciation that are unlikely to cause problems of intelligibility in *lingua franca* interactions and those features that may well do so.

Second, the curriculum would need to focus on how cultures differ and the implications of such differences for cross-cultural communication. The examples of the use of 'facework' and appropriate request schemas are given below. Third, students would need to be taught the communicative strategies that aid successful cross-cultural communication (see Firth, 1996; Meierkord, 2000; and Chapter 11). These strategies include the accommodation of different linguistic and sociolinguistic norms and a range of repair strategies which can be used in the face of misunderstanding. They are underpinned by a mutual desire to cooperate and collaborate and to preserve the face of the participants.

Adopting a *lingua franca* approach would provide the advantages to both teachers and students outlined above for the adoption of an endonormative nativised model. Neither teachers nor students would be asked to aim for an unattainable or inappropriate model. The adoption of a *lingua franca* approach also advantages teachers and learners because the focus and aim of English language teaching shifts. In aiming to teach and learn English in ways that would allow for effective communication across linguistic and cultural boundaries the focus of the classroom moves from the acquisition of the norms associated with a standard model to a focus on learning linguistic features, cultural information and communicative strategies that will facilitate communication.

This approach, which can also be termed a 'bilingual approach', is already being adopted in many multilingual settings. Bilingualism needs to be seen as 'a normal, rather than special, condition' (Graddol, 2006: 117). This should mean that, following Cook (2002), the standards set are L2 or bilingual standards, not unattainable and inappropriate L1 standards. This is not to say these standards are inferior, merely that they are different. L2 and bilingual users should be judged against L2 and bilingual standards. And for the same reasons, speakers of regional varieties of English should be judged against the standards of the varieties they speak. The teaching of English should be framed within the goal of creating bi- and multilingual citizens. 'Schools are very significant contributors towards bilingualism in Europe' (Hoffman, 1996: 54). At the same time, avoiding adopting a native speaker model means that bilingualism in English does not need to equate with learning about British or American culture (Hoffman, 2000). Throughout the chapters of Part B, examples were given of new varieties of English that reflect the cultures of their speakers. And, as I argued above in the context of an ELT curriculum for AEAN countries, English can also provide a medium for the study of many different cultures.

A further possible advantage of an ELF or bilingual approach is that it accommodates cultural conventions and pragmatic norms that differ from Anglo-American norms. For example, the use of 'facework', whereby people tend to delay the introduction of the topic in conversation until after they have talked about the other person's family or given them 'face' in some way (Scollon and Scollon, 1991), is a pragmatic norm that is shared by many Asian cultures. An ASEAN-based *lingua franca* approach would promote the teaching of 'facework' in the ELT classroom, because it is culturally valued in regional cultures. A related example is the Chinese speakers' preference for giving reasons or justifications for a request before making the request, while native speakers prefer to make the requests and then provide justifications for it (Kirkpatrick, 1991, and Chapters 9, 12). This request pattern preference is shared by many other cultures in East and South-East Asia. It would be important therefore to teach this 'reasons for request – request' sequence or schema in the ASEAN ELT classroom. Far from being deviant because they differ from native speaker norms, these 'norms' are culturally appropriate for the learners, as they will, entirely or mostly, be communicating with people from the region.

This focus on cross-cultural communication inherent in an ELF or bilingual approach supports Bamgbose's call that 'Communication across world Englishes has to be seen in terms of accommodation between codes and in a multilingual context' (2001: 359).

I shall conclude this chapter by listing, in the light of the arguments presented above, the skills English teachers in outer and expanding-circle countries need and a set of principles that might underpin relevant English language teacher training courses.

13.4 Requirements for ELT teachers and training courses

English language teachers who wish to work in outer and expanding circle countries should:

- be multilingual and multicultural and ideally know the language of their students and understand the educational, social and cultural contexts in which they are working;
- either be able to provide an appropriate and attainable model for their students or, if they speak another variety, understand that the local variety of English is an appropriate and well-formed variety that is not inferior to their own;
- understand how different varieties of English have developed linguistically and the ways in which they differ phonologically, lexically, grammatically, rhetorically and culturally;
- understand how English has developed in specific contexts and how it has spread across the world;
- understand the role(s) of English in the community and how these interrelate with other local languages;
- be able to evaluate ELT materials critically to ensure that these do not, either explicitly or implicitly, promote a particular variety of English or culture at the expense of others;
- be able to evaluate the specific needs of their students and teach towards those needs; and
- be prepared to contribute to the extra-curricular life of the institution in which they are working.

If these are the skills required of English language teachers, it follows then that the curricula of TESOL courses and the like should be designed to equip teachers with these skills.

A survey of MA TESOL courses offered by institutions across the United States suggests that few courses, at the time of writing, actually did provide their students with these skills (Govardhan, Nayar and Sheorey, 1999). The authors of the survey reported that US MA TESOL courses were generally more suited to those wishing to teach in the United States; they were unable to identify any programme specifically designed for preparing ELT teachers to teach abroad.

A course that prepared English language teachers to teach in outer and expanding-circle countries was the specialist Diploma in Teaching English to Speakers of Asian Languages (Dip TESAL) (Kirkpatrick and Prescott, 1996). While this course focused on Asia, its aims could be adopted by other TESOL courses. The Dip TESAL was designed to produce teachers who:

- have knowledge of the systems of English and how these differ from selected Asian languages;
- are able to analyse the specific linguistic difficulties that speakers of non-Indo-European languages can face in the learning of English and are able to adopt strategies to help their learners overcome these difficulties;
- recognise that English is represented by a range of varieties and that these include varieties that have developed in Asia;
- recognise that these different varieties of English comprise different but complete linguistic systems and represent different cultures;
- understand the importance for English language teachers to be bilingual and multicultural;
- understand the role(s) of English(es) in their teaching community and ensure that this understanding informs their practice; and
- are able to evaluate teaching methods and materials and are able to adapt their teaching styles and methods to suit the needs of different contexts and cultures.

13.5 Conclusion

Governments, ministries and employers, particularly those in outer and expanding-circle countries, need to recognise the advantages associated with multilingual local teachers who are expert users of English. Far from being classified as somehow inferior to native speaker teachers, as is all too often the case at present, these teachers should in fact be held up as strong role and linguistic models for their students. It is these teachers upon whom governments and institutions should be spending their resources to ensure that they receive training and opportunities for professional development. In turn, those providing this training and professional development need to recognise the importance and value of courses that include the components listed above. And while there is always room for the multilingual and culturally aware native speaker teacher, the policy of employing untrained, monolingual native speakers as English language teachers should be systematically opposed by the profession. Well-trained, multilingual and culturally sensitive and sophisticated teachers can best teach today's learners of English, the overwhelming majority of whom are bilingual and who are learning in culturally diverse contexts for an extraordinarily complex range of needs, stretching from local to international.

In the Introduction I listed five key themes that underpinned this book. They were:

(a) that variation is natural, normal and continuous – and that ELT professionals must establish a tolerance and understanding of variation;

(b) that, while prejudice against varieties is likely to occur, these prejudices are simply that – prejudices;

(c) that the differences between all varieties, both native and nativised, are similar and comparable;

(d) that context and learner needs should determine the variety to be taught; and

(e) that multilingual non-native teachers represent ideal teachers in many ELT contexts.

I hope that this book has illustrated these key themes in an approachable and stimulating way and that it has helped develop an understanding of the many complexities surrounding the spread and development of different varieties of English. Above all, I hope that readers can appreciate that English is not solely the property of its native speakers, but that it can, through the processes described in this book, develop new varieties that reflect the cultural norms and meet the functional needs of its speakers. In the teaching of English, therefore, the goals set and the models adopted should be appropriate and relevant to the norms and needs of the learners and users of English.

Appendix – Transcripts of samples of varieties of English

Contents

Chapter 9: Englishes of South-East Asia – colonial descendants?
Track 47: Muhammad Haji Salleh, *On a dry bund*
Track 48: Ghulam-Sarwar Yousof, *The Midnight Satay-Vendor*

Chapter 10: Emerging Englishes: Hong Kong and China
Tracks 49–56: Hong Kong professionals (KT and KC)
Not recorded: Louise Ho, *Hong Kong riots*
Not recorded: Louise Ho, *End of an era*
Not recorded: Agnes Lam, *Yellow flowers on a battlefield*

Chapter 11: English as a *lingua franca*
Track 57: Example 1: A Filipina (P) and a Bruneian (B)
Track 58: Example 2: A Filipina (P), a Bruneian (B) and a Vietnamese (V)
Track 59: Example 3: A Cambodian (C), an Indonesian (I) and a Singaporean (S)
Track 60: Example 4: An Indonesian (I), a Malaysian (M) and a Cambodian (C)

The Transcripts

As a general rule, listeners might like to listen to these excerpts before consulting the transcripts. In this way the relative intelligibility/unintelligibility of these varieties can be better appreciated. Please note that the excerpts here are simply intended to give listeners the opportunity to listen to a selection of different varieties of English. They are *not* supposed to provide listeners with material from which they can make a systematic comparison of, for example, the vowel sounds across varieties of English.

The selections range from informal dialogues (the excerpts in Chapter 6, for example) to poetry readings (the excerpts in Chapter 7, for example). Where I thought it would be helpful, I have provided 'translations' of the excerpts and/or the meanings of some of the vocabulary items.

I would like to acknowledge the help and generosity of the voices here. They include Karen Higgins, Thiru Kandiah, Marion Johnston, 'tope Omoniyi, Sivanes Phillipson, Claudia Sullivan and others who preferred to remain anynymous. Particular expressions of gratitude are reserved for Marion Johnston and 'tope Omoniyi, who provided not only their voices, but also their poems.

Chapter 4: Variation and impurity in British English

Examples of the Doric

When you listen to the examples of the Doric variety on the CD, pay attention to the use of the distinctive phonological, syntactic and lexical features of the variety. In particular, note the use of '-it' as a past tense/past participle marker, the use of initial /f/ where other varieties might use /w/ and the 'new' vocabulary.

Laad O Pairts (cited in Kynoch, D. (1997) *Doric for Swots*, Dalkeith: The Scottish Cultural Press, pp12–13, read by Marion Johnston)

This short story describes a boyhood incident in the life of a local millionaire, called Geordie Peerie. He grew up in a poor home that had only two rooms. If people wanted to wash, they had to use the sink. Geordie has just started to wash.

Laad O Pairts

Track 1

'Nyaakit as the day the howdie skelpit his dowp, Geordie hid ae legit in ower the sink an ae fit in the nammel basin, fin, o a suddenty, there wis a chappin at the door. Fit a fleg he got. Niver myn, he thocht, he widna hae tae ging tae the door. His mither wis ben the hoose. She wid awa tae the door; an wi him in the state he wis in, she widna tak onybody in. He haird her opening the door. "Och, it's yersel, Mr McKillop." (The meenister!) "Come awa in!"

Track 2

Fit wis she thinking aboot? Geordie yarkit his fit oot o the basin, ruggit tee the windae curtains tae hide aa the troke at the sink, grabbit a tool fae the press an his claes aff a cheer an skelpit for aa he wis worth tae the curtaint wardrobe in the far neuk of the livin-room; jinkit ahin't an pullt tee the curtain jist as he saa the meenister's haat comin' roon the door.

Track 3

An there, he dreept and chittert, file the meenister and his mither newsed awa aboot ae thing an another; the kirk and the kyre; the faimily; the loons and their skweel wark. Geordie wis weel able tae spik for himself bit thocht he'd mebbe better nae stick his heid roon the bit cloot hingin in front o him an say "I'm deein fine, thank ye kynly."

Track 4

At laist, the meenister rase, said a gweed-wird or twaa and gaed awa tae gie some ither body a fleg. Geordie's mither, fin she cam back intae the livin-room, wis fair stammy-gastert, fin she saa a near-nyaakit loon faar naebody hid bin afore. "I winnert fit had come ower ye", says she "bit I hidna time tae think ower muckle aboot it."

Track 5

It wis a moment of revalashun. Geordie made up his myn that sic a thing would never happen again. "Gin iver I mak a meelyin", he thocht, "I'm gaan tae get masel a new mither."'

Vocabulary

Laad O Pairts	a versatile, educated (young) man
howdie	midwife
skelpit	belted (note metaphorical use, and use of '–it' past tense marker)
dowp	buttocks
fleg	scare
ruggit tee	tugged closed
troke	stuff, things
jink	avoid
dreep	drip
skweel wark	school work

cloot	cloth
gweed wird	prayer (good word)
stammygaster	an unexpected shock

Translation

Naked as when the midwife slapped his bottom Geordie had a leg in over the sink and a foot in the enamel basin, when, suddenly, there was a knocking at the door. What a fright he got. But never mind, he thought, he would not have to go to the door. His mother was inside the house. She would go (away) to the door; and with him in the state he was in, she would not let anybody in. He heard her opening the door. "Oh, it's you Mr McKillop." (The Presbyterian Minister!) "Come in!"

What was she thinking about? Geordie yanked his foot out of the basin, tugged closed the window curtains to hide all the stuff at the sink, grabbed a tool for the press and his clothes off the chair and belted for all he was worth to the wardrobe in the far corner of the living room; jumped behind it and pulled the curtain to just as he saw the minister's hat come round the door.

And there he dripped and shook while the minister and his mother chatted about one thing and another: the church and the choir; the family; the children and their school work. Geordie was quite able to speak for himself but thought he maybe better not stick his head round the bit of cloth hanging in front of him and say "I'm doing just fine, thank you kindly."

At last, the minister rose, said a prayer or two and went away to give someone else a fright. Geordie's mother, when she came back into the living room, was completely astonished when she saw a near-naked boy where nobody had been before. "I wondered what had happened to you", she said, "but I didn't have time to think too much about it."

It was a moment of revelation. Geordie made up his mind that such a thing would never happen again. "If ever I make a million", he thought, "I'm going to get myself a new mother."

Excerpts from *Gamrie Wis a Magic Place* (written and read by Marion Johnston)

Track 6

'I wrote this because young folk nowadays always say the're bored and we were never bored when we were young. It's called:'

Gamrie Wis a Magic Place

Gamrie wis a magic place tae play fin I was young
But the things t' we'd get up till as yet remains unsung
Bit ah thocht it recht tae tell ye aboot foo we eest tae play
Be it summer or weenter, ere wis nivver a lang aneuch day

Het or caal, rain or shine, we was aye rael well contentit
'n' boret wis a wird't hidnae been inventit.

I quines wis makin milkies ablow i new bank
I loons wis raikin for beg craibs doon aside i shank
Pillars 'n' hardy safties, roddicks 'n' green chats
Pickan thoozins a' buckies, 'n' sailin hame made yaats.

Fishin wis a favourite thing 'ere wis nae occupation tae marra't
A bit a steck fae yer mother's fire 'n' a hyook fae the tin 'n i garrett
Wi twa/three fet a herrin twine, wappit on b'some aal mannie
A limpet for bait, we wis proper set it made a nae bad wannee.

Bit best of aa wis fin we got snaa ah'd be oot o' ma bed lik a rocket
I hale toon gid hushlin mad especially if i road was blockit
I fishermen cudnae get oot o' the toon 'n' snaaploo cudnae get in
It wis oot wi yer sledge 'n' scoor aff i roost 'n' then i fun wid begin

'Er's nae a better feelin wi i frosty ween in yer face
I sparks fae i runners fleein 'n' i runny afore ye lik glaiss
Ah still get hushlin fivver fin i grun's aa' covert wi snaa
Bit ah've still ma sledge in i sheddie ah cudnae gie it awa

It's affa fine t' look back on bit aa'thing comes t' an en'
Oh fit ah wid gie for a 'ear t' dee't aa ower again.

Translation

Gamrie was a Wonderful Place
Gamrie was a wonderful place to play when I was young
But things we used to get up to as yet remain unsung
But I thought it was right to tell you about where we used to play
Be it summer or winter, there was never a long enough day

Hot or cold, rain or shine, we were always very contented
And bored was a word that had not been invented.

The girls were making mud pies below the new bank
The boys were scraping for big crabs beside the slope
Small crabs and other crabs, frog spawn and small haddock
Picking thousands of whelks and sailing home-made yachts.

Fishing was a favourite thing, there was no occupation to match it
A bit of stick from your mother's fire and a hook from the tin in the garret
With two or three feet of herring twine wrapped on by some old man
A limpet for bait and we were ready. It made a good fishing rod.

But best of all was when we got snow, I'd be out of my bed like a rocket
The whole town would go completely mad, especially if the road was blocked

The fishermen could not get out of the town and the snow plough could not get in
It was out with your sled and scour off the rust and then the fun would begin

There's no better feeling with a frosty wind in your face
The sparks of the runners flying and the run in front of you like glass
Ah I still get shaking fever when the ground is all covered with snow
But I've still got my sled in the shed, I couldn't give that away

It's fine to look back on but all things come to an end
Oh what I would give to do it all over again.

Chapter 5: The powerful variety: American English

Examples of English spoken in the southern United States

Karen is a white American female who lives in North Carolina. In these two excerpts, she tells us something about her life. Listeners may find it interesting to compare and contrast her experiences of growing up and her career with those of women in their own cultures.

Karen Higgins (Part 1)

Track 7

My name is Karen Higgins. I live in North Carolina. I er . . . speak with a typical southern accent. I was born and raised in the um central part of North Carolina . . . near Charlotte. I have had people who er tell me that dialects are different from one end of this state to the other, so I've I've not found that to be true myself because um I don't know, I think we all sound the same.

Track 8

Anyway I er I have been many places where my accent was remarked upon. I have had um people in California make fun of the way we talk. . . Of course we are bad to drop our 'gs' and the tireder I get and the more I drink of course the more 'gs' I drop,

Track 9

so we're 'drinkin' instead of 'drinking' . . . I've also er had the experience I've been to New York several times, New York City, and had the experience of er meeting people there who I could hardly understand because they talk so fast. It's true that southerners do talk a little bit slow at times . . .

Track 10

so . . . New York, yeah, I I have had problems with some of those accents. I have um pretty much lived in North Carolina my entire life and worked for a short time in South Carolina but that's the extent of of places I've actually lived . . . I do have a sister who lived in Germany for some years so I have visited ah Germany, Switzerland, Austria, Italy . . . places like that erm . . . where of course my poor attempts at German or my sad attempts at French are erm pretty much laughed at, but people did appreciate the effort. . . .

Track 11

I also have a brother who lives in Hawaii and ah there is a type of dialect there that's a little bit difficult to um understand, actually they they make up some of their own words which is pretty interesting, but erm at least in Hawaii no one ever made fun of my southern accent. . . .

Track 12

I really don't have any anecdotes for you um aside from the um the run-ins I have had with people from California who made fun of my accent. I do um I do realize that I probably . . . talk different when I'm with different people um – I've I've noticed quite a few people do that – I I use proper English more when I'm with people from other areas who do not have the southern accent . . .

Karen Higgins (Part 2)

Track 13

This is Karen Higgins again. I wanted to talk a bit about some of the jobs I've had. The first job I ever had . . . I was six years old and I picked cotton. We . . . got three cents a pound for every pound we picked . . . needless to say not one of my more favourite jobs

Track 14

er I was raised on a farm. We had dairy cows and crops so the um the second job I ever had was . . . probably picking strawberries. The farm work we didn't get paid for but um these were jobs we did for other farmers in the area so picking strawberries I believe if I'm not mistaken we made fifty cents an hour . . .

Track 15

So as time went on ahm probably the worst job I ever had was picking peaches. It was hot and the peaches were fuzzy and the fuzz made you itch – it was just miserable but . . . those were character-building experiences I guess you would say

Track 16

Ah time went on I had a brief career as a Volkswagen mechanic ahm I was living in a place, Grandfather Mountain as a matter of fact, where there were very very few jobs and the jobs that you could get were service jobs cleaning motels uhm had a brief stint making baskets, things like that, and a federal program became available where you could get money to go to technical school.

Track 17

Unfortunately the only er courses you could take were automotive mechanics or machine shop technology so . . . I decided since my Dad and one of my brothers were mechanics that I wanted to learn how to do that . . . went to school for a year and then went to work at Volkswagen and I was the first female Volkswagen mechanic in North Carolina certified to work on Volkswagens. That job ah lasted about a year and a half, got tired of all the grit and grease under my fingernails, so I decided to go back to school . . . and became interested in electronics, the only electronics-er-type course they had at the time was called biomedical electronics which I thought I'd give a go even though I did not like hospitals ah or the way they smelled but this was to learn about working on electronic equipment used in hospitals, which I thought would be very interesting

Track 18

ehm the more I ahm learned the more I liked this because I found out hospitals didn't smell the way that they used to when I was a kid. The disinfectant smell was not so horrible and ah of course we working on equipment didn't have to see some of the grosser things like the nurses do . . . so that's what I ended up doing as my er main career, was being a biomedical electronics technician. Which is really fun and a good thing to do and much much better than picking cotton or peaches or strawberries . . .

An example of 'General' American

Claudia is a white American female who was born in New York, but who grew up in Maine, a state in the north-west of the United States. She has also spent several years of her life as a university lecturer in Singapore. In this excerpt she talks about the prejudices against her Maine accent which she has encountered.

Claudia Sullivan

Track 19

My name is Claudia Sullivan. I was born in New York State, New York City ehm but I was only a year old before we moved to Maine, my parents were moved to Maine, and I learned to talk ehm in Maine . . . where they have they have a what we call a 'down east' accent and until I went away to university . . . in Boston, I spoke like a Mainer.

Track 20

er I did have the advantage of my parents having a New York accent ehm particularly pronouncing 'r's where in Maine we didn't pronounce the 'r's at all, and my sister also had learned to talk in New York so she didn't sound like I did. But I went to Boston University and within twenty-four hours I had adopted my New York accent again because everyone was saying 'Oh isn't that cute', 'Say that again', because they had never heard anyone from Maine before ehm it was very easy for me because I had the background of of New York people.

Track 21

I of course don't think I have an accent ehm I my husband is from Boston and he does seem to have a very strong Boston accent; mine seems to be I think because I'm er more timid or less secure in my language or in myself that I tend to adopt whatever I'm around. Ah as for prejudice with accents I don't I really can't think of any that I feel. I worked in various places in the world in Singapore and in the West Indies and in Hawaii, in Florida, and I never really had any problem with it. The only problem I had with my accent was when I was going to university . . . ehm the accents that I find that are difficult to understand are ehm southern accents when they speak really fast but now that I'm living in the south I'm beginning to pick up on them ehm I don't really . . . I don't really find any other ones difficult to understand.

An example of African American

Tim Kane lives in the northern United States in Pennsylvania but has relatives from the South and has worked in the South. Note how he gives examples of some of the features of southern American speech which were considered in Chapter 5 itself, in particular the lengthening of vowel sounds (Tim uses the term 'voweled out'), and the use of the words 'finnin' and 'fixin to'. When talking to his friends at home, however, he uses a different speech style. For example, when he says "yo bro 'sup?" he is saying something like "Hello brother, what's up?" In this talk he provides more evidence for the existence of the 'identity–communication continuum' (Chapter 1). He speaks a more 'standard' variety at work and two quite distinct varieties when at home in Philadelphia, or with his peers in North Carolina.

Tim Kane

Track 22

My name is Tim Kane. I'm originally from Philadelphia Pennsylvania. My father is a southerner from North Carolina. My mother grew up in Philadelphia but her parents grew up in New England. When I go home I find myself talking with my boys and it's more of a "yo bro 'sup"[1] ehm "how ya doin'?" Everything is everything you know it's er very quick, very casual relaxed sound er quite a bit of a difference between most of the conversation or "conversatin'" that I have to do outside of that in the business but er you do find yourself falling back into it it's a part of the colour of speech it's part of the colour of music music is very big in Philadelphia.

Track 23

I find that when I go down South to visit my family down there it takes actually several hours before I can really understand what they're saying ehm it's a completely different sound, it's voweled out where a simple word like 'had' just lasts for days it seems like. A simple example of that is a phrase like "are you going to go to the store?". In Philadelphia with my boys it would probably be more something like "hey brother you ready to head out?" or er "are you ready to bounce to the store?" and in the South it would be something like "Tim you finnin' to roll to the store?" and that phrase alone [laughs] was enough to send me into confusion. I didn't know what 'finnin' was, but it's 'fixin', sometimes it's er an amalgamation of a few different words er but it all means 'prepared', 'ready', 'set to go'.

Track 24

My father grew up in central North Carolina. He moved to Philadelphia in his late teens early twenties. He still holds very much the southern cadence of his speech I always laugh at him because one of his little expressions you know before we're getting ready for dinner is "er Tim you wash your hand?", making hand a singular er is one of my favourite little things that he does. He also er likes to ask me er "we're going out to the store later on today, I want you to get right" ehm another one of those 'get prepared' you know er "if you fixin' to go to the store you better get right".

---

[1]   Note the shortening in "yo bro' 'sup" where bro' is short for 'brother' and 'sup for 'what's up?'

Track 25

> I went to school in Western Pennsylvania which has a-nother speech pattern that I was unfamiliar with it's not a huge difference but there are other regionalisms and I think it was living out there that made me realize that Philadelphia had its own set of speech patterns and unique phrases. From there, spending time in the South ah in the Virginia Tidewater area and having worked in Jackson Mississippi and in Florida which also has er more of a southern sound than I guess I expected, ehm these experiences introduced me to the idea or at least to a better understanding that your speech can set you apart.

Chapter 6: A younger 'cousin' and an indigenous variety

The first two excerpts come from the Radio Australia programme, 'Australia All Over', which is introduced by Ian Macnamara. His nickname, 'Macca', is a shortened or 'clipped' version of his surname. He is 'I' in these dialogues. In this programme he is interviewing people at a *bush* or country show in a place called Dalgety, which is a small town in New South Wales. In the first dialogue he is talking to a shearer called Malcolm (M) and in the second to a truck driver called Craig (C).

Ian Macnamara (Part 1)

Track 26

I: Good day, what's your name?

M: Malcolm

I: What do you do Malcolm sorry?

M: Oh shearer, labourer, whatever I can find

I: And what are you doing here today?

M: Oh just helping out with the dogs. I'm just out . . . putting the sheep out for the um blokes to work around

I: With their dogs?

M: Yeah

I: And so where do you live?

M: Ah Beloka, about fifteen ks out of out of Dalgety

I: What's that like?

M: Good. Excellent place

I: And where do you go shearing? Just around local or

M: Yeah, just locally. Near Jindabyne, Dalgety, that's about about as far as I go.

I: That's a top hat, that one

M: Ah, it's about buggered now (audience laughter)

I: That's why I say it's a top one, it's great

M: Yeah, they just get comfortable and you've got to throw 'em away.

I: Nice to talk to you.

M: Yeah, nice to talk to you.

Ian Macnamara (Part 2)

Track 27

I: 's Craig. How are you Craig? What What's your story?

C: I come from Cooma, a truck driver ah during the week and got a bit of a block up the back of Adaminaby

I: bit of a block?

C: yeah bit of a bush block, a few horses out there yep

I: And what do you what do you run sheep or

C: a few horses yeah

I: you like riding and stuff

C: yeah you go up the eh up round the back of Adaminaby there yep

I: a bit cool up there I suppose

C: oh yeah we camp out there a fair bit we've had the dam frozen right over and the dog can go skating across that and eh (audience laughter) goes well

I: that's cold

C: yeah it is cold yeah yeah but it's good to see you up here

I: oh it's a pleasure to be er you got em a little house there and stuff have you or?

C: no I live in Cooma got a em got a house in Cooma and live in

I: so go camp you camp up there?

C: yeah camp up there

I: God it must freeze

C: oh it is a bit cool ehm yeah but we have a good time

I: he's the outdoor type Kel he's he's the this bloke's the outdoor type that's a good hat too that one

Track 28

C: yeah so em now we have a good time up there

I: and where do you drive your truck Craig just around the local area?

C: no a Sydney to Canberra er nearly everyday of the week yeah so we keep pretty busy during the week yeah there's no time to rest so

I: is there many prangs on that freeway or hold-ups and stuff?

C: oh yeah now and then they sort of go scrub a bit and yeah

I: there was a big one on ah Friday of course ehm blocked it for a couple of hours but ehm being a truck driver it'd seem to me to be a stressful sort of occupation

C: oh if you can get your sleep in there and sort a you know make sure you get your sleep there and have good rests yeah you should er sort of come good even if a ten minute rest yeah really perks you back up again yeah no worries yeah

I: Craig nice to talk to you

C: thanks Macca for coming up here

I: it's a pleasure please thank Craig and Richard

C: thank you

John Williamson

The excerpt below comes from a Radio National interview with John Williamson for the programme 'The Children of the Bush'. John Williamson is a well-known Australian folk singer, and *True Blue* is one of his most famous songs.

Track 29

'The most important images of Australia, to me, are the natural ones ehm and I'm talking about the colour, for instance, the red ochre, the shape of gum leaves, ah. Gum trees themselves which are completely unique to this country, and ah, they're evergreen, um. To me there's so much more colour in gumtrees than than the first Europeans realized er. And they are very much a part of a my psyche now as a as a sixth-generation Aussie I really feel I'm starting to eh feel the spirit of the land that the Aborigines obviously have felt for thousands of years.

Track 30

Hey true blue, don't say you've gone
Say you've knocked off for a smoko and you'll be back later on
Hey, true blue

I find urban Aussies um I perform to as more urban Aussies than I do to anybody else um and even when it comes to big towns in the country and ahum because they're all very similar now everything's they all get their Coles and they all got their Targets and they've all got their McDonalds and they've all got the same TV programs they watch, but I think one thing that Australians have in common is is that most of 'em have some sort of connection with the bush and I think they like like to think they have, I mean if they know a farmer that's out in the bush that they can go and visit that's important to them.

Track 31

ehm I'd I'd say the majority of Australians find it very important to have that that bush er connection or or escape and I I think it's important to Australians that we've got that wide horizon. I think that's the difference between an Australian and a European is that that we know that we can just drive for hours and it's in our psyche that we can just get in a car and drive for hours without running eh without needing a passport.'

Chapter 7: Englishes of the subcontinent

These examples are Sri Lankan poems or excerpts of poems read by the Sri Lankan scholar Thiru Kandiah. He first introduces the poems and then reads them. Of the four poems, the first two are by the female poet Yasmine Gooneratne and the second two are by Lakdasa Wikkramasinha. Gooneratne is one of Sri Lanka's finest poets and she uses the standard language to accommodate Lankan experiences. The first poem, *Menika* is the name of a domestic servant. The poem talks about an arranged marriage or match, which remains typical, especially in the villages. In the final verse the poet talks about a girl's coming of age. This is a very important occasion in Sri Lanka and a time that is very important for the girl's mother.

Thiru Kandiah: introduction

Track 32

'I've chosen the poems I'm going to read not only because I like them and because I think they are good poems in their own right, but because I think they will help dispel a common misconception about new Englishes like Lankan English. The misconception is that such Englishes may be seen as some kind of minimalist entities defined by those odd exotic-sounding unusual forms which are simply suited to the expression of minimal thoughts and simple everyday experience in pure colloquial settings. These poems will, I hope, demonstrate that Lankan English is a versatile entity which has a strong systematic nature which gives an important place to both everyday spoken and formal standard modes of expression and which is also adapted immediately to a range of complex imaginative, emotional and intellectual experience.'

(Some feminists might find the poem unacceptable as the woman never blames the man; but she does stand tall and prevails over her unfortunate circumstances.)

Track 33

Menika by Yasmine Gooneratne

Deft-handed, swirling rice-grains in clear water,
pouring the white stream from pot to pot
she said:
I would like to go back to the village next week
There is a court case
I am reclaiming my children, two daughters, from their father
He has another woman.

Neat-handed, kneading coriander and cumin
on the smooth stone
she said:
My father made the marriage
There were good fields and much fine property

My father inspected the fields, my brother went with him,
They all agreed it was a good match
Two weeks after the marriage he brought her back to the house

The pestle rising, falling, in her practised hands
the grain in the mortar crumbling to powder
she said:
We lived eighteen years in that house
My children with me in one room, she with him in the other
One day a relation of his came in, asking for a measure of rice
I did not think to refuse it
That night he came home drunk, and said I was giving away the household goods

Spreading the grain in the sun to dry
she said:
When he beat me before the neighbours I sent for my father
He came and took me away
When we signed the register at the Police Station
the Sergeant said: What a man is this,
To make such a shameful to-do over a measure of rice!
She looks after my children well, they tell me
But they are daughters, can I allow them to become women
And far away from me?

On the day of the court case, her skin smoothly powdered,
a crimson sari knotted at her neat waist, her hair
combed into shining coils on her slender neck
She said:
He is a good man
There is no fault in him

The second poem is an extract from a long poem by Gooneratne. The lizard referred to is the house lizard or ghekko. Many superstitions are built around it. For example, if one is leaving the house and the ghekko chirps one is advised to come back into the house and only go out again sometime later. The first two and final stanzas are written in standard while the rest of the poem is in colloquial Sri Lankan English. 'King Kong' is the derisive nickname given by a junior to his boss. In this poem, Gooneratne is dealing with the decline of Sri Lanka into decadence and chaos.

Track 34

From *The Lizard's Cry* by Yasmine Gooneratne

Slowly
light dies.
Gently

breath recedes.
Where then shall we turn?
To whom are we to render our petition?

Somewhere along a corridor of files
six floors up above a seething city
a bell rings
a voice replies

   What is this I say can't get a call
   you fellows talking talking all
   the time on this phone you're telling me
   this is Government business Ha ha ha
   Look here Head Office rang up complaints being made
   about those missing items Then some foreigners it seems paid
   a visit here (our chaps also) and they have said
   we should do something about the lava-
   tory too Trouble is I say that Silva is
   a soft chap never moves from his chair His
   people can't be controlled naturally This
   is your problem Melvin not ours
   I think you better advise the chap Just tell
   Head Office rang up tell they'll give us hell
   if things don't improve Bad for us no Melvin all this talk What? Can you hear
   me I say another thing just
   now I heard them say your section must
   shift into Grandpass I can fix it yes
   but you must also ha ha ha remember
   us Good good good Glad to help a friend
   Goodlooker your boss has got himself Congratulations
   boy I'd like to give her some dictation myself Send
   her along sometime So how's the
   wife and kids Regarding
   the other matter No need to tell I told I say King
   Kong on line son I'll be hanging
   up now Cheer-o cheer-o Yes sir Morning sir
   All the mail in order sir Unlock
   the files Watch the clock
   Grease a palm Pass the buck
   Our responsibility stops here

Watchman of evil, confessor of our present anguish,
where then shall we turn?

As crowding beasts, clawing each other down,
snarl for the fading light as for a bone,
to what god can we render our petition?

The next two poems are by the late poet, Lakdasa Wikkramasinha. He had an instinctive feel for everyday language and liked to used Lankan names in his poems. Note 'Haniketta' and 'Iddamalgoda' in the first poem and the woman's name, 'Dunkiriniya', in the second, for example.

The first poem is about a farmer who is also a poet. 'Walauva' refers to a feudal house and 'yala' is the smaller of the two annual harvests reaped in Sri Lanka.

Track 35

From *The Life of the Folk-Poet Ysinno* by Lakdasa Wikkramasinha

Ysinno cut the bamboo near Haniketta,
And from those wattles made his hut
And had nothing to cover it with, nothing
Like a hundred and sixty
Bales of straw

So he made his way to the Walauva at Iddamalgoda
And to the Menike said how poor he was,
And how from his twenties he had made those lines of song
Swearing before her all his fealties.
So she said, Wait for the yala
Harvest and take the straw

Ysinno said, O the rains are coming near,
My woman fretting, her kid will get all wet.

Then the kind Menike said, O then
You take what straw you need from the behind shed.
And Ysinno being a folk poet, and his lines being not all dead,
The benison of the Menike of Iddamalgoda
Lives even today.

In his second poem Lakdasa Wikkramasinha writes about a cobra who has killed a woman. The cobra is venerated in Sri Lanka, even though it is poisonous and capable of killing people. In the poem the cobra is killed after killing the woman, and people from surrounding villages come to see it. The real beauty and sadness of the poem lies in the last three lines when we learn who has died.

'Paramitas' are the disciplines Buddhists are expected to observe on their way to Nirvana.

Track 36

The Cobra by Lakdasa Wikkramasinha

Your great hood was like a flag
hung up there
in the village.
Endlessly the people came to Weragoda -
watched you (your eyes like braziers),
standing somewhat afar.
They stood before you in obeisance. Death,
the powers of the paramitas, took you to heaven
however.

The sky, vertical, is where you are now
shadowing the sun, curling round and round my mind.
They whisper death-stories –
but it was only my woman Dunkiriniya,
the very lamp of my heart,
that died.

Chapter 8: Voices from Africa

Two quite distinctive examples of African Englishes are provided here. The first is of White South African in conversation with an Australian radio presenter and the second is of the Nigerian scholar and poet, 'tope Omoniyi, reading his own poetry

The first excerpt is an interview with a Soweto Flying Squad (SFS) policeman whose first language is English. Soweto (South West Township) is a black suburb of Johannesburg. The interview was conducted by Pieta O' Shaughnessy (POS), for Curtin University's Radio 6NR.

In the interview, a white South African police officer talks about his job. He is a Soweto Flying squad officer who has come over to a university in Australia to work with students and staff during a brief visit as a visiting lecturer.

Note that the speaker uses a standard variety of English, as he wants to communicate with people from outside his own community. By simply listening to the interview the listener can determine the relative intelligibility of the speaker's *accent*, however. Some listeners may find this variety of English particularly difficult to understand until they gain some familiarity with it.

Interview with a Soweto Flying Squad (SFS) policeman, conducted by Pieta O'Shaughnessy (POS)

Track 37

SFS: The students on the Social Sciences body, the Department, we invite actively involved in a role play with them, the role plays and scenarios, which we've depicted for the people which we've set out for them and it's to you know it's just to get to know the guys and to show them how how the things are done being active being an active participant

POS: Can you can you give us an example of a role play say, just er give er outline for me a role play you might do with the students in this way?

Track 38

SFS: OK the ones one of the ones the role play that we did on Tuesday was a scenario in Orlando West. We'd have er a landlord with seven shacks in the back with all the tenants there as well and you'd have illegal immigrants staying there and there was a squabble apparently with one of the tenants and the landowner and ehm and er the er on the rent and the electricity issue and there was a a fight ensued and she was beaten up severely or she was stabbed and he was also beaten up. And I have to get all the people together a hostile crowd the ANC activists and erm your community leaders and things like that. So everyone it's it's a debate where every-one comes together and you you know everyone just just climbs in and you see how you how the policing is done as such

Track 39

POS: So how long have you been in the police force, in the Flying Squad?

SFS: Ehm I've been in the force for three and a half years and in Soweto itself for three years

POS: Why did you join the police force in the first place, was it has it always been some-thing you wanted to do?

SFS: Yes definitely I've always been I've always wanted to help people and it's well I've had brothers who were in the police as well so it's you know I think it's pretty it comes down that way

Track 40

POS: What would be the most rewarding aspect of your work?

SFS: It's just you see people appreciate the work you do and . . . and to help someone who really does need help . . . and ehm that's basically it it's just you know to ren-der a service to the people a good service

POS: And what would be the most challenging or perhaps frightening aspect of what you do?

SFS: It's the that your life is always at risk, there's a a big a big risk involved, you never know when or what's going to happen when it's going to happen that's the biggest fear that you might lose your life in the line of duty

POS: How many how many officers for example have lost their lives in the line of duty in the Soweto Flying Squad in the last four months?

SFS: None in the last four months. A lot of a lot of the guys have committed suicide due to the stress and stress-related incidents. We've lost ehm in the last in our relief in the last eight months we've lost two guys to suicides and two guys have died in accidents and things like that

Track 41

POS: Have you had any ehm perception of the fact that those people have been under such stress? I mean what kind of incidents would have concerned them to that degree that they might commit suicide?

SFS: I mean it's all . . . everything you see . . . I mean you you think you can cope with it, but you can't really. It's it's it's in your subconscious most of the time and you think you're a strong character you can handle it I mean you see it everyday of your life and one day you just er I don't know you just snap and it's everything just happens from there. You become depressive and I mean a person you think you're tough you can handle it but you can't. It's I mean it's you need psychological help and that type of thing

Track 42

POS: How old are you?

SFS: er twenty-two

POS: How do you feel?

SFS: About what?

POS: I mean do you feel that you're in any way stressed or that you're under that kind of strain?

SFS: I do feel that I am stressed but I've been to a psychologist a couple of times and he explained to me OK what your problem is and give you a bit of counselling and that. Nothing to be disgraced about I'm only I'm not embarrassed about it. I mean it helps me in my work as well it pertains to my work so it's it definitely helps me

POS: Have you have you felt like you ever wanted to do anything else?

SFS: What do you mean another type of career? No not at all. I love my work it's I enjoy it thoroughly. I mean to provide a service for the people it's great. It's it's funny a lot of people aren't too they don't derive a lot of job satisfaction from their work and their careers. Actually that's the most important thing it's the job satisfaction

The next excerpts are examples of Nigerian English and are read by the Nigerian scholar and poet 'tope Omoniyi. He reads four of his own poems, from his 2001 collection *Farting Presidents and Other Poems*, Ibadan: Kraft Books.

Track 43

Let them who have ears hear by 'tope Omoniyi

Let them who have ears hear
feed them from fibres of history
on the graveless end of tyrants

teach them from signs of the times
that these are not rumours and murmurs
but the war cries of distressed gods
targeting bullet vendors
and two-kobo Generals

let them who have ears hear
in the barracks and Government House
that only dogs destined to stray
defy the hunter's rally

those who wrestle with the gods
contend with the Unseen
the Mighty Sigidi, spirit warrior
making a mockery of letter bombs
and tanks

for a nation on cliff-edge
only a half-tilt will quench the appetite
of angry gods
the mightiest will fall to a pulp
commoners will stretch their creases
and wait for coronation next season.

Track 44

I do not know anymore by 'tope Omoniyi

I do not know what to do with the leaders of my clan
I do not know what to make of their pacifism
all night long they preach the gospel of non-violence
but they hang at dawn
and are buried at noon

I do not know what to do about the rage in my veins
I do not know what to make of this rebel urge
all night long I hatch plans of assault against the enemy
then bow to elderly wisdom
and carry coffins

I do not know what to do anymore
to rouse the world
I do not know how to mould
their bashful threats into bombs
all night long they warn these sons of a gun
but daybreak serenades an unholy swoon
and raises a toast to enemies of our moon

I do not know anything anymore
but one – we're a tribe of warriors
when my time comes
my crimson stream will join the ritual flow
    I shall embrace their gallows with a smile
    and a prayer that our passing brings
    strength and defiance to pall bearers.

Track 45

Midwives or a deluge? by 'tope Omoniyi

we have witnessed gross abominations
we have seen the castration of justice
on court-room slabs
we have swallowed fat frustrations
at the coronation of falsehood

    but now
    gales and floods of cleansing
    or promises of them
    flood through our land
    parting anal feathers
    and exposing the foul frames

    of vicious uniformed contrivances!
    fixed forensic findings revealed
    vindicate victims of tutored miscarriage
    after the savaging of Ogoni
    fresh hunt now for stale villains
    royal victims craving judicial rebirth

but how long more
these gales and floods of cleansing?
how potent this royal injunction
for the burnishing of courtrooms?

our stables still fetid with mess
from unbridled stallions on patrol
horrid stench of stillbirths
clench still to Wisdom Wigs

and so several yet languish
    for innocence
    perhaps in Kirikiri
    many more are hounded in the streets and parks
    in homes and pubs
    from Benin to Birnin Kebbi

and as we approach the end
of our generation's tether
we wonder

> if commissioned midwives can deliver us
> from the miscarriage of Wigs and goons
> and the tragic innocence of folks

or our stables must wait for a cleansing deluge.

Track 46

The dogs of Baidoa by 'tope Omoniyi

daily
my innerwards turn
at the ghastly
sight
of their savagery
on kith and kin

these dogs of Baidoa
court my hate
with their bumper
health and crease-free
suits
besides kinsmen
on death row
chestbones, skulls and all
covered with thin slices
of death satin skin

dogs want to be
presidents in Baidoa
but do they have
courage to sit over a
parliament of ghosts
> for their clansmen
> have departed in hunger
> starved beyond the
depths of catacombs
they raise a voice
for the union of the dead
some day soon
the whirl of enraged spirits
unearthed will choke

the barking dogs
of Baidoa
and castrate their dreams.

Chapter 9: Englishes of South-East Asia – colonial descendants?

Poetry again provides the examples here. Two Malaysian poems are read by Sivanes Nadarajan, a Malaysian-Indian academic. The first is by Muhammad Haji Salleh and the second is by Ghulam-Sarwar Yousof. Both come from the collection *Insights*, compiled by Malachi Edwin Vethamani and published in 2003 by Maya Press.

Track 47

On a dry bund by Muhammad Haji Salleh

i cycled on a dry bund
back
to my childhood.
its world was open and green:
thick nipahs half-cut
wild and dusty jeruju
caught trouser cuffs or claves,
fierce beluntas spread out their thorns
to the swamp sun,
and the channels in mud
slowly find their courses to the sea.

memories return again,
the acrid berembang on a child's morning tongue,
gentle sweetness of young nipah fruits,
grease from dredge and the smell of engines,
they give life to my citified senses.

Track 48

The Midnight Satay-Vendor by Ghulam-Sarwar Yousof

he cuts a sorry figure, the solitary vendor
among the sleeping bungalows
pedalling up the stubborn
aristocratic slopes of jesselton heights

  satay
    satay
      satay

i can see him wiping his sweaty brow
can smell piquant in the air the aroma

of chicken and *cincang*
as he fans the fire
beneath the sizzling rows of skewers

at home in the *kampong* a wife and children
await the meagre day's collection:
some *ringgits* and a few *sen*
that go nowhere
in these days of *inflasi*; and the election
too, with its promise, come and gone

but life must not stop for the likes of him,
so at *pasar malam* and along the night's inclines
wiping his migraines off his forehead
he returns to the embers
his children amidst their *kurang ajar* yawns
prepare tomorrow's *ketupat* and cucumbers

    satay
      satay
        satay

i wish at times I could trade places with him
the midnight vendor, if only as a game
surrender for once a so-called elegance

but education tells me I am *halus*, he *kasar*
for don't you see I'm a shakespeare-*wallah*
with this degree that clings to me like a vise
and a middle-class airconditioned nose?

Vocabulary

Poem 1

nipah	a kind of palm
jeruju	a plant with sharp leaves
beluntas	a plant/tree
berembang	a brown fruit

Poem 2

cincang	meat sauce
kampong	Malay village
ringgits/sen	Malaysian currency (dollars and cents)
inflasi	inflation
pasar malam	night market
kurang ajar	cheeky, disrespectful
ketupat	sticky rice cakes

halus	upper class
kasar	lower class
wallah	person with a specified role

Chapter 10: Emerging Englishes: Hong Kong and China

In this excerpt, the longest on the CD, two multilingual Hong Kong professionals talk about their experiences with English. Note that, although these speakers occasionally use non-standard forms, they understand each other perfectly. I think listeners will also find that they can understand them. Listeners might like to consider how intelligible these speakers are, compared with the Australian and South African speakers.

Hong Kong professionals

Track 49

KT: Actually both of us are like a product of Hong Kong. We er born and we grew up and basically we have education in Hong Kong. So can you tell me exactly how you started to learn English and what what was your feeling?

Track 50

KC: er I started learning English when . . . I when I was in primary two I think (ehm) aged er aged six. (ehm) so I learned er English as a school subject (ehm) I think among er er seven to eight school subjects in my primary school

Track 51

KT: Even in primary school? (yeah) You mean teaching that subject in English?

KC: I er learned the subject of English er (wow) I think er all primary school kids (ehm) did er most primary school kids do nowa nowadays (ehm) so er er and then I was switched to a secondary school using English as the medium of instruction (ehm) er where most of the subjects were taught in English (ehm) so that er I think that lasted for seven years until I entered er university which er is an English-speaking university where most er lectures examinations er reading assignments were all in English. er so I /f/ I recall that I think the er the biggest er difficulty for me is really when switching from primary school setting in which Chinese is the medium of instruction er to a secondary school using English as a medium of instruction. I still remember that was er quite a shock actually. I got a er an English speaking er er class teacher. er the principal was an English er nearly all the lessons er were taught in English except perhaps physical education or of course Chinese. er so I I think it had taken me maybe two to three years to adjust to that. (ehm) yeah so that er that wasn't very pleasant experience, I would say, in er in learning in my learning of English. But I I think eventually er I got over that and then has since used English er as the er medium of learning in universities in postgraduate work and and now in in my workplace I think where English is er is really used as the bus as the language of communication with er with er the er /s/ with the senior management ehm and and a large number of colleagues (ehm)

Track 52

KT: Well I had a very similar experience. Like you I I would say that I was quite dumb when I entering er my secondary school which is also an um English [?] um stroke a school with English as the medium of instruction. Like you I I thought it was it was to me it's a terrible experience. I had two years in a row going to the assembly week-ly really without knowing what's going on – laugh – and I er really lost confidence in myself. But like again like you I have my er headmistress many teachers who are expatriates there there really was no choice for us to speak Chinese at all and through that well maybe it's a forced situation but I think that actually was the way I was brought up er looking back I thought the experience was in fact very positive to become a multilingual person

Track 53

KC: so er so er do you recall whether whether you really liked English as a er a school subject or or English as a language right for for your your own daily use er?

KT: well English as a subject to me is is just like er part of the game you know if you want to survive if you want to like lead er er er a life that er will allow you to move up the social ladder. er when I was young I already realised that you actually have to speak good English. Why I say so . . . because ehm I recall that I have many class-mates who were very brilliant learners great in arts music what have you or Chinese. But only because my English was better again looking back I know that I have really a better life than you know what they have too. so to me er learning English is something I feel OK but I also er have a strong feeling of the fact that er you know the language is always put in a political context it's a sociological context. it actually means at least in Hong Kong something to do with your future. So stu-dents have to learn ehm very diligently. When I have grown up there's another observation I had, that is you know being a multilingual person I I would say that learning English is not that political (laugh). In fact I think it it's also an element of respect of other people. As you said English is really the language of communication these days not only in the work place but I think just as as a person. I have who have extensive international experience English is the only language that you can speak and communicate people as the I think the only common platform in the world. So when I come across situations where there are expatriates around and there are many Chinese around, I am always very conscientious that speaking English is real-ly a matter of respect for other people ehm in the audience or ehm you know in that that gathering . . . so what is er your observation?

Track 54

KC: well er in my er secondary school days I I /f/ er recall that I had never ident identi-fied myself as someone good in English (laugh) there were classmates I think er who have much er better English training I think in the primary school days. They could er speak pretty well, very good pronunciation, (ehm) and er I think they were well-liked by their English teachers because they they always gave correct answers so er there were groups of classmates I think mainly mainly girls er who er like English literature. (ehm) er I still remem I remembered that I hated English literature (laugh) right. I had no I did not find any interest er in reading er literary works. I I was never er interested in in reading Shakespeare (laugh). er I was er punished by not being able to memorise the er poems (laugh) of English er poets. I I so er in those days it was copying a hundred times the poem of a certain poet which er make me made me hate really the er such learning right of er of English. And so I actually found people who were interested in English literature a bit strange OK – laugh – I (laugh)

Track 55

KT: did they did you actually find that most of them are very like snobbish people? (laugh)

KC: well they er this I could not understand why they could become interested in it (laugh) OK so but anyway I think perhaps my exposure for example in – cough – with er non-Chinese-speaking professors in er in the university and my er later my overseas studies in Canada in er in Australia, and er so er of course there there were still some times where I I was not very sure OK about what my English prof my professors were referring to. (ehm) There were some th I think th differences all right there were some er daily English which they have thought was very /s/ very common for them OK (ehm) but actually might not be understood OK by me as a foreign student. (ehm) er of course there were sometimes the the problem accents for example in I think particularly in er Australia (ehm) er in Scotland (ehm) and then I realised er er it was sometimes it might not be just a problem for a foreign student because even people who spoke English as their first language they sometimes had difficulty in understand er er each other. (ehm) So so er generally of of course I think the English used by academics right I think they they have survived so long I think – laugh – in that field so they I think they tend to speak a kind of English still that er is more easily understood among that er that er professional field. (ehm) But I do not the same feeling OK when when er it was to the in the for the common folks in in bars or coffee shops (laugh) er er of course sometimes it's difficult to it's not easy to understand OK. I still remember having er dinner in a pub where the er the er northern English were watching a soccer game (laugh) OK between Manchester United and another another team. And I could not understand what er many words OK. They were so expressive they were so er so I felt I'm I was a foreigner (laugh) OK? a complete foreigner (ehm) during that er

Track 56

KT: even though you can speak English

KC: yeah in that evening yeah. So er so sometimes I think we we had that feeling when travelling er in the in the /s/ the we the type of English OK I think still is spoken by common folk sometimes it's er still difficult to understand by by I find it difficult to understand

KT: thank you

The following three poems, two by Louise Ho and one by Agnes Lam, are reprinted here as additional examples. Please note, though, that they are not recorded on the accompanying CD.

Hong Kong riots by Louise Ho

At five this morning
The curfew lifted.
Receding it revealed
Shapes that became people
Moving among yesterday's debris
Stones, more so than words,
Are meaningless,
Out of context

End of an era by Louise Ho

End of era
Or change of chapter
Smaller than a speck on the map
A nerve centre in the world
Miniscule place
Global space
Several vortices
Suspended by their own velocity
Drive cogwheels that orbit like planets

Yellow flowers on a battlefield by Agnes Lam

You ask me what is happiness
You ask me what is success
I once was young like you
Like you, I needed answers.

You tell me learning is difficult
in circumstances like yours.
Your teachers know that too.
I couldn't agree more.

There are not enough books,
not enough tapes or videos,
not enough teachers,
not enough anything.

How can I talk to you
about English on the Net

when there's only one computer
for each department?

Six days I have taught you.
Six days you have all come.
Always eager, always trying,
ever listening and asking.

You ask me for my poems.
You ask me for my photo.
You ask me for my signature.
My dear students, I am but a teacher.

Tomorrow I shall fly away
back to my office where I work
from eight to eight and I shall miss
your thirst for learning, your welcome.

I wish so much
You would be happy,
That you would find
Meaning and success.

But all I can leave you
are but another's words –
zhan di huang hua fen wai xiang.
On a battlefield, yellows flowers are
sweeter than ever

[The final two lines of the final poem translate the previous line of standard *putonghua*.]

Chapter 11: English as a *lingua franca*

These examples are all taken from conversations between people from different countries in ASEAN, using English as a *lingua franca*. The nationality of each of the speakers is given at the beginning of each excerpt.

Example 1: a Filipina (P), a Bruneian (B) and a Thai (T)

The bold type indicates where one speaker anticipates what the other is going to say and provides an example of shared understanding. Listeners will also be able to hear the syllable-timing of these speakers.

Track 57

P: and the parents are well educated whereas {T: eh hm} those coming from the public
er {B: school} should come the lower er

B: **income**

P: **income families** {F+T: ehm yeah} that's why er during our national exams this ah children coming from the private schools they get higher scores than the ones who are {F+T: ehm} in the government in the elementary {F+T: ehm} school except for some science high schools {B: ehm} and the University of the Philippines {B: yes} system students [they get high grades

B: for our high school] we get good results because we {F: ehm} we after standard six or primary six they primary school they go to a secondary {T: correct} school so our school is a government school and we get students from private school {T: yes} and students from the government school {F: eh hm} so and ehm these people who've who are who are from the government er the private school usually do better {T: ehm} and they will continue **doing**

P: **better**

B: **better** until {T: right} er ['O' levels {V: yeah yeah} or or high school {Fx2 +T: yeah} at the end of the high school year

Example 2: a Filipina (P), a Bruneian (B) [the same participants as in example 1] and a Vietnamese (V)

Note the Vietnamese speaker's pronunciation of 'taught', her use of both /θ/ and /t/ and her addition of an 's' to 'future' and 'children'. None of this causes any misunderstanding.

Track 58

P: er what have you done in Vietnam about teacher education?

V: ehm well ehm for in terms of ehm teaching grammar ehm as I mentioned this morning ehm (..) er we have er the at university we have the two like er two stages. The first one is for the first year so the students ehm will be **/t?tʃ/** all the basic er rules like like I I mean this for the er for the sub for the grammar subject itself it's not for interpretative skills {F: ehm} so ehm after the first years er we move to the second year and the **th/θ/ird** year for more ehm like er more academic {B: more academic yes} more **/t/eoretical** {B: oh ok} (..) what because we believe that ehm because our teacher won't be teacher of English in the future**s** so they will teach [ehm

B: young] young children

V: young children**s** {T: ehm} so they must like master grammar very well so that they can you know they are able to ehm teach them? the rules [so

Example 3: a Cambodian (C), a Indonesian (I) and a Singaporean (S)

Note how the Cambodian makes himself easily understood and how the Singaporean suggests an alternative word ('benefits' for 'good things'), which he then adopts. The question in bold is actually a rhetorical question, so when the Indonesian tries to answer it, the

Cambodian speaker continues his rhetorical 'game' until all the participants understand. The excerpt ends in shared laughter.

Track 59

C: in the future I hope that er (..) er more and more (..) Cambodians will speak English because erm we we understand about the advantages of English. We cannot erm live erm without English because {S: ok} we have to contact the world {S: eh hm} we have erm to do business with the world we have to {I: ehm} yeah we have to develop our country with the world. {S: ehm} So nearly all nearly all nearly all factors of develop-ment we have to (..) erm interdependent {S: eh hm} yeah we have to interdependent between one {S: eh hm} country and another country. So we have to use English in communi[cation

I: ah yes of] course yes

C: so Cambodian people rely and I will I will tell Cambodians I will tell them about the advantage advantages of English and ehm er (..) motivate them to learn English because I know the the the **good things** of English

S: the **benefits**

C: yeah the benefit **you want to travel the world**?

I: well you [can you

C: you you] have to speak English

I: you [can

C: you] want to do business with er {I: ehm ehm} other country you have [to

S: you have] to use English

I: yeah

C: use] English

I: yeah yeah ok

C: you want to do research? (I: laugh)

S: you have to do it in English

C: you have to (S+I: laugh) to do in English (general laughter)

Example 4: an Indonesian (I2), a Malaysian (M) and a Cambodian (C2)

These are different participants from those above. I discuss this excerpt in Chapter 11 itself. I have bolded the linguistic features that are discussed there. The reason why the Indonesian speaker does not mark the past tense on 'pick' is almost certainly phonological, but phonology cannot explain the lack of past tense markings on 'sit', 'check', and 'take'.

Track 60

I2: er I **I waited]** for the official **who picked** (/pik/) me up ok er and **then I tried** to look for the official but because er er **the plane you know landed** so early so (ehm uh oh) the **official hasn't come yet** (C2: ehm) yeah

M2: what a pity (laugh)

I2: er er I I **I had to stay** in the airport and **then did nothing** (C2: ehm) **just sit and I check the placard** of (ehm) RELC (M2: ehm) ok and er and **I couldn't see that's why I just sit and take a rest**…what about you what time

C2: how long **have you waits** for them

I2: just an hour

C2: an <u>hours</u> (I2: an hour) oh oh

I2: ok **I enjoyed** the arcades you [know

M2: and] then **how did you get here**

I2: er no the official

M: **came late**

I2: er **that I met** ok the er **came late** (laugh) yeah because **the flight was earlier** than the (eh) schedule (oh) so ok **I just er waited** for him an hour in the airport yeah er finally I **met him** (ehm) at one o' clock (laughter) **that's it**

M2: luckily **you arrived** [safely

C2: I] **also arrived** <u>earliers</u> than the exact time (I: oh ok) as the **one** <u>that's pick</u> me up (ehm) **said but luckily I mets him** (laugh)

References

Achebe, C. (1975/2005) 'The African writer and the English language', in: Jenkins, J. (2005) *World Englishes*, London: Routledge, pp169–72.

Adamson, B. (2002) 'Barbarian as foreign language: English in China's schools', *World Englishes*, 21(2): 231–43.

Adamson, B. (2004) *China's English. A History of English in Chinese Education*. Hong Kong: Hong Kong University Press.

Ahulu, S. (1994) 'How Ghanaian is Ghanaian English?', *English Today*, 38 10(2): 25–9.

Aitken, A. J. (1979) 'Scottish speech: A historical view, with special reference to the Standard English of Scotland', in: Aitken, A. J. & McArthur, T. (eds.) (1979) *Languages of Scotland*, Edinburgh: Chambers, pp85–118.

Aitken, A. J. & McArthur, T. (eds.) (1979) *Languages of Scotland*, Edinburgh: Chambers.

Algeo, J. (2003) 'The origins of Southern American English', in: Nagle, S. J. & Sanders, S. L. (eds.) (2003) *English in the Southern United States*, Cambridge: Cambridge University Press, pp6–16.

Ammon, U. (1996) 'The European Union. Status change during the last 50 years', in: Fishman, J., Conrad, A. & Rubal-Lopez, A. (eds.) (1996) *Post-imperial English*, Berlin: Mouton de Gruyter, pp241–67.

Ammon, U. (2000) 'Towards more fairness in international English: Linguistic rights of non-native speakers?, in: Phillipson, R. (ed.) (2000) *Rights to Language: Equity, Power and Education*, Mahwah, New Jersey: Lawrence Erlbaum Associates, pp111–16.

Awoniyi, A. (1995) 'Determining language in education policy. The dilemma in Africa', in: Owalabi, K. (ed.) (1995) *Language in Nigeria: Essays in Honour of Ayo Bamgbose*, Ibadan: Group Publishers, pp441–54.

Baikolo, A. (1995) 'A stylistic analysis of some of the novels of Achebe and Beti', in: Owalabi, K. (ed.) (1995) *Language in Nigeria: Essays in Honour of Ayo Bamgbose*, Ibadan: Group Publishers, pp380–94.

Bailey, G. (1997) 'When did Southern American English begin?', in: Schneider, E. W. (ed.) (1997) *Englishes Around the World. Studies in Honour of Manfred Görlach*, Amsterdam: John Benjamins, vol. 1, pp255–76.

Bailey, G., Maynor, N. & Cukor-Avila (eds.) (1991) *The Emergence of Black English: Text and Commentary*, Amsterdam: John Benjamins

Bailey, R.W. (1996) 'Attitudes towards English: The future of English in South Asia', in: Baumgardner, R. J. (ed.) (1996) *South Asian English: Structure, Use and Users,* Urbana: University of Illinois Press, pp40–52.

Bailey, R.W. & Görlach, M. (eds.) (1982) *English as a World Language,* Ann Arbor: University of Michigan Press.

Bamgbose, A. (1982) 'Standard Nigerian English: Issues of identification', in: Kachru, B. B. (ed.) (1982/1992) *The Other Tongue: English Across Cultures,* Chicago: Illinois University Press, pp99–111.

Bamgbose, A. (1996) 'Post-imperial English in Nigeria', in: Fishman, J., Conrad, A. & Rubal-Lopez, A. (eds.) (1996) *Post-imperial English,* Berlin: Mouton de Gruyter, pp357–72.

Bamgbose, A. (1998) 'Torn between the norms and innovations in World Englishes', *World Englishes,* 17 (1): 1–14.

Bamgbose, A. (2001) 'World Englishes and globalization', *World Englishes,* 20(3): 357–64.

Bamiro, E. O. (1994) 'Lexico-semantic variation in Nigerian English', *World Englishes,* 13(1): 51–64.

Bartlett, F. C. (1932) *Remembering. A Study in Experimental and Social Psychology,* Cambridge: Cambridge University Press.

Baumgardner, R. J. (ed.) (1996) *South Asian English: Structure, Use and Users,* Urbana: University of Illinois Press.

Bautista, M. L. (ed.) (1997a) *English is an Asian Language: The Philippine Context,* Sydney: Macquarie Library.

Bautista, M. L. (1997b) 'The lexicon of Philippine English', in: Bautista, M. L. (ed.) (1997a) *English is an Asian Language: The Philippine Context,* Sydney: Macquarie Library, pp49–72.

Bautista, M. L. (2004) 'Special articles on Philippine English: Guest editor's introduction', *Asian Englishes,* 7(2): 4–7.

Bautista, M. L. (2005) 'Investigating the putative features of Philippine English, with cross reference to other Englishes', Paper given at the 15th conference of the International Association of World Englishes (IAWE), Purdue University, 21–23 July.

Bernard, J. R. L. (1988) 'Australian Pronunciation', in: *The Macquarie Dictionary,* pp18–27.

Berns, M. (1995) 'English in the European Union', *English Today,* 43, 11 (3): 3–11.

Bernstein, C. (2003) 'Grammatical features of southern speech: *yall, might could,* and *fixin' to',* in: Nagle, S. J. & Sanders, S. L. (eds.) (2003) *English in the Southern United States,* Cambridge: Cambridge University Press, pp106–18.

Biakolo, A. (1995) 'A stylistic analysis of some of the novels of Achebe and Beti', in: Owalabi, K. (ed.) (1995) *Language in Nigeria: Essays in Honour of Ayo Bamgbose,* Ibadan: Group Publishers, pp380–94.

Bickerton, D. (1981) *Roots of Language,* Ann Arbor: Karoma.

Bisong, J. (1995) 'Language choice and cultural imperialism. A Nigerian perspective', *ELTJ* 49(2): 122–32.

Biswas, G. (2004) 'Language policy in Southeast Asia: A case study of India', in: Mansoor, S., Meraj, S. & Tahir, A. (eds.) (2004) *Language Policy, Planning and Practice: A South*

Asian Perspective, Karachi: Aga Khan University and Oxford University Press, pp106–11.

Blake, N. F. (ed.) (1992) *Cambridge History of the English Language, Vol 2: 1066–1476,* Cambridge: Cambridge University Press.

Blake, N. F. (1996) *A History of the English Language,* London: Macmillan.

Bloomfield, L. (1933) *Language,* London: George, Allen and Unwin.

Bokamba, E. (1982) 'The Africanisation of English', in: Kachru, B. B. (ed.) (1982/1992) *The Other Tongue: English Across Cultures,* Chicago: Illinois University Press, pp77–98.

Bolton, K. (2000) 'The sociolinguistics of Hong Kong and the space for Hong Kong English', *World Englishes,* 19(3): 265–86.

Bolton, K. (2003) *Chinese Englishes: A Sociolinguistic History,* Cambridge: Cambridge University Press.

Bolton, K. & Lim, S. (2000) 'Futures for Hong Kong English', *World Englishes,* 19(3): 429–43.

Boyle, J. (1997) 'Imperialism and the English language', *Journal of Multilingual and Multicultural Development,* 18(3): 169–81.

Braine, G. (ed.) (1999) *Non-Native Educators in English Language Teaching,* Mahwah, New Jersey: Lawrence Erlbaum Associates.

Briguglio, C. (2005) 'The use of English as a global language in multinational settings: Implications for business education', PhD Dissertation, Curtin University of Technology, Perth, Australia.

Brown, A. (1988) 'Staccato effect in the pronunciation of English in Malaysia and Singapore', in: Foley, J. (ed.) (1988) *New Englishes. The Case of Singapore,* Singapore: National University of Singapore Press, pp115–25.

Brown, A. & Deterding, D. (2005) 'A checklist of Singapore English pronunciation features', in: Deterding, D., Brown, A. & Low. E. L. (eds.) (2005) *English in Singapore: Phonetic Research on a Corpus,* Singapore: McGraw Hill, pp7–14.

Brutt-Griffler, J. (2002) *World English. A Study of its Development,* Clevedon: Multilingual Matters.

Brutt-Griffler, J. (2005) 'Globalisation and Applied Linguistics: Post-imperial questions of identity and the construction of applied linguistics discourse', *International Journal of Applied Linguistics,* 15(1): 133–115.

Buchan, P. & Toulmin, D. (1989) *Buchan Claik,* Edinburgh: Gordon Wright Publishing.

Burchfield, R. (1985) *The English Language,* Oxford: Oxford University Press.

Burchfield, R. (1994a) 'Introduction', in: Burchfield, R. (ed.) (1994b) *Cambridge History of the English Language, Vol 5: English in Britain and Overseas. Origins and Development.* Cambridge: Cambridge University Press.

Burchfield, R. (ed.) (1994b) *Cambridge History of the English Language, Vol 5: English in Britain and Overseas. Origins and Development.* Cambridge: Cambridge University Press.

Butler, S. (1997) 'Corpus of English in Southeast Asia: Implications for a regional dictionary', in: Bautista, M. L. (ed.) (1997a) *English is an Asian Language: The Philippine Context,* Sydney: Macquarie Library, pp.103–24.

Butler, S. (2002) 'Language, literature and culture – and their meeting place in the dictionary', in: Kirkpatrick, A. (ed.) (2002b) *Englishes in Asia: Communication, Identity, Power and Education*, Melbourne: Language Australia, pp143–168.

Canagarajah, S. C. (1994) 'Competing discourses in Sri Lankan English poetry', *World Englishes*, 13 (3): 361–76.

Canagarajah, S. C. (2000) 'Negotiating ideologies through English', in: Ricento, T. (ed.) (2000) *Ideology, Politics and Language Policies. Focus on English*, Amsterdam: John Benjamins, pp121–32.

Canagarajah, S. C. (2005) 'Reconstructing local knowledge, reconfiguring language studies', in: Canagarajah, S. C. (ed.) (2005) *Reclaiming the Local in Language Policy and Practice*, Mahwah: Lawrence Erlbaum Associates, pp3–24.

Carrell, P., Devine, J. & Eskey, D. (eds.) (1988) *Interactive Approaches to Second Language Reading*, Cambridge: Cambridge University Press.

Carrell, P. & Eisterhold, J. (1988) 'Schema theory and ESL reading pedagogy', in: Carrell, P. , Devine, J. & Eskey, D. (eds.) *Interactive Approaches to Second Language Reading*, pp73–92.

Cenoz, J. & Jessner, U (eds.) (2000a) *English in Europe: The Acquisition of a Third Language*, Clevedon: Multilingual Matters.

Cenoz, J. & Jessner, U. (2000b) 'Expanding the scope: sociolinguistic, psycholinguistic and educational aspects of learning English as a third language in Europe', in: Cenoz & Jessner (eds.) (2000) *English in Europe: The Acquisition of a Third Language*, Clevedon: Multilingual Matters, pp248–60.

Cheshire, J. (ed.) (1991) *English Around the World. Sociolinguistic Perspectives*, Cambridge: Cambridge University Press.

Chick, J. K. (2002) 'Intercultural miscommunication in South Africa', in: Mesthrie, R. (ed.) (2002) *English in South Africa*, Cambridge: Cambridge University Press, pp258–75.

Clyne, M. (2003) *Dynamics of Language Contact*, Cambridge: Cambridge University Press.

Collard, K., Fatnowna, S., Oxenham, D., Roberts, J. & Rodriguez, L. (2000) 'Styles, appropriateness and usage of Aboriginal English', *Asian Englishes*, 3(2): 82–97.

Collins, P. & Blair, D. (eds.) (1989) *Australian English*, Brisbane: Queensland University Press.

Comrie, B., Matthews, S. & Polinsky, M. (1996) *The Atlas of Languages*, London: Quarto Books.

Conrad, A. (1996) 'The international role of English: The state of the discussion', in: Fishman, J., Conrad, A. & Rubal-Lopez, A. (eds.) (1996) *Post-imperial English*, Berlin: Mouton de Gruyter, pp13–36.

Cook, V. J. (1999) 'Going beyond the native speaker in language teaching', *TESOL Quarterly*, 33(2): 185–210.

Cook, V. J. (2001) (3rd edition) *Second Language Learning and Teaching*, London: Arnold.

Cook, V. J. (2002) 'Language teaching methodology and the L2 user perspective', in: Cook, V. J. (ed.) (2002) *Portraits of the L2 User*, Clevedon: Multilingual Matters, pp327–43.

Cook, V. J. (ed.) (2002) *Portraits of the L2 User*, Clevedon: Multilingual Matters.

Cook, V. J. & Newson, M. (1996) (2nd edition) *Chomsky's Universal Grammar*, Oxford: Blackwell.

Cooke, M. (1995) 'Aboriginal evidence in the cross-cultural courtroom', in: Eades, D. (ed.) (1995) *Language in Evidence*, Sydney: Sydney University Press.

Crane, G. (1994) 'The English language in Brunei Darussalam', *World Englishes*, 13(3): 351–60.

Crystal, D. (1995) 'Documenting rhythmical change', in: Windsor Lewis, J. (ed.) (1994), *Studies in General English and Phonetics: Essays in Honour of Professor J. D. O'Connor*, London: Routledge, pp174–9.

Crystal, D. (1997/2003) *English as a Global Language*, Cambridge: Cambridge University Press.

Crystal, D. (2004) *The Stories of English*, London: Allen Lane.

Cukor-Avila, P. (1997) 'Change and stability in the use of verbal –s over time in AAVE', in: Schneider, E. W. (ed.) (1997) *Englishes Around the World. Studies in Honour of Manfred Görlach*, Amsterdam: John Benjamins, vol. 1, pp295–306.

Cukor-Avila, P. (2003) 'The complex grammatical history of African-American and white vernaculars in the South', in: Nagle, S. J. & Sanders, S. L. (eds.) (2003) *English in the Southern United States*, Cambridge: Cambridge University Press, pp82–105.

D'Souza, J. (1997) 'Indian English: Some myths, some realities', *English World-wide*, 18(1): 91–105.

D'Souza, J. (2001) 'Contextualising range and depth in Indian English', *World Englishes*, 20(2): 145–59.

Dalby, A. (2002) *Language in Danger*, London: Allen Lane.

Dare, A. S. (1999) 'English and the culture of Yoruba', *English Today*, 57, 15 (1): 11–16.

David, M. (2000) 'Status and roles of English in Malaysia: Ramifications for ELT', *English Australia Journal*, 18(1): 41–9.

David, M. & Yong, J. (2002) 'Even obituaries reflect cultural norms', in: Kirkpatrick, A. (ed.) (2002b) *Englishes in Asia: Communication, Identity, Power and Education*, Melbourne: Language Australia, pp169–78.

Davies, A. (1991) *The Native Speaker in Applied Linguistics*, Edinburgh: Edinburgh University Press.

Davies, A. (1996) 'Ironising the myth of linguicism', *Journal of Multilingual and Multicultural Development*, 17 (6): 485–96.

Davies, A. (1999) 'Standard English: Discordant voices', *World Englishes*, 18(2): 171–86.

Davies, A. (2003) *The Native Speaker: Myth and Reality*, Clevedon: Multilingual Matters.

de Ersson, E.O. (2005).The uses of the progressive construction in Indian English. Paper given at the International Association of World Englishes conference, Purdue University, 21–23 July.

de Klerk, V. & Gough, D. (2002) 'Black South African English', in: Mesthrie, R. (ed.) (2002) *English in South Africa*, Cambridge: Cambridge University Press, pp356–78.

Delbridge, A. (1999) 'Standard Australian English', *World Englishes*, 18(2): 259–70.

Desai, A. (1996) 'A coat of many colours', in: Baumgardner, R. J. (ed.) (1996) *South Asian English: Structure, Use and Users*, Urbana: University of Illinois Press, pp221–30.

Desai, G. (1993) 'English as an African language', *English Today*, 34, 9 (2): 4–11.

Deterding, D. (2000) 'Potential influences of Chinese on the written English of Singapore', in: Brown, A. (ed) (2000) *English in Southeast Asia*, Singapore, National Institute of Education, pp201–209.

Deterding, D. (2006) 'Deletion of final /t/ and /d/ in BBC English: Implications for teachers in Singapore', *STETS Language & Communication Review*, vol 5, No. 1, pp21–3.

Deterding, D., Brown, A. & Low. E. L. (eds.) (2005) *English in Singapore: Phonetic Research on a Corpus*, Singapore: McGraw Hill.

Deterding, D. & Kirkpatrick, A. (2006) 'Intelligibility and an emerging ASEAN English lingua franca', *World Englishes*, 25 (3): pp391–410.

Deterding, D. & Poedjosoedarmo, G. (1998) *The Sounds of English: Phonetics and Phonology for English Teachers in Southeast Asia*, Singapore: Prentice Hall.

Dillard, J. L. (1992) *A History of American English*, London: Longman.

Dixon, R. M. W. (1993) 'Australian Aboriginal Languages', in: Schulz, G. (ed.) (1993) *The Languages of Australia*, Canberra: Australian Academy of the Humanities, pp71–82.

Dixon, R. M. W., Ramson, W. S. & Thomas, M. (1990) *Australian Aboriginal Words in English*, Melbourne: Oxford University Press.

Dollerup, C. (1996) 'English in the European Union', in: Hartmann, R. (ed.) *English in Europe*, pp24–36.

Du, R. & Jiang, Y. (2001) 'Jin ershi nian 'Zhongguo yingyu' yanjiu shuping' ('China English' in the Past 20 Years), *Waiyu jiaoxue yu yanjiu (Foreign Language Teaching and Research)*, 33(1), 37–41.

Dubois, S. & Horvath, B. (2003) 'Creoles and Cajuns', *American Speech*, 78(2): 192–207.

Eades, D. (1991) 'Communicative strategies in Aboriginal Australia', in: Romaine, S. (ed.) (1991) *Language in Australia*, Cambridge: Cambridge University Press, pp84–93.

Ellis, A. J. (1890) *English Dialects. Their Sounds and Homes*, London: English Dialect Society and Paul, Trench and Trubner.

Fenton, A. (2005) *Buchan Words and Ways*, Edinburgh: Berlin.

Ferguson, C. A. (1996) 'English in South Asia: Imperialist legacy and regional asset', in: Baumgardner, R. J. (ed.) (1996) *South Asian English: Structure, Use and Users*, Urbana: University of Illinois Press, pp29–39.

Fernando, C. (1996) 'The ideational function of English in Sri Lanka', in: Baumgardner, R. J. (ed.) (1996) *South Asian English: Structure, Use and Users*, Urbana: University of Illinois Press, pp206–17.

Firth, A. (1996) 'The discursive accomplishment of normality: On 'lingua franca' English and conversation analysis', *Journal of Pragmatics*, 26: 237–59.

Fisher, O. (1992) 'Syntax', in: Blake, N. (ed.) (1992) *Cambridge History of the English Language, vol. 2: 1066–1476*, Cambridge: Cambridge University Press, pp 207–408.

Fishman, J. (1996) 'Summary', in: Fishman, J., Conrad, A. & Rubal-Lopez, A. (eds.) (1996) *Post-imperial English*, Berlin: Mouton de Gruyter, pp623–41.

Fishman, J., Conrad, A. & Rubal-Lopez, A. (eds.) (1996) *Post-imperial English*, Berlin: Mouton de Gruyter.

Foley, J. (ed.) (1988) *New Englishes. The Case of Singapore*, Singapore: National University of Singapore Press.

Flynn, S. (1984) 'A universal in L2 acquisition based on a PBD typology', in: Eckman, F., Bell, L. & Nelson, D. (eds.) (1983) *Universals of Second Language Acquisition*, Rowley, Mass.: Newbury House, pp75–87.

Garcia, E. A. (1997) 'The language policy in education', in: Bautista, M. L. (ed.) (1997a) *English is an Asian Language: The Philippine Context*, Sydney: Macquarie Library, pp73–86.

Giles, H. & Powesland, P. (1975) *Speech Style and Social Evaluation*, London: Academic Press.

Goethals, M. (1997a) 'NELLE: Portrait of a European network', *World Englishes*, 16(1): 57–63.

Goethals, M. (1997b) 'English in Flanders (Belgium)', *World Englishes*, 16(1): 105–14.

Gonzalez, A. B. (1991) 'Stylistic shifts in the English of the Philippine print media', in: Cheshire, J. (ed.) (1991) *English Around the World. Sociolinguistic Perspectives.* Cambridge: Cambridge University Press, pp333–63.

Gonzalez, A. B. (1997) 'The history of English in the Philippines', in: Bautista, M. L. (ed.) (1997a) *English is an Asian Language: The Philippine Context*, Sydney: Macquarie Library, pp25–40.

Görlach, M. (ed.) (from 1991) *Varieties of English Around the World*, Amsterdam: John Benjamins.

Görlach, M. (1994) 'Innovations in New Englishes', *English Worldwide*, 1994 15(1): 101–26.

Görlach, M. (1997) 'Language and nation: The concept of linguistic identity in the history of English', *English Worldwide*, 18(1): 1–34.

Görlach, M. (2002) *Still More Englishes*, Amsterdam: John Benjamins.

Gough, D. (n.d.), 'English in South Africa. The introduction to the Dictionary of South African English' (www.rhodes.ac.za/affiliates/dsae/GOUGH.HTML).

Govardhan, A., Nayar, B. & Sheorey, R. (1999) 'Do US MATESOL programs prepare students to teach abroad?', *TESOL Quarterly*, 33 (1): 114–25.

Graddol, D. (2006) *English Next*, London: The British Council.

Green, L. J. (2002) *African American English*, Cambridge: Cambridge University Press.

Gupta, A. F. (1988) 'A standard for written Singapore English', in: Foley, J. (ed.) (1988) *New Englishes. The Case of Singapore*, Singapore: National University of Singapore Press, pp27–50.

Gupta, A. F. (1997) 'Colonisation, migration and functions of English', in: Schneider, E. W. (ed.) (1997) *Englishes Around the World. Studies in Honour of Manfred Görlach*, Amsterdam: John Benjamins, vol. 2, pp147–58.

Gupta, R. S. & Kapoor, K. (eds.) (1991) *English in India: Issues and Problems*, New Delhi: Academic Foundation.

Guy, G. & Vonwiller, J. (1989) 'The high rising tone in Australian English', in: Collins, P. & Blair, D. (eds.) (1989) *Australian English*, Brisbane: Queensland University Press, pp21–34.

Halliday, M. A. K. (1978) *Language as Social Semiotic*, London: Edward Arnold.

Halliday, M. A. K., McIntosh, A. & Strevens, P. (1964) *The Linguistic Sciences and Language Teaching*, London: Longman.

Harkins, J. (2000) 'Structure and meaning in Australian Aboriginal discourse', *Asian Englishes*, 3(2): 60–81.

Hartmann, R. (ed.) (1996) *The English Language in Europe*, Oxford: Intellect.

Hashim, A. (2002) 'Culture and identity in the English discourses of Malaysians', in: Kirkpatrick, A. (ed.) (2002b) *Englishes in Asia: Communication, Identity, Power and Education*, Melbourne: Language Australia, pp75–94.

Hing, B. (2005) 'Taking the Mickey', *The Diplomat*, 4(3): 56–8.

Ho Wah Kam & Wong, R. (eds.) (2003) *English Language Teaching in East Asia Today*, Singapore: Eastern Universities Press.

Hockett, C. F. (ed.) (1970) *A Leonard Bloomfield Anthology*, Bloomington: University of Indiana Press.

Hoffman, C. (1996) 'Societal and Individual Bilingualism with English in Europe', in: Hartmann (ed.) *English in Europe*, pp47–60.

Hoffman, C. (2000) 'The spread of English and the growth of multilingualism in Europe', in: Cenoz, J. & Jessner, U. (eds.) (2000) *English in Europe: The Acquisition of a Third Language*, Clevedon: Multilingual Matters, pp1–21.

Hogg, R. (ed.) (1992) *Cambridge History of the English Language, Vol 1: The Beginnings to 1066*, Cambridge: Cambridge University Press.

Holm, J. (1989) *Pidgins and Creoles. Volume 2. Reference Survey*, Cambridge: Cambridge University Press.

Holm, J. (2000) *An Introduction to Pidgins and Creoles*, Cambridge: Cambridge University Press.

Honna, N. & Takeshita, Y. (1998) 'On Japan's propensity for native speaker English: A change in sight', *Asian Englishes*, 1(1): 117–37.

Honna, N. & Takeshita, Y. (2000) 'English language teaching for international understanding in Japan', *English Australia Journal*, 18(1): 60–78.

Hosali, P. (2005) 'Butler English', *English Today*, 81, 21 (1): 34–9.

Hu, X. (2005) 'China English, at home and in the world', *English Today*, 83, 21(3): 27–38.

Hung, E. (ed.) (1988) *Renditions (29/30) Special Issue on Hong Kong.* Hong Kong: Chinese University of Hong Kong.

Hung, E. & Pollard, D. (eds.) (1997) *Renditions (47/48). Special Issue on the Hong Kong Nineties*, Hong Kong: Chinese University of Hong Kong.

Hung, T. T. N. (2000) 'Towards a phonology of Hong Kong English', *World Englishes*, 19(3): 337–56.

Hung, T. T. N. (2002) 'English as a global language: implications for teaching', *The ACELT Journal* 6(2): 3–10.

Ihalainen, O. (1994) 'The dialects of England since 1776', in: Burchfield, R. (ed.) (1994b) *Cambridge History of the English Language, Vol 5: English in Britain and Overseas. Origins and Development.* Cambridge: Cambridge University Press, pp197–274.

Jackson, H. (1981) 'Contrastive analysis as a predictor of error', in: Fisiak, J. (ed.) (1981) *Contrastive Linguistics and the Language Teacher*, Oxford: Pergamon, pp195–206.

Jacques, M. (2005) 'No monopoly on modernity', *The Guardian Weekly*, Vol. 172 No. 8 Feb 11–17, p16.

James, A. (2000) 'English as a European lingua franca: Current realities and existing dichotomies, in: Cenoz, J. & Jessner, U. (eds.) (2000) *English in Europe: The Acquisition of a Third Language,* Clevedon: Multilingual Matters, pp22–38.

Jenkins, J. (2000) *The Phonology of English as an International Language,* Oxford: Oxford University Press.

Jenkins, J. (2002) 'A sociolinguistically based, empirically researched pronunciation syllabus for English as an international language', *Applied Linguistics,* 23 (1): 83–103.

Jenkins, J. (2005) *World Englishes,* London: Routledge.

Jenkins, J., Modiano, M. & Seidlhofer, B. (2001) 'Euro-English', *English Today,* 68, 17 (4): 13–21.

Johnson, R. K. (1994) 'Language policy and planning in Hong Kong', *Annual Review of Applied Linguistics,* 14: 177–99.

Johnstone, B. (2003) 'Features and uses of southern style', in: Nagle, S. J. & Sanders, S. L. (eds.) (2003) *English in the Southern United States,* Cambridge: Cambridge University Press, pp189–207.

Jones, G. M. (1996) 'Bilingual education and syllabus design', *Journal of Multilingual and Multicultural Development,* 17 (2–4): 280–93.

Jordan, J. (1985) *On Call. New Political Essays 1981–85,* Cambridge: South End Press.

Jowitt, D. (1994) 'The English of Nigerian newspapers', *English Today,* 40, 10 (4): 23–8.

Kachru, B. B. (ed.) (1982/1992) *The Other Tongue,* Chicago: Illinois University Press.

Kachru, B. B. (1983) *The Indianization of English,* New Delhi: Oxford University Press.

Kachru, B. B. (1985) 'Standards, codification and sociolinguistic realism: The English language in the Outer Circle', in: Quirk, R. & Widdowson, H. (eds.) (1985) *English in the World,* Cambridge: Cambridge University Press, pp11–30.

Kachru, B. B. (1992a) 'Teaching World Englishes', in: Kachru, B. B. (ed.) (1982/1992) *The Other Tongue: English Across Cultures,* Chicago: Illinois University Press, pp355–66.

Kachru, B. B. (1992b) 'Models for non-native Englishes', in: Kachru, B. B. (ed.) (1982/1992) *The Other Tongue: English Across Cultures,* Chicago: Illinois University Press, pp48–74.

Kachru, B. B. (1995) 'The speaking tree: A medium of plural canons', in: Tickoo, M. L. (ed.) (1995) *Language and Culture in Multilingual Societies,* Singapore: SEAMEO Regional Language Centre, pp1–20.

Kachru, B. B. (1996) 'South Asian English: Toward an identity in diaspora', in: Baumgardner, R. J. (ed.) (1996) *South Asian English: Structure, Use and Users,* Urbana: University of Illinois Press, pp9–28.

Kachru, B. B. (1997) 'English as an Asian language', in: Bautista, M. L. (ed.) (1997a) *English is an Asian Language: The Philippine Context,* Sydney: Macquarie Library, pp1–25.

Kachru, Y. (1991a) 'Speech acts in World Englishes: Toward a framework for research', *World Englishes,* 10(3): 299–306.

Kachru, Y. (1991b) 'Writings in the other tongue. Expository prose', in: Gupta, R. S. & Kapoor, K. (eds.) (1991) *English in India: Issues and Problems in Indian English,* Delhi: Academic Foundation, pp227–46.

Kachru, Y. & Nelson, C. (2006) *World Englishes in Asian Contexts.* Hong Kong: Hong Kong University Press.

Kahane, H. (1992) 'American English: From a colonial substandard to a prestige language', in: Kachru, B. B. (ed.) (1982/1992) *The Other Tongue*, Chicago: Illinois University Press, pp. 229–36.

Kamwangamalu, N. M. (2002) 'The social history of English in South Africa', *World Englishes*, 21(1): 1–8.

Kandiah, T. (1991) 'South Asia', in: Cheshire, J. (ed.) (1991). *English Around the World. Sociolinguistic Perspectives*. Cambridge: Cambridge University Press, pp271–87.

Kandiah, T. (1998) 'Epiphanies of the deathless native user's manifold avatars: A post-colonial perspective on the native speaker', in: Singh, R. (ed.) (1998) *The Native Speaker. Multilingual Perspectives*, New Delhi: Sage, pp79–110.

Kandiah, T. (2001) 'Whose meanings? Probing the dialectics of English as a global language', in: Goh, R. B. H. (ed.) (2001) *Ariels – Departures and Returns: A Festschrift for Edwin Thumboo*, Singapore: Oxford University Press, pp102–21.

Kay, W. (1988) *Scots – the Mother Tongue*, Edinburgh: Grafton Books.

Kirkpatrick, A. (1991) 'Information sequencing in Mandarin letters of request', *Anthropological Linguistics*, 33(2): 183–203.

Kirkpatrick, A. (1995) 'Chinese Rhetoric: Methods of argument', *Multilingua*, 14 (3): 271–95.

Kirkpatrick, A. (1996) 'Topic-comment or modifier or modified. Information structure in Modern Standard Chinese', *Studies in Language*, 20 (1): 93–113.

Kirkpatrick, A. (2002a) 'ASEAN and Asian cultures and models: Implications for the ELT curriculum and teacher selection', in: Kirkpatrick, A. (ed.) (2002b) *Englishes in Asia: Communication, Identity, Power and Education*, Melbourne: Language Australia, pp213–24.

Kirkpatrick, A. (ed.) (2002b) *Englishes in Asia: Communication, Identity, Power and Education*, Melbourne: Language Australia.

Kirkpatrick, A. (2006a) 'Which model of English: native speaker, nativised or lingua franca?', in: Rubdy, R. & Saraceni, M. (eds.) (2006) *English in the World: Global Rules, Global Roles*, London: Continuum Press, pp71–83.

Kirkpatrick, A. (2006b) 'Oral Communication and Intelligibility among ASEAN speakers of English', in: Foley, J. (ed.) (2005) *New Dimensions in the Teaching of Oral Communication*, Singapore: Regional Language Centre Anthology Series No. 47: 33–52.

Kirkpatrick, A. (2007) 'Linguistic imperialism? English as a global language', in: Hellinger, M. & Pauwels, A. (eds.) (2007) *Language and Communication: Diversity and Change. Mouton Handbooks of Applied Linguistics*. Berlin: Mouton de Gruyter.

Kirkpatrick, A. & Prescott, D. (1996) 'The changing face of English language teaching: Principles and practice', *Conference proceedings of the international conference on Higher Education in the 21st Century. Mission and challenge in developing countries*, Hanoi: Royal Melbourne Institute of Technology and the Vietnam National University, pp357–73.

Kirkpatrick, A. & Xu, Z. (2002) 'Chinese pragmatic norms and "China English"', *World Englishes*, 21(2): 269–80.

Kirkpatrick, A. & Saunders, N. (2005) 'The intelligibility of Singaporean English: A case study at an Australian university', in: Deterding, D., Brown, A. & Low. E. L. (eds.) (2005) *English in Singapore: Phonetic research on a corpus*, Singapore: McGraw Hill, pp153–62.

Koch, H. (2000) 'Central Australian Aboriginal English: In comparison with the morphosyntactic categories of Kaytetye', *Asian Englishes*, 3(2): 32–59.

Krasnick, H. (1995) 'The role of linguaculture and intercultural communication in ASEAN in the year 2020: Prospects and predictions, in: Tickoo, M. L. (ed.) (1995) *Language and Culture in Multilingual Societies*, Singapore: SEAMEO Regional Language Centre, pp81–93.

Kretzschmar, W. A. Jr. (1997) 'American Englishes for the 21st century', in: Schneider, E. W. (ed.) (1997) *Englishes Around the World. Studies in Honour of Manfred Görlach*, Amsterdam: John Benjamins, vol. 1, pp306–23.

Kubota, R. (1998) 'Ideologies of English in Japan', *World Englishes*, 17 (3): 295–306.

Kynoch, D. (1997) *Doric for Swots*, Edinburgh: Scottish Cultural Press.

Labov, W., Ash, S. & Boberg, C. (2005) 'A National Map of the Regional Dialects of American English', www.ling.upenn.edu/phono_atlas/home.html

Labrie, N. & Quell, C. (1997) 'Your language, my language or English?', *World Englishes*, 16(1): 3–26.

Lass, R. (1999) 'Phonology and Morphology', in: Lass, R. (ed.) (1999) *The Cambridge History of the English Language, Vol III: 1476–1776*, Cambridge. Cambridge University Press, pp56–186.

Lass, R. (2002) 'South African English', in: Mesthrie, R. (ed.) (2002) *English in South Africa*, Cambridge: Cambridge University Press, pp104–26.

Le Page, R. B. (1984) 'Retrospect and prognosis in Singapore and Malaysia', *International Journal of the Sociology of Language*, 45: 113–26.

Le Page, R. B. & Tabouret-Keller, A. (1985) *Acts of Identity. Creole-based Approaches to Language and Ethnicity*, Cambridge: Cambridge University Press.

Lee, S. K. (2004) 'I speak in my mother-alien tongue', in: Mukundan, J., Abidin, D. Z. & Singh, D. (eds.), *ELT Matters 2: Development on English Language Learning and Teaching*, Serdang: Universiti Putra Malaysia Press, pp 114–25.

Li, C. (ed.) (1976) *Subject and Topic*, London: Academic Press.

Li, C. & Thompson, S. (1976) Subject and topic: A new typology of language', in: Li, C. (ed.) (1976) *Subject and Topic*, London: Academic Press, pp457–89.

Li, D. C. S. (2000) 'Hong Kong English. New variety of English or interlanguage?', *English Australia Journal*, 18(1): 50–59.

Li, D. C. S. (2002a) 'Pragmatic dissonance: The ecstasy and agony of speaking like a native speaker of English', in: Li, D. C. S. (ed.) (2001) *Discourses in Search of Members. In Honor of Ron Scollon*, Lanham, Maryland: University Press of America, pp. 559–95.

Li, D. C. S. (2002b) 'Hong Kong parents' preference for English-medium education: Passive victim of imperialism or active agents of pragmatism', in: Kirkpatrick, A. (ed.) (2002b)

Englishes in Asia: Communication, Identity, Power and Education, Melbourne: Language Australia, pp28–62.

Lin, J. (2005) 'Which is better in China, a local or a native English teacher?', *English Today*, 83, 21 (3): 39–46.

Lippi-Green, R. (1997) *English with an Accent. Language, Ideology and Discrimination in the United States*, London: Routledge.

Lo Castro, V. (1987) 'Aizuchi: A Japanese conversational routine', in: Smith, L. E. (ed.) (1987) *Discourse Across Cultures*, New York: Prentice Hall, pp101–13.

Lowenberg, P. (1991) 'Variation in Malaysian English: The pragmatics of language in contact', in: Cheshire, J. (ed.) (1991) *English Around the World. Sociolinguistic Perspectives*. Cambridge: Cambridge University Press, pp364–75.

Luke, K. K. & Richards, J. C. (1982) 'English in Hong Kong: Status and functions', *English Worldwide*, 3(1): 47–64.

Mackay, G. (1996) *The Land Still Speaks*, Canberra: Australian Government Printing Services.

Malcolm, I., Haig, Y., Konigsberg, P., Rochecouste, J., Collard, G., Hill, A. & Cahill, R. (1999) *Two-way English*, Perth: Education Department of Western Australia.

Mansoor, S., Meraj, S. & Tahir, A. (eds.) (2004) *Language Policy, Planning and Practice: A South Asian Perspective*, Karachi: Aga Khan University and Oxford University Press.

Martin, I. P. (2002) 'Canon and pedagogy: The role of American colonial education in defining standards for Philippine literature', in: Kirkpatrick, A. (ed.) (2002b) *Englishes in Asia: Communication, Identity, Power and Education*, Melbourne: Language Australia, pp201–11.

Martin, P. (2005) 'Talking knowledge into being in an upriver primary school in Brunei', in: Canagarajah, S. C. (ed.) (2005) *Reclaiming the Local in Language Policy and Practice*, Mahwah: Lawrence Erlbaum Associates, pp225–46.

Matsuda, A. (2003) 'Incorporating World Englishes in teaching English as an international language', *TESOL Quarterly*, 37(4): 719–28.

Mazrui, A. (1973) 'English language and African nationalism', in: Bailey, R. W. & Robinson, J. L. (eds.) (1973) *Varieties of Present Day English*, New York: Macmillan, pp56–76.

McArthur, T. (1998) *The English Languages*, Cambridge: Cambridge University Press.

McArthur, T. (2002) *The Oxford Guide to World Englishes*, Oxford: Oxford University Press.

McClure, J. D. (1994) 'English in Scotland', in: Burchfield, R. (ed.) (1994b) *Cambridge History of the English Language, Vol 5: English in Britain and Overseas. Origins and Development*. Cambridge: Cambridge University Press, pp23–93.

McClure, J. D. (2002) *Doric: the dialect of North-East Scotland*, Amsterdam: John Benjamins.

McIntosh, A. (1952) *An Introduction to a Survey of Scottish Dialects*, Edinburgh: Thomas Nelson & Sons.

McKay, S. M. (2002) *Teaching English as an International Language*, Oxford: Oxford University Press.

McLellan, J. (2005) 'Malay-English Language Alternation in Two Brunei Darussalam On-Line Internet Chatrooms', PhD Dissertation, Curtin University of Technology.

Medgyes, P. (1994) *The Non-Native Teacher*, London: Macmillan.

Mehrotra, R. R. (1998) *Indian English: Texts and Interpretation*, Amsterdam: John Benjamins.

Mehrotra, R. R. (2000) 'Indian Pidgin English: Myth and reality', *English Today*, 63, 16 (3): 49–52.

Mehrotra, R. R. (2003) 'A British response to some Indian English uses', *English Today*, 75, 19 (3): 19–25.

Meierkord, C. (2000) 'Interpreting successful lingua franca interaction: An analysis of non-native/non-native small talk conversations in English', available online at: http://www.linguistik-online.de/1_00/MEIERKOR.HTM

Meierkord, C. (2004) 'Syntactic variation in interactions across international Englishes', *English Worldwide*, 25(1): 109–32.

Melchers, G. & Shaw, P. (2003) *World Englishes*, London: Arnold.

Mencken, H. L. (1965) *The American Language* (4th edition), New York: Knopf.

Mesthrie, R. (ed.) (2002) *English in South Africa*, Cambridge: Cambridge University Press.

Mesthrie, R. (2002) 'From second language to first language: Indian South African English', in: Mesthrie, R. (ed.) (2002) *English in South Africa*, Cambridge: Cambridge University Press, pp339–35.

Moag, R. F. (1992) 'The life cycle of non-native Englishes: A case study', in: Kachru, B. B. (ed.) (1982/1992) *The Other Tongue*, Chicago: Illinois University Press, pp233–44.

Mufwene, S. (1991) 'Is Gullah decreolizing? A comparison of the speech sample of the 1930s with a sample of the 1980s', in: Bailey, G., Maynor, N. & Cukor-Avila (eds.) (1991) *The Emergence of Black English: Text and Commentary*, Amsterdam: John Benjamins, pp213–30.

Mufwene, S. (2001) *The Ecology of Language Evolution*, Cambridge: Cambridge University Press.

Mufwene, S. (2003) 'The shared ancestry of African-American and American-White Southern Englishes: Some speculations dictated by history', in: Nagle, S. J. & Sanders, S. L. (eds.) (2003) *English in the Southern United States*, Cambridge: Cambridge University Press, pp64–81.

Mulhausler, P. (1982) 'Tok Pisin in Papua New Guinea', in: Bailey, R.W. & Görlach, M. (eds.) (1982) *English as a World Language*, Ann Arbor: University of Michigan Press, pp439–66.

Munoz, C. (2000) 'Bilingualism and trilingualism in school students in Catalonia', in: Cenoz, J. & Jessner, U. (eds.) (2000) *English in Europe: The Acquisition of a Third Language*, Clevedon: Multilingual Matters, pp157–78.

Murison, D. (1979) 'The historical background', in: Aitken, A. J. & McArthur, T. (eds.) (1979) *Languages of Scotland*, Edinburgh: Chambers, pp2–13.

Nagle, S. J. & Sanders, S. L. (eds.) (2003) *English in the Southern United States*, Cambridge: Cambridge University Press.

Naik, M. K. & Narayan, S. A. (2004) *Indian English Literature 1980–2000: A Critical Survey*, New Delhi: Pencraft International.

Ngugi wa Thiong'o (1986/2005) 'The language of African literature', in: Jenkins, J. (2005) *World Englishes*, London: Routledge, pp172–7.

Nihalani, P., Tongue, R. K., Hosali, P. & Crowther, J. (2004) (2nd edition) *Indian and British English: A Handbook of Usage and Pronunciation*, New Delhi: Oxford University Press.

Norton, B. (1997) 'Language, identity and the ownership of English', *TESOL Quarterly*, 31(3): 409–29.

Okudaira, A. (1999) 'A study on international communication in regional organizations: The use of English as the "official" language of ASEAN', *Asian Englishes*, 2(1): 91–107.

Oladipo, O. (1995) 'African world, Western concepts', in: Owalabi, K. (ed.) (1995) *Language in Nigeria: Essays in Honour of Ayo Bamgbose*, Ibadan: Group Publishers, pp396–407.

Owalabi, K. (ed.) (1995) *Language in Nigeria: Essays in Honour of Ayo Bamgbose*, Ibadan: Group Publishers.

Pankratz, K. (2004) 'Philippine English vs the TOEFL', *Asian Englishes*, 7 (2): 74–103.

Parakrama, A. (1995) *De-hegemonising Language Standards. Learning from Postcolonial Englishes about 'English'*, Basingstoke: Macmillan.

Pena, P. S. (1997) 'Philippine English in the classroom', in: Bautista, M. L. (ed.) (1997a) *English is an Asian Language: The Philippine Context*, Sydney: Macquarie Library, pp87–102.

Pennycook, A. (1998) *English and the Discourses of Colonialism*, London: Routledge.

Phillipson, R. (1992) *Linguistic Imperialism*, Oxford: Oxford University Press.

Phillippson, R. (1997) 'Realities and myths of Linguistic Imperialism', *Journal of Multilingual and Multicultural Development*, 18(3): 238–47.

Phillipson, R. (2002) 'Global English and local language policies', in: Kirkpatrick, A. (ed.) (2002b) *Englishes in Asia: Communication, Identity, Power and Education*, Melbourne: Language Australia, pp7–28.

Platt, J. (1991) 'Social and linguistic constraints on variation in the use of two grammatical variables in Singapore English', in: Cheshire, J. (ed.) (1991) *English Around the World. Sociolinguistic Perspectives*. Cambridge: Cambridge University Press, pp376–87.

Platt, J. & Weber, H. (1980) *English in Singapore and Malaysia. Status, Features, Functions*, Kuala Lumpur: Oxford University Press.

Platt, J., Weber, H. & Ho, M. L.(1984) *The New Englishes*, London: Routledge.

Poplack, S. & Tagliamonte, S. (1991) 'There's no tense like the present', in: Bailey, G., Maynor, N. & Cukor-Avila, P. (eds.) (1991) *The Emergence of Black English: Text and Commentary*, Amsterdam: John Benjamins, pp274–324.

Poynton, C. (1989) 'Terms of address in Australian English', in: Collins, P. & Blair, D. (eds.) (1989) *Australian English*, Brisbane: Queensland University Press, pp55–69.

Quayum, M. A. (ed.) (2003) *Petals of Hibiscus: A Representative Anthology of Malaysian Literature in English*, Petaling Jaya: Pearson.

Raheem, R. & Ratwatte, H. (2004) 'Invisible strategies, visible results: Investigating language policy in Sri Lanka', in: Mansoor, S., Meraj, S. & Tahir, A. (eds.) (2004) *Language Policy, Planning and Practice: A South Asian Perspective*, Karachi: Aga Khan University and Oxford University Press, pp91–105.

Ramly, R., Othman, N. A. & McLellan, J. (2002) 'Englishisation and nativisation in the context of Brunei Darussalam: Evidence for and against', in: Kirkpatrick, A. (ed.) (2002b) *Englishes in Asia: Communication, Identity, Power and Education*, Melbourne: Language Australia, pp113–24.

Rampton, B. (1990) 'Displacing the native speaker: Expertise, affiliation and inheritance', *English Language Teaching Journal*, 44 (2): 93–101.

Ransom, W. (1987) 'The historical study of Australian English', in: *The Macquarie Dictionary. Second Revision*, Sydney: The Macquarie Library, pp37–42.

Richardson, M. (1984) 'The Dictamen and its influence on 15th century English prose', *Rhetorica*, 2 (3): 207–26.

Saghal, A. (1991) 'Patterns of language use in a bilingual setting in India', in: Cheshire, J. (ed.) (1991). *English Around the World. Sociolinguistic Perspectives*, Cambridge: Cambridge University Press, pp299–307.

Saro-Wiwa, K. (1985) *Sozaboy: A Novel in Rotten English*, Port Harcourt: Saros International.

Schaeffer, R. P. & Egbokhare, F. O. (1999) 'English and the pace of endangerment in Nigeria', *World Englishes*, 18(3): 381–91.

Schmied, J. (ed.) (1989) *English in East and Central Africa* 1, Bayreuth: Bayreuth University Press.

Schmied, J. (1991) *English in Africa*, London: Longman.

Schmied, J. (ed.) (1992) *English in East and Central Africa* 2, Bayreuth: Bayreuth University Press.

Schneider, E. W. (ed.) (1997) *Englishes Around the World. Studies in Honour of Manfred Görlach* (2 vols), Amsterdam: John Benjamins.

Schneider, E. W. (2003a) 'The dynamics of new Englishes: From identity construction to dialect rebirth', *Language*, 79(2): 233–81.

Schneider, E. W. (2003b) 'Evolution(s) in global English(es)', in: Peters, P. H. (ed.) (1993) *From Local to Global English. Proceedings of the Style Council 2001/2*, pp3–24, Sydney: The Dictionary Research Centre, Macquarie University.

Scollon, R. and Scollon, S. (1991) 'Topic confusion in Asian English discourse', *World Englishes*, 10(2): 113–25.

Seidlhofer, B. (2001) 'Closing a conceptual gap: The case for a description of English as a lingua franca', *International Journal of Applied Linguistics*, 11(2): 133–57.

Seidlhofer, B. (2004) 'Research perspectives in teaching English as a lingua franca', *Annual Review of Applied Linguistics*, 24: 209–39.

Sidhwa, B. (1996) 'Creative processes in Pakistani English fiction', in: Baumgardner, R. J. (ed.) (1996) *South Asian English: Structure, Use and Users*, Urbana: University of Illinois Press, pp231–40.

Skutnabb-Kangas, T (2000) *Linguistic Genocide in Education or Worldwide Diversity and Human Rights?*, Mahwah, NJ: Lawrence Erlbaum Associates.

Smith, G. (2002) 'Kissing cousins? The relationship between English and Tok Pisin in Papua New Guinea', in: Kirkpatrick, A. (ed.) (2002b) *Englishes in Asia: Communication, Identity, Power and Education*, Melbourne: Language Australia, pp113–23.

Smith, L. E. (1992) 'Spread of English and issues of intelligibility', in: Kachru, B. B. (ed.) (1982/ 1992) *The Other Tongue: English Across Cultures*, Chicago: Illinois University Press, pp75–90.

Sonntag, S. K. (2003) *The Local Politics of Global English: Case Studies in Linguistic Globalisation*, Lanham, Maryland: Lexington Books.

Sridhar, K. K. (1991) 'Speech acts in an indigenised variety: Sociocultural values and language variation', in: Cheshire, J. (ed.) (1991) *English Around the World. Sociolinguistic Perspectives*, Cambridge: Cambridge University Press, pp308–18.

Srivastava, R. N. & Sharma, V. P. (1991) 'Indian English today', in: Gupta, R. S. & Kapoor, K. (eds.) (1991) *English in India: issues and problems*, New Delhi: Academic Foundation, pp189–206.

Stanlaw, J. (2004) *Japanese English: Language and Culture Contact*, Hong Kong: Hong Kong University Press.

Strang, B. (1970) *A History of English*, London: Methuen.

Strevens, P. (1992) 'English as an international language: Directions in the 1990s', in: Kachru, B. B. (ed.) (1982/1992) *The Other Tongue: English Across Cultures*, Chicago: Illinois University Press, pp27–47.

Swales, J. (1993) 'The English language and its teachers: Thoughts, past present and future', *English Language Teaching Journal*, 47 (4): 283–91.

Swales, J. (1997) 'English as Tyronnosaurus Rex', *World Englishes*, 16(3): 373–82.

Sweeting, A. & Vickers, E. (2005) 'On colonising colonialism: The discourses of history of English in Hong Kong', *World Englishes*, 24(2): 113–30.

Tay, M. (1991) 'Southeast Asia and Hong Kong', in: Cheshire, J. (ed.) (1991) *English Around the World. Sociolinguistic Perspectives*, pp319–32.

Thomas, E. R. (2003) 'Secrets revealed by Southern vowel shifting', *American Speech* 78 (2): 150–70.

Thompson, R. T. (2003) *Filipino English and Taglish: Language switching from multiple perspectives*, Amsterdam: John Benjamins.

Tillery, J., Bailey, G. & Wikle, T. (2004) 'Demographic change and American dialectology in the twenty-first century', *American Speech*, 79(3): 227–49.

Titlestad, P. J. H. (1998) 'South Africa's language ghosts', *English Today*, 54, 14(2): 33–9.

Todd, L. & Hancock, I. (eds.) (1986) *International English Usage*, London: Croom Helms.

Tosi, A. (ed.) (2003) *Crossing Barriers and Bridging Cultures. The Challenges of Multilingual Translation for the European Union*, Clevedon: Multilingual Matters.

Trudgill, P. (1990). *The Dialects of England*. Oxford: Basil Blackwell.

Tsuda, Y. (1997) 'Hegemony of English vs. ecology of language: Building equality in international communication', in: Smith, L. E. & Forman, M. L. (eds.) (2000) *World Englishes*, Honolulu: Hawaii University Press pp21–31.

Valentine, T. M. (1991) 'Getting the message across: Discourse markers in Indian English', *World Englishes*, 10(3): 325–334.

van Essen, A. (1997)' English in mainland Europe: A Dutch perspective', *World Englishes*, 16(1): 95–103.

Vethamani, M. E. (ed.) (2003) *In-sights: Malaysian Poems*, Petaling Jaya: Maya Press.

Viereck, W. (1996) 'English in Europe: Its nativisation and use as a lingua franca', in: Hartmann, R. (ed.) (1996) *The English Language in Europe*, Intellect: Oxford, pp16–23.

Vittachi, N. (2000) 'From Yinglish to sado-mastication', *World Englishes*, 19(3): 405–14.

Wang, R. (1994) 'Shuo dong dao xi hua yingyu (Talking about English)', Beijing: Waiyu jiaoxue yu yanjiu chubanshe (Foreign Language Teaching and Research Press).

Watson, D. (2003) *Death Sentence: The Decay of Public Language*, Sydney: Knopf.

White, L. & Genesee, F. (1996) 'How native is near-native? The issue of ultimate attainment in adult second language acquisition', *Second Language Research*, 12(3): 233–265.

Widdowson, H. (1997) 'EIL, ESL, EFL: Global issues and local interests', *World Englishes*, 16 (1): 135–46.

Widdowson, H. (2003) *Defining Issues in English Language Teaching*. Oxford: Oxford University Press.

Williams, J. M. (1975) *Origins of the English Language*. New York: Macmillan.

Wiwa, K. (2005) 'In the name of my father', *The Observer Review*, 6 November, pp1–2.

Wolf, H.-G. (2001) *English in Cameroon*, Berlin: Mouton de Gruyter.

Wolfram, W. (2003) 'Language variation in the American South', *American Speech*, 78(2): 123–9.

Xu, X. (2000) 'Writing the literature of non-denial', *World Englishes* 19(3): 415–28.

Xu, Z. (2005) 'Chinese English. What is it and is it to become a regional variety of English?', PhD Dissertation, Curtin University of Technology, Perth, Australia.

Yoshikawa, H. (2005) 'Recognition of world Englishes: Changes in Chukyo University's students' attitudes', *World Englishes*, 23 (3): 351–60.

Zhang, H. (2002) 'Bilingual creativity in Chinese English: Ha Jin's 'In the Pond', *World Englishes*, 21(2): 305–15.

Author index

Subject index